The Dismal Battlefield

The
Dismal
Battlefield

MOBILIZING FOR
ECONOMIC CONFLICT

John C. Scharfen

Naval Institute Press
Annapolis, Maryland

Library of Congress Cataloging-in-Publication Data
Scharfen, John C., 1925–
    The dismal battlefield : mobilizing for economic conflict / John
C. Scharfen.
            p.   cm.
    Includes bibliographical references and index.
    ISBN 1-55750-769-4 (permanent paper)
    1. Economic sanctions.   2. United States—Economic policy.
3. United States—Military policy.   I. Title.
HF1413.5.S32   1995
337.73—dc20   95-11420

Printed in the United States of America on acid-free paper ∞

02 01 00 99 98 97 96 95   9 8 7 6 5 4 3 2

First printing

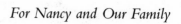
For Nancy and Our Family

IN MEMORIAM

John Charles and Margaret Cole Scharfen
Maxine Scharfen Dauffenbach
A. Harold Schulz
Lieutenant Colonel Jack D. Spaulding, USMC
Major General Edward A. Wilcox, USMC
Major General Richard C. Schulze, USMC
Dr. A. Budd Fenton

Contents

Figures and Tables

———■————————————————

Figures

Tables

Preface

—■————————————————————

This book focuses on the United States and the use of economic force to achieve national security objectives. Nevertheless, it is a subject that has universal interest and application to other nations, to international bodies, and to other uses of economic force as well.

Writings on the subject are scarce.[1] However, there is a wealth of information relevant to economic conflict buried in the reporting, analysis, and discussion of most issues associated with U.S. national security events. In the last few decades there have been few international crises in which the United States was involved when the use of the economic instrument was not contemplated, threatened, or employed.

A central postulate of this work is that the economic instrument most often fails because it is neither understood nor properly employed. It fails because users have not organized, planned, or been educated or trained to use it. Because it is inadequately understood, it is often employed when the chances for success are low. Nor has any user rationalized the use of economic force to permit the generation of policy, doctrine, strategy, or tactics of economic conflict.

I am not one of the nation's 116,000 economists. This is both an advantage and a disadvantage. It is an advantage in that being outside that select fraternity relieves one of carrying the burden of biases that go with such an association. Economists are committed to making the system work. However, the use of economic force subverts and often does lasting harm to the system—anathema to economists, who therefore seem to have quarantined the study of the use of economic force. The disadvantage that comes with being outside this fraternity has been compensated for by seeking advice, counsel, and input from a wide range of professionals. The study of the use of economic force to achieve national security objectives is about the dynamics of the use of force, not the dynamics of international economics. This work draws on my thirty years of experience in the organization of government, policy analysis, and strategic planning in the use of force at the most senior levels of government.

The work represents over fifteen years of research and study on the subject. It grew out of a series of concept papers that have been reviewed extensively within the federal bureaucracy, and out of oral presentations made to senior officials in the U.S. Congress and in the departments and agencies of the federal government. The book reflects the valuable advice and encouragement provided by these officials. It has also benefited from discussions generated in classes I have given on the subject in the U.S. Congress Legislative Studies Institute. These discussions have contributed valuable insights into the dynamics of economic conflict. Several newspaper articles written over the years on the subject of economic conflict, as well as an article on the principles of economic war (coauthored with William R. Ball and published in 1983 in the U.S. Naval Institute *Proceedings*), also elicited valuable input from diverse sectors.[2]

Personal encouragement and critical comment have been provided along the way by Lieutenant General B. E. Trainor, Dr. Roger Barnett, Dr. Jeffrey Salmon, Colonel John J. Grace, Colonel Gerard P. O'Keefe, Mr. Gregor Peterson, Mr. R. Richard Newcomb, Mrs. Kristine S. Wilcox, the Honorable Kazuhiko Togo, Mr. Jeff Schulze, and Mr. Andrew McClintock. I am indebted to Ms. Linda Eady for her help in generating the graphics used here and to Dr. Morrie Roesch for his assistance in statistical analysis.

A special thanks is due to Mary Yates for her editorial advice and assistance.

TITAN Applications, a firm doing valuable work for both the

government and private sectors, provided a stimulating environment conducive to the study of the economic instrument. Mr. Donald Shaw of TITAN was particularly helpful in reviewing drafts and making substantial input. Mr. Edward Knauf, president of TITAN Systems, was always encouraging.

While I welcome this opportunity to acknowledge my debt to all those whose assistance has been critical to this project, the responsibility for the conclusions and such errors as appear in these pages are mine alone.

The Dismal Battlefield

Chapter 1

Introduction

—————————————————————————■——

**To launch economic sanctions without a careful
examination of all these factors would be like launching
a military campaign without military analysis.**

Johan Galtung

magine a nation using military force without a battle plan; without exercising, training, or educating its armed forces; without
adhering to—or even knowing—the basic principles of military
warfare; with no one in charge; with no hierarchy of command;
without organizing its forces; with no systematic study of relative
strengths and vulnerabilities. Or imagine a nation committing its
political assets when embarking upon important international
negotiations without thorough planning or clearly defined objectives; without organizing and preparing its political and diplomatic
forces. Absurd, you say? Of course it is absurd. Yet this is exactly how
nations, alliances, and world bodies are managing and employing
their economic power today.

Purpose and Approach

The purpose of this book is to analyze the dynamics of economic conflict. It offers suggestions on how to engage in such conflict. It provides a seminal examination of some principles of the use of economic force to achieve national objectives. Maritime forces can play a significant role in the application of economic force and are given special attention.

It will be argued here that while economic force is increasingly being relied upon to achieve national, alliance, and world organization objectives, it is an instrument that is poorly understood, poorly planned, and poorly employed. Likewise, the issue of seapower to enforce economic proscriptions receives little attention in the priorities of structuring and training naval forces.

While it is hoped that this work will interest and prove valuable to the journalist and the academic, it does not purport to be journalism or an academic treatise. Rather, this book is a primer. It addresses an area of conflict that for a number of reasons has largely been ignored by academic, strategic, and industrial economists. The reader will find, therefore, that much attention is devoted to the fundamentals of economic conflict. This work also analyzes why this instrument is being poorly employed. It is a practical, procedural prescription.

These pages are aimed at advisers, analysts, policymakers, and decision makers who employ the economic instrument to further national objectives (i.e. the executive and legislative branches of government, to include legislators, their aides, department and agency officials, and military officers). The work should also have relevance for the directors of international and multinational corporations. It is hoped that it provides grist for the mills of analysts of international relations as well as journalists, academics, and informed, concerned citizens.

Included are recommendations as to how the United States might better prepare for a twenty-first century when economic force could become both a threat and a preferred weapon in the U.S. national arsenal.

It will be shown that basic principles of economic conflict can be postulated, just as there are postulates as to the basic principles of military war. There are universal conceptual and systemic voids in the use of economic force where the circumstances warrant the same kind of paradigm we find in military doctrine. The language of economic conflict must be refined, and relevant terms are defined. Because of the similarity of the economic and military conceptual frameworks, the language of economic conflict used here will often draw upon the vocabulary anointed by centuries of the study of military force.[1] Nevertheless, the dynamics of military and economic force are distinct.

While there are many forms of economic conflict that may be waged at many levels of society, to include individuals, pressure groups, and corporations (see table 1), this work focuses on national and multinational conflicts.

One can imagine no international use of the economic instrument that would not be accompanied by a concurrent use of either military or political force (or both).[2] Throughout this work references will be made to events that reflect the use of two or more forms of national power. To help in discussion of the complex employment of force, the following convention will be used: when the military instrument is the primary tool and the economic and political are secondary, it will be written MILITARY-*economic-political;* when the economic and political instruments only are used and the economic is dominant, it will be written ECONOMIC-*political;* and so forth.

And now a few words about what this work is not. It does not deal with the fine points of international economic relations. Rather, it is a treatise on the use of force to achieve national objectives, with an emphasis on national security objectives, employing the economic instrument as one of several options.

This work is not intended to fault economists or their science for the deplorable condition of the study and understanding of the use of economic force. The science of economics is oriented toward maximizing the wealth of humankind. Economists are devoted to making the system work. To many economists, subverting the system through the use of force to gain national advantage is anathema.[3]

This is not an appeal for the use of more or less force in international competition, be it military, diplomatic, or economic. It acknowledges, however, that with (*inter alia*) the decline in the willingness to use military force, economic force may be used more frequently.

The arguments presented here are not judgments on the morality of economic conflict. Economic force produces casualties. The collateral damage is most always indiscriminate, affecting an entire population including the very young, the old, the sick, and the defenseless. While the question of the Just Economic War is raised, it is not answered here. That will take more study and debate than can be squeezed into these few pages.

This is not an evaluation of the successes and failures of the use of economic force. That task has been competently accomplished by the team of Hufbauer, Schott, and Elliot, and what is presented here is indebted to their good work.[4] As this is being written, however, there are major developments taking place that provide insights into economic conflict that have not been thoroughly analyzed. These developments include the economic collapse of the Soviet Union, the United Nations' imposition of economic pressures upon Iraq and Haiti, and the political and social conversion of South Africa. Such events are instructive and may best be used in the future to illustrate points in the discussion of the utility of economic force.

Neither is this a treatise on seapower. That subject must be left to the classic writings of the Corbetts and Mahans and to contemporaries such as Colin Gray and Roger Barnett. This work addresses seapower only as it relates to its contribution to the use of economic power.

Finally, what follows does not propose that economic force is a panacea for the resolution of international conflict. Nor is it proposed that economic force can supplant other forms of national force in the competition between nations. Rarely will economic force be used effectively without the concurrent use of diplomatic or military force, a fact that often makes an appraisal of its effectiveness difficult.

The Eight Postulates of Economic Conflict

This analysis of economic conflict is based upon the following postulates:

1. There is a spectrum of economic activities that ranges from economic support to economic competition and economic conflict. Economic conflict includes both economic coercion and economic war. (See figure 4.)

2. Economic force is being and will be used with increasing frequency in lieu of or in concert with other forms of national power.

3. The United States is poorly prepared to use or defend against the use of the economic instrument in international relations. Specifically:

—There is no department, agency, or staff within the federal bureaucracy that has responsibility or is organized for the overall management of the economic instrument.
—There are no education or training programs to prepare the U.S. bureaucracy to employ or defend against the use of economic force.
—There are few published works that analyze the use of economic force and none that focuses on its dynamics.
—There is no standard vocabulary to describe the dynamics of economic force.
—There is no doctrinal foundation for the examination of the use of economic force in the pursuit of national objectives.

4. Economic force has many facets. The use of the economic instrument covers a broad spectrum from the awarding of economic incentives to the deprivation of economic essentials. The users and targets of economic force range from world bodies through entities such as nations, cartels, and multinational corporations to individuals.

5. There are principles of economic conflict, just as there are principles of military war; however, with a single exception, these principles have been neither enunciated nor analyzed.[5]

6. A legislative framework is needed for the proper management of economic force.

7. There is a requirement for a doctrinal and organizational framework for the proper management of U.S. economic force.

8. Institutionalizing a national apparatus to study, plan and train for, and control the use of economic force could evoke dangerous, hostile reactions from a nation's allies and adversaries.

Chapter 2

The Language of Economic Conflict

Language, the first and most basic tool of culture, is also its truest mirror. Any culture worthy of consideration will have created language to reflect its special preoccupations. Eskimos, it's said, have a hundred words for snow.

Richard Ben Cramer

Before there can be a serious study of and debate about the dynamics of economic conflict, it is important that there be an agreed-upon definition of terms. Unfortunately there is no such agreement nor any compendium of definitions available. This should come as no surprise, for, in general, economic discourse takes place in a Tower of Babel. Robert Passell, a journalist who writes on economics for the *New York Times,* has written about the difficulties in economic language: "One group of specialists barely speaks the same language as the Ph.D's across the hall."[1]

In 1960 Robert Loring Allen wrote that there is "no satisfactory definition which exists for economic war." The 1991 edition of *The Harper Collins Dictionary, Economics* fails to provide a definition of *economic warfare* or *economic conflict*.[2] *Economic war* implies aggression on the part of those who employ the economic weapon.[3] It is a term favored by the target of that force and those moralists who would class the use of the economic instrument as unscrupulous. *Economic sanctions* is a milder term and one favored by those employing the instrument.

The use of such euphemisms is not unique to the discussion of economic force. The U.S. War Department has become the Department of Defense and the secretary of war the secretary of defense. In diplomatic language the term *incursion* is preferred by the offensive force while *invasion* is favored by the defender. During the Korean hostilities a war became a "police action" and a "conflict." During President John F. Kennedy's Cuban missile crisis the U.S. naval blockade of the island became a "quarantine." In 1993 the Clinton blockade of Haiti was termed an "embargo." During the fall of 1994 the U.S. invasion of that country was termed an "insertion" by the State Department. Wars have been described as "conflagrations." In 1989 Japan's Emperor Hirohito referred to World War II as the "unfortunate past." To the paramilitary agent his activity is "unconventional warfare," to the victim it is "terrorism."

Some of the most innovative jargon is found in the federal budget, which James K. Glassman has exposed as "essentially a fraud." It is a process that Representative Martin Hoke of Ohio refers to as "the dark alchemy of baseline budgeting." The smoke and mirrors of the federal budget process permit our executive and legislative branches to predict and claim savings when such savings are in reality increased expenditures. George Orwell warned us fifty years ago that "political language is designed to make lies sound truthful and murder respectable, and to give an appearance of solidity to pure wind."[4]

According to William Lutz, there are four ways to avoid the harsh realities of events through language. One is the use of the euphemism (e.g. "unlawful deprivation of resources" for "starvation"). Another is professional jargon (such as "economic incentives" for "bribery"). A third is bureaucratese. Lutz cites this example of economic bureaucratese as being typical: "It is a tricky problem to find the particular calibration in timing that would be appropriate to stem the acceleration in risk premiums created by falling incomes without prematurely aborting the decline in the inflation generated risk premiums." The language of economics seems to be a particular quagmire, as confirmed by Alan Greenspan, chairman of the Federal Reserve, when he began a speech, "I guess I should warn you, if I turn out to be particularly clear, you've probably misunderstood what I have said." Finally, according to Lutz, is the category of inflated language. Lutz cites the description of the 1983 Grenada military operation as a "predawn vertical insertion" rather than an "invasion."[5]

The most troublesome term in the lexicon of economic force is *economic war*. Adler-Karlsson alleged that the refusal to acknowledge the pervasiveness of acts of economic war is due to "a conspiracy of silence."[6] It is a term assiduously avoided by politicians, economists in particular, and academics in general. Absent the circumstances of general war, it is a term seldom used by those who are the users of economic force but one favored by those who are the targets.

However, we should not devalue the political utility of the euphemism. The use of a euphemism can at times free a leadership to rationalize the use of force when its employment might otherwise be challenged. As we shall see, a blockade has a certain meaning under international law that implies a state of belligerency between nations. Several times in the past few decades the United States felt compelled to invoke a blockade against a hostile target (Cuba and Iraq) but did not want to declare that a state of belligerency existed. It therefore opted to call the Cuban blockade a quarantine and the Iraqi blockade an interdiction. Each term served the purpose. For sound political reasons the U.S. leadership has avoided using the term *economic war* in its peacetime commitment to the use of economic force. The preferred term is *economic sanctions*. Academics and the media have followed suit.

Admitting to the conduct of an "economic war" can impose much unwarranted baggage on a leadership. First, it raises questions as to the authority to declare war and the way in which relevant legislation impinges on such use of force. Second, the term *war* implies a level of hostility and violence that can be a burden to an administration that is seeking international or domestic support or wants to avoid being labeled an aggressor. So there may be good reason to use euphemisms in the diplomatic language that is used during the course of economic conflict. However, in discussions such as those presented here, it is important that such subterfuges be recognized for what they are, and that they not cloud rational fact-finding and discourse. Third, if economic war should be formally declared, the case may be made that such declaration demands that the moral principles of the just war be invoked. (See chapter 5.)

In September 1976 a group of prominent economists and scholars of international relations met for a singularly productive series of meetings on this subject. Because the term *economic war* conjured a violence the group was reluctant to endorse, they settled on the alternative *economic conflict*.[7] Miroslav Nincic and his colleagues used the term *economic coercion* in their study of the subject.[8] There are other terms, such as *economic leverage, economic sanctions* (which is the favorite), *economic imperialism, economic nationalism, trade warfare, managed trade,* and *economic guerrilla warfare*. Some terms imply more violence than *economic conflict*. Others imply less. To some extent the choice of terms reflects the prejudice of the user.

In 1989 some Japanese were not reluctant to use the term *economic war,* as evidenced in the manuscript *The Japan That Can Say No* authored by Ako Morita (chairman of the Sony Corporation) and Shintaro Ishihara (a former Japanese minister of transport). Their book contains this threat: "There is no hope for the U.S., economic warfare is the basis for the existence of the free world."[9]

The U.S. ambassador to Japan, expressing his concern for the significance and the impact of language, told a group of Japanese reporters at the Japan National Press Club, "Choice of language is

worth attention," and he cited the Japanese use of terms such as *war,*
attack, and *counterattack* as being dangerous in the context of economic and political relations.[10] Michael Sekora, former Pentagon
analyst, alleges that the Japanese practice capitalism with military
discipline, using terms such as *frontal attack, flanking attacks,* and *total
envelopment.* Sekora believes that the Japanese language of international commerce connotes *war.*[11]

Many Japanese argue that they are merely being realistic. What
was it if not a form of war when, in 1988, the United States inflicted
drastic economic punishment on Panama in efforts to remove
strongman Manuel Antonio Noriega from power? The Panamanian
legislature, the National Assembly of Representatives, demonstrated
its preference of terms when it passed a December 1989 resolution
that "the Republic of Panama is declared to be in a state of war
while the aggression [U.S. sanctions] lasts." Noriega pointed out that
Ronald Reagan had imposed the sanctions under the provisions of
the War Powers Act.[12]

Spokesmen for the Soviet Union have characterized the state
of U.S.-Soviet economic relations during the long years of the cold
war as one of "economic warfare."[13] In 1982 the Soviet foreign
trade minister, Nikolai Patolichev, charged the United States with
conducting an economic war against the Soviet Union and called
for the U.S. government "once and for all to cease using trade as a
weapon."[14] In May 1981, at a major KGB conference in Moscow,
an ailing Leonid Brezhnev, general secretary of the Communist
Party, alleged that Ronald Reagan had committed to "a further
expansion of the arms race...to erase the gains of international
socialism through provocations...[and] economic warfare." In 1983
Vladimar Kryuchkov, head of the KGB's First Service, expressed
serious concern about the U.S. strategy of "economic warfare."[15]
The *New Encyclopaedia Britannica* registered concurrence when it
described the cold war as an "economic war." However, in 1984
Richard Perle, then assistant secretary of defense for international
security policy, wrote, "The Reagan Administration has no desire to

conduct economic war against the Soviet Union or Warsaw Pact countries." Nevertheless, throughout this same article Perle took the economic offensive, calling for a revision of the Export Administration Act "providing for sharper definitions and tougher sanctions" and citing the need "to overhaul and modernize the existing system of controlling military relevant Western technology."[16] In 1982 the U.S. Office of Technology Assessment characterized the administration's call for a Western embargo of Soviet gas and oil equipment "tantamount to economic warfare." In retrospect Roger Robinson, credited with being the principal author of national security decision directive 66 (NSDD-66), has characterized that Reagan administration document as "tantamount to a secret declaration of economic war on the Soviet Union."[17]

In 1991 Friedman and Lebard wrote, "The American penchant for engaging in economic warfare to solve conflicts has a long history."[18]

In 1980 Bani-Sadr, Iran's foreign minister, announced that Iran intended to withdraw all its money from U.S. banks. The U.S. response indicated its interpretation of the Iranian initiative to be "tantamount to a declaration of economic warfare against the United States."[19]

In mid-1994, when the United States was threatening to use economic force to persuade the North Koreans to abandon their plans to develop nuclear weapons, the North Koreans issued the statement that they viewed invoking sanctions as equivalent to declaring war.

Sanctions is the most widely used term in the lexicon of economic force, yet the least descriptive, least meaningful one. Nevertheless, the term has great utility for the statesman and the media, for through common usage it has come to represent the full panoply of economic-force activity. It is so entrenched in the vocabulary that it is likely to survive, if only in the short term. However, since it means everything, in analytical terms it means nothing, which of course gives it utility in the language of diplomacy. There are problems with the word itself, since it is one of the few con-tranyms in the English language; that is, it has two opposing defin-itions. On the one hand, we use *sanction* to indicate "authoritative approval or permission"; on the other, the term is used to denote an instrument of disapproval employing "coercive action."[20] Although the word has utility in less probing, less analytical undertakings, it will be avoided in these pages whenever possible.

At the end of this text there is a glossary of terms that relate to our subject. The definitions are designed to provide a consistency within the context of this effort and to serve serious students of eco-nomic conflict. The following terms, extracted from the glossary, are particularly significant:

—*economic power:* the capacity to influence the course of events using economic instruments
—*economic force:* the application of economic power
—*economic support:* the award of economic benefits to influence the recipient's behavior, to reward it, or for humanitarian reasons
—*economic competition:* the natural contention between nations, car-tels, and international industries and corporations to acquire mar-kets and goods for national or commercial benefit
—*economic coercion:* a limited use of economic force to achieve a limited objective, normally accompanied by the use of political force
—*trade warfare:* the use of the economic instrument by two adver-saries whose objectives are economic, normally accompanied by the use of political but not military force
—*economic warfare:* a major use of economic force to change the behavior of or extract an advantage from an adversary, normally accompanied by the use of political force and sometimes by the use of military force
—*economic conflict:* a state that includes either economic coercion, trade warfare, or economic warfare or any combination of the three

The term *force* is commonly associated with the use of the military. As the term is used here, force can be exerted through the use of any one of the instruments available to an international power. These instruments may include the military, the diplomatic, and the economic. (They may also include the psychological or the social, depending upon how the instruments of power are defined.)

Terms used for centuries to describe military activities have found their way into the lexicon of other instruments of force. Paul Kennedy has written, "The language used to describe international trade and investment has become increasingly military in nature; industries are described as 'coming under siege'; markets are 'captured' or 'surrendered'."[21]

The reliance on military terminology in these definitions has several advantages. For one, after centuries of being filtered through analytical studies, military terminology has become precise. Not only is it explicit, but it also has the advantage of being familiar to a wide segment of the concerned population.

Throughout this work the terms *political* and *diplomatic* may appear to be used interchangeably. However, distinctions are made. The term *political* is used when describing a force or power, as in "political force." The term *diplomatic* may be used when describing an activity, as in "diplomatic initiatives." Some academics seem to favor the term *diplomatic* as being most relevant and descriptive in both cases.[22] However, there is a meaningful difference between the terms that justifies using them in their proper contexts.

Economic statecraft has also been used to define the dynamics of international political activity that impinges on the use of economic force.

The definitions proposed in the glossary often depart radically from those found in the contemporary literature. For example, Nincic and Wallenstein define *economic warfare* as "purely economic actions directed to a military objective." The definition provided in these pages does not limit economic warfare to a specific objective, military or otherwise. Nincic and Wallenstein define *economic coercion* as the "imposition of pain by one government on another in order to gain some potential goal."[23] The definition of *economic coercion* provided here does not limit either the user or the target to a government (either may be a multinational body, such as the United Nations, or a multinational corporation). Nor does it limit the activity to only a political goal (it could be economic).

The common element found in figure 4 (chapter 3) across the categories of economic support, competition, coercion, and war is that each to some degree relies upon the use of the economic instrument to achieve an objective. However, only in economic competition and the trade war is the objective purely economic. In economic support, coercion, and war, the objective routinely transcends economics and will include political, military, and possibly even social goals.

Chapter 3

The Problem

———————————————■———

Happy is the city which in time of peace thinks of war.

Inscription in the armory of Venice.

The United States has been derelict in preparing for and in employing economic force. While the country devotes much of its national energy and treasure to preparing for and conducting military and political conflict, the leadership has done little to prepare to engage in economic conflict, either in defense or in offense. Because it is poorly understood, poorly taught, and poorly employed, economic force, once committed, often has been ineffectual.

It is not as if the nation has not used economic force or does not intend to use it or should not prepare defenses against economic aggression. It has been used often, and there is a growing consensus among knowledgeable observers that as public discomfort with the

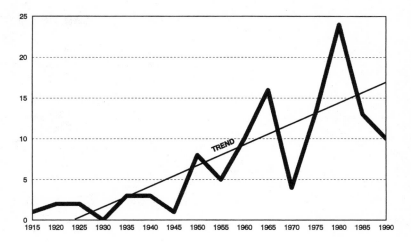

Figure 1
Number of Sanctions Episodes Initiated, 1915–90

Source: Data from Hufbauer, Schott, and Elliot, *Economic Sanctions Reconsidered*, 2d ed., 33.
Note: Does not include U.S.-UN versus Iraq.

use of military force and covert action in international competition has grown, economic force has become a more palatable option. Certainly there has been a major shift in the relationships between the old cold war adversaries. In 1993 a senior Clinton adviser was quoted as saying, "Economics has replaced traditional military security as the centerpiece of U.S.-Russia relations."[1] While the current U.S.-Russian accommodation does not signal the end of the utility of U.S. military force, it does change the nature of that utility, and it does enhance the global potential of the economic instrument.

Increasing Use of Economic Force

Gary Clyde Hufbauer, Jeffrey J. Schott, and Kimberly Ann Elliot, having carefully traced the evolution of the use of economic "sanctions," concluded that "sanctions have been deployed more frequently with each passing decade." (See figures 1 and 2.) Former U.S. commerce secretary C. William Verity has said, "What's going

18

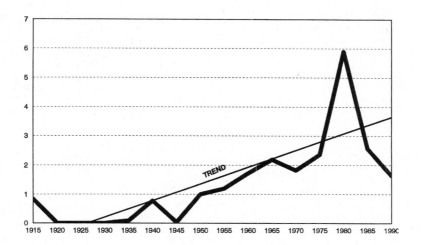

Figure 2
Aggregate Annual Cost to the Target Countries of Sanctions Initiated, 1915–90 (each fifth year, billions of 1990 dollars)
Source: Data from Hufbauer, Schott, and Elliot, *Economic Sanctions Reconsidered*, 2d ed., 33.
Note: Does not include U.S.-UN versus Iraq.

to happen in the 1990's is economic warfare." Les Aspin, former chairman of the House Armed Services Committee and former secretary of defense, has said, "In the new world, economics is power, whereas military power used to be power. You will see a school of thought emerging that the organizing principle of policy ought to be nationalistic economics: how we organize ourselves, how we organize our military, debt, foreign policy."[2]

Scholars Drew Christiansen and Gerard Powers, of the Office of International Justice and Peace, wrote in 1993, "Nuclear weapons were the weapons of choice for the superpowers during the cold war; economic sanctions seem to be the weapon of choice to the United Nations in its aftermath." Edward N. Luttwak agrees: "Patient investment capital is replacing firepower, the development of civilian products is displacing military innovation and the penetration of markets is displacing military garrisons on foreign soil."[3]

While he served as secretary of defense, Caspar Weinberger

laid down five rules that should be followed prior to the commitment of U.S. military force. The fifth rule was that "a determination must be made that all other means short of [military] force have been tried and found wanting."[4] The Weinberger rules were widely accepted among military strategists, including the chairman of the Joint Chiefs of Staff, Colin Powell, and are still considered by many to provide thresholds that should be crossed before committing military force. This fifth rule dictates that economic force must always be considered and, if practical, used in lieu of or prior to military force.

Naval strategist James Stavridis has warned that as long as there is a wide economic disparity between countries of the industrialized Northern Hemisphere and those of the Southern, there will be "economic conflict." He envisions third world countries sponsoring terrorists and using unconventional economic instruments to discomfit the West, generating economic wars. He foresees a war between Japan and other Pacific Rim nations occurring before a U.S.-Japanese confrontation.[5]

In 1993 James Carville, a senior adviser to the Clinton administration, predicted a "modern economic war." Futurist Paul Kennedy, in his advice on preparing for the twenty-first century, wrote, "With the Cold War over, many writers now argue that military rivalries and arms races are being replaced by economic rivalries, technology races, and forms of commercial warfare." In 1993 Mike Moore editorialized, "In cases where nations must act forthrightly against other nations, sanctions offer an option short of war."[6] James Ngobi, secretary of the UN Sanctions Committees, insists that there is a growing appreciation that economic force can provide a medium to promote the commonweal of the international community through "peaceful" means.

In early 1994 it seemed obvious that the sitting president was reluctant to use military force until other options had been exhausted. In the words of columnist Jim Hoagland, "To be blunt, Clinton is trying to buy off the Ukrainians and North Koreans [in his efforts to stem nuclear proliferation]. He dangles ensnaring deals instead of issuing bold ultimatums and organizing international coalitions." Hoagland held that Bill Clinton was merely reflecting the temper of his constituency "because Congress and the American electorate prefer not to accept the costs and responsibility of enforcing global ultimatums now that the Soviet threat has disappeared."[7]

Senator John Glenn, a member of the Armed Services and Intelligence Committees, counseling that America's relations with China were at a critical crossroads in late 1993, proposed that the United States should undertake seven initiatives. Five of the seven involved the use of economic force.[8]

In 1991 the Japanese magazine *Mainichi* published an article that warned, "The voices of those who say the end of the gulf war will herald the beginning of a war between the U.S. and Japan are growing louder. ... This time the war will not be military but economic."[9]

One sure sign that a national threat is in the public consciousness is when it becomes the central plot of contemporary novels. There were at least four popular novels in the 1992–94 time frame that focused on economic conflict: Larry Bond's *Cauldron,* Michael Crichton's *Rising Sun,* Jack Anderson's *The Japan Conspiracy,* and Tom Clancy's *Debt of Honor.*[10]

In 1990 the chairman of the Senate Intelligence Committee, David L. Boren, warned that the United States risks losing its superpower status unless it refocuses its attention on the problems of exercising economic vis-à-vis military power. Columnist Jim Hoagland has written, "Sanctions are the policy tool of choice in the new World Order."[11]

Senator Carl Levin, chairman of the Senate Armed Services Subcommittee on Conventional Forces and Alliance Defenses, has said, "The economic battlefield is going to be the next major battle." Senator Jesse Helms has predicted that food exports "probably will be our main foreign policy lever." Journalist Bruce W. Nelan, writing in *Time* magazine, predicts, "Just as wars—two World Wars and equally important, the cold war—dominated the geopolitical map of the 20th century, economics will rule the 21st."[12]

These quotations are but a few of dozens made by contemporary policymakers and scholars. There is a growing consensus that economic force is becoming increasingly useful in the exercise of national power.[13] In some instances economic force is the principal instrument being used to influence an adversary. In others it may play a supporting role where military or political forces dominate.

Notwithstanding the strength of these trends, the consensus that the use of economic force will become more important and useful is not complete. George McGovern, former senator from South Dakota and Democratic candidate for president in 1972, calls embargoes of little states "self-defeating" and "anachronisms of the now dead Cold War."[14] In addition there is a countervailing movement abroad that seeks to promote "international commercial disarmament." The movement puts greater emphasis on less hostile competition between nations than on international economic conflict, but the disarmament does impinge on the use of economic force as well. The December 1988 Uruguay Round of the General Agreement on Tariffs and Trade negotiations specifically addressed trade disarmament issues. A member of the U.S. GATT delegation for the Uruguay Round wrote, "There is growing consensus that if we can defuse the trade weapons that encourage trade conflict, this in itself will create a better environment for peace, and prosperity based on growth." He characterized the Uruguay Round as a "good start in the direction of commercial disarmament."[15]

The U.S. leadership appears to be of two minds on the issue of international economic relations. On the one hand there appears to be a continuing effort to encourage "free trade" and eliminate barriers that impede that goal. There appears to be a consensus that trade warfare, as contrasted with economic coercion, is destructive for all parties involved. On the other hand the leadership finds the use of economic force in pursuit of national security objectives to be useful and preferable to more violent options.

On balance there appears to be sufficient evidence to support the postulate that the use of economic force to achieve national security objectives has increased substantially over the past half century. Whether or not it will continue to be employed with increasing frequency will depend upon the kind of world order there will be in the 1990s and beyond, and the willingness of major economic powers to use economic coercion. Testing of this aspect of the postulate should proceed from an analysis of U.S. requirements for and the utility of all forms of national power, not just the economic.

The Study of Economic Conflict

There are dozens of schools and universities dedicated to teaching the art of military warfare, including the National War University with its component National War College and the Industrial College of the Armed Forces. Many private and state universities host army, navy, and air force ROTC programs. The Department of State has its Foreign Service Institute to educate and train diplomats and soldiers in the arts of the employment of international diplomatic force. There are many schools of international relations. However, there is not a single U.S. school, large or small, dedicated to the study of the use of economic force. Nor is there even a single comprehensive course of study in any government or private institution dedicated to this important subject. The school where one would be confident that the subject would be taught is the Industrial College of the Armed Forces. In fact no such course is now offered. In 1950 and 1951 there was one brief period of instruction offered on economic war. However, it was a superficial treatment that has been abandoned.[16]

Not only is the subject of the employment of economic force not studied; neither is it practiced (gamed). The Pentagon and other agencies of government have engaged in hundreds of major political-military games. The armed services conduct extensive war games to hone their military skills. However, there has apparently never been a dynamic economic war game played anywhere. Nor are the economic dimensions of international conflict routinely played in multidisciplinary war games.

In 1990 Milner and Baldwin prepared an annotated bibliography of writings on this subject and concluded that the study of "the political economy of national security can be described as nascent." Clinton administration economic guru Laura Tyson wrote a lengthy scholarly book on "trade conflict" with only passing references to "sanctions" and trade "retaliations."[17]

In 1979 the academic Martin Shubik wrote, "It is surprising how small the literature is on economic warfare of any sort, involving hot or cold wars. One is hard put to find twenty books. Many of them are of the era of World War II."[18] Shubik's assessment may be dated, and too harsh. A bibliography is presented here that identifies more capable works than he would lead us to believe have been written. Nevertheless, his judgment as to the paucity of good analysis and reporting on the subject is supportable. In the ten years between Shubik's assessment and the time of this writing, there have been few meaningful contributions from any source. For example, there was not a single title on economic war in the 1989 issue of *The Reader's Catalog.* Gunnar Adler-Karlsson, in his comprehensive study *Western Economic Warfare, 1947–1967,* wrote, "In the author's attempt to break this conspiracy of silence, the great lack of previous writings has of course been an obstacle."[19]

Economist Robert J. Samuelson reviewed the best books on economics for 1989. Of the seven that made his list, not one displayed even a remote concern for the impact of economic conflict on U.S. national security. In 1958 professor of economics Thomas C. Schelling of Yale produced a valuable work, *International Economics,* that addressed, *inter alia,* "economic warfare and strategic trade controls." One of the best analyses of the dynamics of economic force was written by Johan Galtung in 1967.[20] However, none of these worthy efforts provides the sound intellectual footing required for the employment of and defense against economic force that is the objective of this work.

Hufbauer, Schott, and Elliot's excellent analysis of the use of "sanctions" by nations during this century was published in 1985, with an updated second edition in 1990. It is a valuable contribution, and this author is greatly indebted to it. However, it does not address the concerns of the doctrine, morality, tactics, strategy, or principles of economic conflict—the concerns of this effort. Barry Carter's *International Economic Sanctions* provides valuable analyses and recommendations on the legislative requirements for the effective use of the economic tool. The volume *Power, Economics, and Security: The United States and Japan in Focus,* funded by the Pew Charitable Trust, provides some insights but not the basic analysis sought here. Professor Yuan-li Wu's 1952 *Economic Warfare* made a significant contribution, but it was a pioneer effort. Klaus Knorr's *The Power of Nations* sheds insightful and valuable but too little light on the economic component of international power for the practitioner of the art. Thomas Schelling's "Economic Warfare" chapter in his *International Economics* is helpful.[21] Notwithstanding these noteworthy contributions, the art of economic conflict is poorly understood, poorly analyzed, and poorly reported.[22]

Although official statements of national strategy invariably cite the importance of the nation's economy to the national welfare, statements of national strategy consistently fail to address the role of economic force. State Department counselor Robert B. Zoellick put it best when he said to Congress, "Economic policy...must become an increasingly critical component of the United States foreign policy strategy." Henry Kissinger has written, "The United States must recognize the need for a deliberate [economic] strategy."[23]

The significance of economic power is generally recognized. Kissinger, Knorr, Schelling, and others agree. But power and force are two different commodities. National power—to include economic power—is a potential, just as the tons of water being captured by a dam has energy potential. Force is the application of that power, just like the water that, released from behind the dam, rushes down spillways to turn turbines that generate electricity. In our rubric, force equates to economic coercion, trade wars, and economic warfare.

There has been virtually nothing of consequence written about the strategy of economic conflict. There has been even less written about the tactics of the application of this force. There are no theories on the best way to apply economic force when pursuing national objectives. There are no road maps as to the how, when, where, and why of the use of economic force.

A sound strategy is based on concepts, detailed planning, and an appreciation of the situation. Sound tactics are based on the identification of requisite implementing skills. A fifteen-year search of the relevant literature has failed to elicit a single substantive work that addresses either the strategy or tactics of economic conflict. Columnist Jim Hoagland said it well: "The expanding use of sanctions has not been accompanied by concentrated thought and discussion about the long-term effect, and effectiveness, of trade embargoes that have a greater ability than ever before to devastate the country and people they are supposed to rescue."[24]

Economic conflict is a complex subject. It has seldom been analyzed and rationalized as a major instrument to achieve national objectives. With rare exceptions those good works that have been published have been devoted to condemning or ignoring the use of the economic instrument. Few works have prescribed how the instrument should be used or have appraised its potential. This work will attempt to fill some of those voids.

The Study of Seapower in Economic Conflict

There has also been little written about the role of seapower as a military component of economic war. It enjoys but a passing reference in U.S. Navy doctrinal publications at both the strategic and the tactical level. However, historically seapower has played a prominent and at times quintessential role in economic conflict. As long as the oceans remain the principal highways for transport of the great bulk of international commerce, as long as only limited port, harbor, and passage choke points are available to ocean-borne commerce, seapower will be an important instrument in enforcing economic mandates. With the growth of commercial air transport between nations, seapower may lose the near monopoly on the role of enforcer of economic investments it enjoyed a century ago. However, seapower—which of course may also have a powerful air component—remains the military tool of choice to enforce the mandates imposed during economic hostilities.

Doctrine

Through the centuries there have been many great military philosophers. They include Thucydides, Sun Tzu, Julius Caesar, Karl von Clausewitz, Antoine Henri Jomini, Alfred Thayer Mahan, Frederick the Great, and Helmuth von Moltke, to name a few. There are many brilliant contemporary military analysts, such as Liddell Hart and John Keegan, writing on the subject of military force for a wide audience in dozens of professional journals, newspapers, and books. Likewise, there have been scores of international political theorists, among them Niccolò Machiavelli, Alighieri Dante, Hugo Grotius, Robert Strausz-Hupe, Halford Mackinder, Harold and Margaret Sprout, and Ho Chi Minh. The long list of contemporary international political theorists includes Morton Halperin, Herman Kahn, Henry Kissinger, Morton Kaplan, Hans Morgenthau, and Harold Lasswell. Paul Smith authored a tract *On Political War* in 1990.[25] However, when we turn our attention to economic force, it is impossible to find a single scholar of the stature of any of these historic figures whose name is associated with a philosophy of economic force.[26] Neither Karl Marx, Vladimir I. Lenin, nor Friedrich Engels qualifies. They were moralists seeking secular salvation through economic liberation who gave little thought to employing the economic instrument as a weapon. Other economic theorists such as Adam Smith, Richard

Cobden, and John Stuart Mill advocated free trade as the alternative to international conflict, not the use of trade as an instrument of force. There are no Sun Tzus, Adam Smiths, or Machiavellis of economic conflict. (See table 1.)

The lack of such an intellectual heritage deprives the United States (and others) of a basis for building a doctrinal foundation for the examination of the use of economic force in the pursuit of national objectives. There can be no progress made in establishing the essential frameworks for the use of the economic instrument until the dynamics of such utility are adequately studied and rationalized.

U.S. Organization for Economic Conflict

The Department of Defense's primary authority and responsibility for managing and employing military force are clearly defined. Likewise, the Department of State's primary authority and responsibility for managing and employing U.S. political force in international relations are clearly defined. The United Nations has sanctions committees. However, there is no department or agency within the U.S. federal government that has the primary responsibility for managing and employing economic force. In this respect the U.S. bureaucracy is singular, for as Sony chairman Akio Morita has been quoted as saying that America is the only industrial nation without a Department of Industry.[27]

Many countries have special bureaus to manage special trade commodities. For example, Australia and Canada have wheat boards, Russia has Exporthleb, Poland has Rolinplex, Iran has EKTA, and Japan has a food agency. The United States has no such bureau.[28]

During World War II the United States did organize for the employment of economic force in a fundamental fashion. The Board of Economic Warfare was activated, and future director of the Central Intelligence Agency William Casey, then a junior naval officer, was one of its consultants. Herb Meyer, former president of the

Table 1

The Study, Management, and Practice of Economic versus Political and Military Conflict

	Political	Military	Economic
Doctrine, strategy, and tactics	Aristotle, Machiavelli, Ho Chi Minh (*inter alia*)	Sun Tzu, Thucydides, Clausewitz, (*inter alia*)	?
Education	Universities, Foreign Service Institute	Universities, war colleges, skill schools	?
Training and practice	Political/military games	Political/military games, operational training exercises	?
Responsible	Department of State	Department of Defense	?

Rand Corporation, credits Casey with practically inventing this "American concept of warfare when he served with the Economic Warfare Board."[29]

In large measure because of the magnitude of its operations, its operational orientation, and its freer access to discretionary funds, the Department of Defense has probably allocated more resources to the study of economic force than all the resources committed by the Departments of State, Commerce, and Treasury and the National Security Council combined. In the early 1980s Defense maintained an International Trade and Security Policy staff (under-secretary of defense for policy) that, by charter, had an interest in economic conflict. It is apparent, however, that their role was to monitor economic activity and that they were not disposed to take initiatives to define or clarify policies or initiate actions related to economic conflict.

In 1989, citing a new emphasis on economic issues, the international policy staffs of the Pentagon were reorganized under a deputy undersecretary of defense for strategy and resources.[30] The undersecretariat was organized with what was described as a "strong economic component." However, the charter of the economic component reportedly would focus on armaments cooperation and technical competitiveness "as well as other broad issues."

While the Department of Defense (DoD) appears to have best organized its resources to study the use of economic force, both its legitimate jurisdiction and its proclivity appear to inhibit real progress in the training and organization for economic conflict. Nevertheless, the entry of DoD into the economic policy arena is the occasion for serious concern among those departments and agencies whose charters give them jurisdiction in such matters. The Departments of Commerce, Treasury, and State find the economic impact and influence of the Advanced Research Projects Agency, the Defense Science Board, and the Office of the Secretary of Defense for International Security Policy to be intrusive in areas where they have principal authorities. An article in the *Journal of Commerce* makes this point: "The size of [DoD's] financial resources and the deference paid to its judgments about national security needs make it all too easy for the Pentagon to act on such [economic] matters while the rest of official Washington debates." The article goes on to press the point that international economic issues are "matters of commercial policy" not properly within the purview of DoD.[31]

William Safire has recommended the creation of a "council on economic intervention" as a way to "turn up the economic heat when appeals to conscience or international organizations fail."[32]

In 1989 the Central Intelligence Agency made a major commitment to analyze the threat of economic coercion. In September of that year CIA director William Webster warned of the threat of Soviet high-technology espionage. He also identified the increased integration of international financial markets and drug cartels as being national security risks for the United States. "Along with the globalization of international finance has come the greater use of the financial system by government and groups whose objectives threaten our national security interests." Webster continued, "The international narcotics money laundering industry, as well as terrorist activities, gray arms purchases, technology transfer and nuclear proliferation, are often funded through the world's financial networks." As to the extent of the agency's commitment, Webster said, "Intelligence on economic developments and other issues has never been more important."[33]

By June 1990 the U.S. National Security Agency (NSA) had begun planning to focus its global electronic capability on the world economy. This agency of the Department of Defense, faced with the perception of the reduction of the Soviet military threat and the recognition of the increasing importance of economic conflict, prepared to reorient against the most likely, rather than the most destructive, threat to U.S. national security.[34]

The American businessman may not be enthusiastic about NSA's focus on the world economy, fearing that the agency could abuse its charter in a way that would be contrary to American business. As businessman Gregor Peterson has written, "If NSA can monitor the activities of foreign governments and businesses, it can certainly monitor domestic business as well."[35] It seems safe to conclude, however, that whatever the quality or magnitude of the CIA or NSA analyses of other nations' economic conditions and the nature of the economic threats they pose to the United States, the value of these products is negligible if there are no dedicated users of them.

Within the federal bureaucracy there are mechanisms to manage implementation of details of relevant laws that limit select exports and imports. Most important, there is the Office of Foreign Asset Control (FAC) Directorate of the Treasury Department, known as the "watchdog of U.S. sanctions." There is also the management of the Munitions Control List administered by the State Department. There is the management of the Commodity Control List administered by the Commerce Department. The United

States participated in the informal organization the Coordinating Committee (COCOM), composed of certain NATO countries dedicated to limiting exports of equipment and materials to the Soviet Union. There is the State Department's Overseas Security Advisory Council, made up of several hundred U.S. corporations and a few government agencies. However, these activities are accounting and enforcement programs, not policy advocates. An embryonic National Economic Commission is focused on promoting the national economy in peaceful competition, not economic conflict.

The Role of Economic Conflict in National Strategy

An integrated national strategy must include three components: military, political, and economic. In part because responsibility is fixed for the military and political components of U.S. strategy, they are thoroughly addressed in statements of national strategy.

Currently there is no tool of international relations that is more widely employed or discussed—albeit seldom in analytic terms—than economic force. On any given day the world's leading newspapers consistently deliver one or more leading articles that report on details of the subject. Each edition of professional journals oriented toward international relations has at least one article that refers to an economic-conflict event. The widespread use of economic force and the widespread debates about it have shaped how we think about international relations.

While the economic component may be addressed in statements of national strategy, it is only in terms of economic ends and means. The economic component has never been addressed in terms of the application of and defense against the use of economic force to achieve national objectives. The United States lacks an integrated national strategy because it has failed to address a basic, important element of such a strategy.

One critical barometer of the degree of a government's commitment to an instrument of power is the allocation of resources.

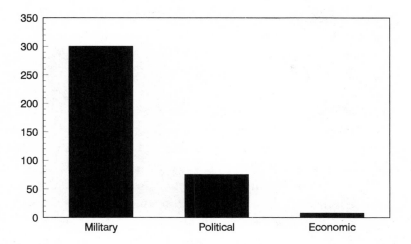

Figure 3
Relative Investments for the Employment of Force (billions of U.S. dollars)

The United States routinely spends some $300 billion a year preparing to use or deter the use of military force. Calculating the resources allocated to the use of political force is more difficult. However, the State Department's budget is about $4 billion. the budget for the Office of Foreign Asset Control is a mere $2.5 million annually. Notwithstanding how one accounts for the U.S. resources authorized for the use of economic force, one must conclude that they are so small, compared with the resources devoted to the military and political components, that they cannot be measured. (See figure 3.)

The Ubiquity of Economic Conflict

Economic force has many facets. The use of the economic instrument covers a broad spectrum from the awarding of economic incentives to the deprivation of economic essentials. The users of economic force range from world bodies through entities such as nations, cartels, multinational corporations, and individuals both legal and illegal (i.e. drug cartels, the Mafia, warlords, smugglers, etc.). Suffering from the misnomer of the popular, comprehensive term *sanctions,* economic force is universally viewed as a simple, single-faceted instrument. In fact economic force is polymorphic and more complex than the term *sanctions* implies.

The nation is not the only entity that may engage in economic conflict. A multinational organization—for example, the League of Nations or the United Nations—may engage in economic war, as may multinational corporations or cartels. Individual consumers may use the economic instrument to protest a policy or activity of a firm or a nation, as did many, for example, in their boycott of South African products. National leaders may use economic force against their populace, as in the example of China inflicting economic punishment on families for producing more than the allotted number of children. A matrix of possible users and targets of economic conflict is presented in table 2.

Economic conflict is not limited to the international scene. It can also be waged in intranational conflict (civil war). In 1990 the Soviet Union, faced with a Lithuanian declaration of independence, wielded the economic instrument against that Baltic republic in an attempt to force the Lithuanians to renounce their separatist intentions. That confrontation provided a classic example of the interplay among the three most commonly used, most potent national instruments: military, political, and economic force. One of the Soviets' first reactions to the Lithuanian declaration was to march their tanks through Vilnius in a display of military force. Economic pressure was subsequently initiated against the "rebel" state with the imposition of "sanctions." The USSR waged political war against the Lithuanians on a broad front, from President Mikhail Gorbachev's personal appeal to the Lithuanian populace, to Soviet diplomatic initiatives to mitigate damage in East–West relations. The Soviet crisis came at a critical time when U.S.–Soviet trade relations were about to be recast. Significantly, the most potent, reasonable response

Table 2

The Ubiquity of Economic Conflict

TARGET

USER	Nation	Individual(s)	World body	Corporation	Munic./state govt.
Nation	U.S. vs. Cuba, 1960–[1]	U.S. vs. Haitian leaders, 1993–[2]	U.S. vs. UN, 1984–85[3]	Levi Strauss vs. China, 1993[4]	USSR vs. Baltic states 1991[5]
Individual(s)	China vs. Chinese, 1993–[6]	Irish tenants vs. Capt. Boycott, 1880[7]	Butch Reynolds vs. IAAF, 1993[8]	Eishiro Saito vs. Japanese steel corporations, 1993[9]	San Francisco vs. table grape farmers, 1988[10]
World body	League of Nations vs. Greece, 1925[11]	UN vs. Bobby Fischer, 1993[12]	[13]	[14]	[15]
Corporation	Arab League blacklisting firms trading with Israel, 1948[16]	Legal firm vs. Pan Am 103 victims 1993[17]	International grain merchants vs. UN, 1968–75[18]	VW vs. GM, 1993[19]	Table grape farmers vs. San Francisco, 1988[20]
Munic./state govt.	Lithuania vs. USSR, 1990[21]	Celebrities vs. Colorado, 1992[22]	[23]	San Francisco vs. table grape farmers, 1988[24]	D.C. vs. Virginia and Maryland, continuing[25]

Notes:

1. United States invoked embargo upon Cuba in August 1960, which has been expanded and extended into 1995. Purpose is to limit Cuban exportation of revolution and to overthrow communist regime.

2. In June 1993 the United States imposed specific penalties on Haitian military leaders, government officials, and businessmen, freezing their financial assets and banning them from doing commercial business in the United States. Purpose was to return Aristide to presidency.

3. On 31 December 1984 the United States terminated its membership in the United Nations Educational, Scientific and Cultural Organization for that organization's "endemic hostility towards the institutions of a free society." The United States had been supplying one-quarter of UNESCO's funding.

(*continued*)

4. In 1993 the Levi Strauss Corporation decided to terminate its operations in China to protest that country's "pervasive violations" of human rights.

5. In 1991 the Soviet Union conducted what some termed "economic war" against the Soviet states Latvia, Estonia, and Lithuania when they agitated for their independence from Moscow.

6. China's family-planning program coerces couples into limiting the number of children they produce or suffer a fine or loss of their jobs.

7. In 1880, in protest over threats of eviction, Irish tenants, suffering through a famine, boycotted any communications with landlord manager Captain Charles Cunningham Boycott, who was then forced to import workers from Ulster to harvest the crops.

8. Track and field's world governing body, the IAAF, barred U.S. 400-meter star Butch Reynolds from international competition, alleging illegal use of steroids. Reynolds imposed one of the individual's most potent economic weapons on the IAAF by filing suit in a U.S. federal court. He was awarded a $27.3 million judgment. The IAAF refused to comply with the court's finding. Reynolds did collect $700,000 from Mobil Oil Co., a sponsor of the event, in a separate suit.

9. On 7 April 1993 Eishiro Saito, a steel importer from Osaka, Japan, sent a letter to American steel companies accusing Japan's steel producers of rigging steel prices through a private cartel. A spokesman for the Japanese steel industry denied the accusation.

10. In 1988 the city of San Francisco supported a ban on table grapes, which posed an economic hardship on both individual farmers and their cooperatives. The ban backfired, for the agricultural associations retaliated by blacklisting San Francisco as a convention center, costing the city some $45 million in convention revenue.

11. In a border conflict of 1925 Greece occupied Bulgarian territory. The League of Nations demanded withdrawal of the Greek military and threatened to use economic force under Article 16. The Greeks evacuated Bulgaria.

12. In May 1992 the United Nations imposed an economic embargo on Serbian-controlled Yugoslavia. Bobby Fischer, world chess champion, violated those strictures by competing in a chess match against Boris Spassky in Belgrade. The United States, as a UN member and representative, indicted Fischer for "trading with the enemy."

13. While it is possible that one world body could bring economic force against another, no such event was identified in this search.

14. Since the nation is normally interposed between a corporation and a world body, it seems unlikely—but not impossible—that two such entities would engage in economic conflict.

15. Since a nation is normally interposed between a municipal or state government and a world body, it seems unlikely—but not impossible—that two such entities would engage in economic conflict.

16. From before the creation of the state of Israel, the Arab League has blacklisted and graylisted firms doing business with the Israelis.

the United States could have used against the USSR to support Lithuania's independence was the withholding of certain economic privileges about to be extended to the Soviet Union (another use of economic force).

The term *economic civil war* has been used to describe the conflict between separate states of the United States when competing for the location or creation of industry. The weapons employed in

---

Notes continued

17. The law firm Hughes, Hubbard and Reed, on behalf of the Libyan government, offered an economic incentive (carrot) to the families of the victims of the terrorist attack on Pan Am 103 to facilitate a deal with the United States to lift its boycott/embargo.

18. In 1968 the United Nations passed Resolution 253, which embargoed Rhodesian exports. Grain merchants effectively circumvented the embargo, shipping an estimated 1.6 million tons of white maize from Rhodesia to countries such as Japan and Belgium during the period 1968 to 1975.

19. While the allegations are still unproven, a dispute between General Motors and Volkswagen provides an excellent example of corporation-versus-corporation economic conflict. When senior executive Jose Ignacio Lopez de Arriortua and seven other senior executives left GM for VW in 1993, it was alleged that they were guilty of industrial espionage in that they took crates of confidential GM papers with them to the German operation.

20. See comment number 10.

21. In 1990 the Lithuanian state, making a bid for independence from the USSR, responded to Russian economic pressures with a boycott and threat to produce its own currency.

22. Hollywood celebrities boycotted the ski resorts of Colorado in protest over a November 1992 anti-gay rights measure passed by the state's voters.

23. See comment number 15.

24. See comment number 10.

25. Intense competition to attract new industries to states within the United States has generated mini-economic wars, also called "bidding wars," characterized by the promise of tax and other incentives. An example of a different kind of economic coercion is the District of Columbia's 1992 proposal to levy a commuter tax on suburban (read Virginia and Maryland) commuters. Fairfax County (Virginia) officials promised to steal business from the district should the D.C. proposal be implemented. In 1993 Virginia's governor-elect, George F. Allen, immediately after his election pledged to "seek a competitive edge" in economic development. He characterized the interstate competition he expected to face as "a war."

such interstate economic conflicts are tax relief and other incentives that may be proffered to a favored industry.[36]

The Spectrum of International Economic Relations

There is a spectrum of international economic activities. The spectrum ranges from economic support (the most benign) to economic warfare (the most aggressive). In between are the categories of economic competition, economic coercion, and trade war.[37] (See figure 4.)

The spectrum represented by the figure is present in both unilateral and multilateral relations between states. It is possible, for example, for a European Community to engage in an economic or trade war (but unlikely for a United Nations). It is very likely that a European Community or a North American Free Trade Agreement block could engage in economic competition (but again, unlikely for an Organization of American States). The trend is toward multilateral use of economic force and away from use by a single nation. There is also a trend to seek the approval and sponsorship of the United Nations. A UN mandate promotes international cohesion (promoting the principle of unity—see chapter 8) and resolves the questions of possible violation of Article 2(4) of the UN Charter, which outlaws the use of force to resolve international disputes (see chapter 5).

Economic support is the carrot, characterized by such economic assistance efforts as the Marshall Plan and Harry Truman's Point Four program. It is used in both national altruism and self-interest. It is often used to reward a nation for supportive behavior (e.g. the U.S. 1990 award of economic benefits to Turkey and Egypt for support of U.S. and UN objectives in the Middle East).

Economic competition is the most common relation between modern industrial states. This portion of the spectrum is also characterized by cooperation and conciliation, with the objective of making the international trade system work better for the benefit of all.

THE ECONOMIC SPECTRUM

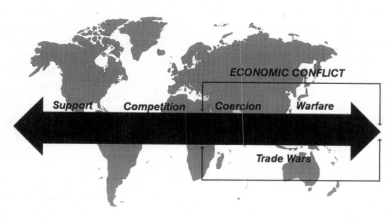

Figure 4
A Spectrum of Economic Activities

The economic competition portion of this spectrum has been submitted to much more detailed analysis and soul searching than has been given to economic conflict. Competitive national economies have been studied by American government, industry, and academia with interesting and sometimes beneficial results.[38] The focus of such efforts has been to determine how the United States can regain its competitive edge over Japanese and European industry.[39]

An example of economic competition that seems meaningful here is the U.S.-Japanese competition for air routes. The United States holds that its airline industry is fighting a series of protectionist initiatives by France, Germany, and Japan. The Japanese view is that the United States has access to more than its share of slots at Tokyo's Narita Airport. Worse, the Japanese complain that American carriers are flying from the United States to Tokyo and Osaka, boarding passengers, and carrying them to Australia and other Asian destinations contrary to agreement.[40]

International economic competition is seldom limited to economic activity, as it may also involve political or even military considerations. The 1993 Saudi decision to purchase $6 billion worth of commercial jets from Boeing and McDonnell Douglas Corporation rather than the European Airbus was made not purely on economic or technological grounds but for political and military reasons as well. Political suasion was generated by President Jimmy Carter to King Fahd personally. Implicit in the negotiations was the continued U.S. military commitment to the integrity and security of Saudi Arabia.[41]

In the early days of the Clinton administration there was much talk about the United States embracing "managed trade" policies. According to Robert Samuelson, managed trade, as described by the Clinton economic spokesmen, is a euphemism for coercing the Japanese to guarantee the import of U.S. products. The danger, says Samuelson, is that such aggressive trade practices could move U.S. relations with Japanese allies from economic competition to trade warfare.[42]

The next step in this progression to maximum economic aggression exhibits two phenomena. One is, for want of a better term, "trade warfare." The other is economic coercion. The distinction between the two is important to this effort. *Trade warfare* is an imprecise, misleading term that is nonetheless widely used in the media. It is the conflict between nations for economic advantage employing economic and, sometimes, political instruments. The military instrument may also be employed in trade warfare, but it would be a relatively nonaggressive supporting weapon. An example of a full-blown mini–trade war—termed the "cod war" in the Polish press—was set off when Danish fishermen were caught by the Polish Coast Guard trawling in Polish waters.[43] In retaliation, Danish boats blocked their Polish neighbors from selling their catches at the Danish port in Bornholm. The Poles responded by blocking Danish boats from selling in Polish ports.

As used here, the term *trade warfare* is imprecise and misleading because it may involve the use of financial or resource instruments in lieu of, or in addition to, trade measures. It also implies an uncharacteristic degree of belligerency—implicit in the term *war*—that should be reserved to describe the condition of economic war. However, the term *trade war* has the advantage of common usage.

A popular scenario as to how a trade war could start was bandied about during the July 1993 Group of Seven Summit. The scenario postulates that the United States, frustrated by Japan's unwillingness to take the drastic economic steps necessary to right the trade imbalance, enacts import thresholds for Japan and uses its economic muscle to impose high tariffs on Japanese auto imports. Japan retaliates with its own tariff barriers. There is popular resentment and a perception of unfair practices in both countries. The United States withdraws some of its military support for Japan from the Western Pacific. Japan rearms and poses a threat to its Asian neighbors not unlike that of the 1930s.

Some would describe the contemporary fight for shares of the world's steel markets a "trade battle," and perhaps even a "trade war." Steel producers from every part of the world are competing ferociously for a dwindling steel market. The United States, Canada, Mexico, Europe, Taiwan, and Japan have each imposed economic strictures on foreign steel they charge has been "dumped" on the international market at prices pegged unfairly low. The European Community imposed punitive tariffs on steel tubing from Eastern producers in November 1992. The EC maintained that since the East European steel plants were owned by the governments, they must be government-subsidized and, by definition, unfair.

The steel controversy is one of the world's most persistent problems. The industry has drastically overproduced, yet countries plagued by high unemployment are reluctant to close steel mills. Hence they have been dumping their steel products on the international market with impunity, violating American trade laws. There are no effective international laws or courts to deter this dumping.

Therefore the United States has relied on its own laws and has imposed economic penalties on offending nations.

On the other hand, Michael Schrage, a columnist for the *Los Angeles Times,* contends that major technology firms have been so intent on forging "strategic alliances" that the interdependence of international industrial commerce makes trade wars an anachronism. Schrage predicts that concerns for the flow of intellectual and financial capital will soon replace concerns for trade deficits and the flow of tangible goods. Gregor Peterson has written, "If 'global' business is indeed a reality, it means old concepts like the trade balance are no longer meaningful. What is domestic? (Are Toyota cars manufactured in the U.S. domestic production?) What is foreign? (When HP manufactures subcomponents in Singapore and ships them to the U.S., are they foreign imports?)"[44]

Economic coercion is the use of the economic instrument by one nation against another to achieve a national objective. The objective of economic coercion is generally not economic; the objective is more likely to be to protect human rights, to undermine a political system, or to encourage an end to a more violent hostility.

Economic war is the ultimate "stick," the use of economic and other forms of force to disrupt an entity's infrastructure so seriously as to force it to accommodate the objectives of the wielding power.

Trade wars characteristically involve two nations or blocs wielding the economic weapon. Economic coercion characteristically implies one state wielding force against a victim that has limited capability to respond with economic force. A trade war is *lex talionis,* tit for tat. Economic coercion is "Take that, and that, and that!" A trade war is likely to inflict greater casualties and exact higher costs from the combatants and the international system of commerce. Economic coercion is generally more focused, having clearer, more limited objectives. Trade wars are accidents of escalating events. Economic coercion is deliberate. Trade wars are more likely to be waged between industrial powers (e.g. Japan vs. the European Community). Economic coercion is more likely to be imposed by a major industrial power against a lesser power (e.g. the United States vs. Uganda). Trade wars are most likely to be resolved by negotiations, in compromise and mutual changes in economic policy. Economic coercions are most likely to end in capitulation or defeat. For the industrial nation, economic coercion can be a useful tool; a trade war is likely to be disaster. A nation would not threaten a trade war for deterrent effect but would use the threat of economic coercion as a deterrent.

Brown-John, in his treatise on international law and "sanctions," wrote, "A major distinction that may, or should, exist between sanctions and economic warfare is that sanctions utilized as an enforcement action should provide no accrued benefit to the states imposing sanctions. That is, the imposing states would not usually derive long-term strategic, economic, or other advantages over the target states. Economic warfare, on the other hand, should be designed to devolve substantial benefit upon the state(s) employing the techniques."[45] This distinction is interesting in that it agrees with the proposition represented in figure 4 that the distinctive feature of economic war is that it represents a higher level of aggressive activity than do "sanctions" (or economic coercion). However, the Brown-John definition is made in terms of the employing state only. If one assumes that the contest between the parties is not a zero-sum affair—that is, that the damage to the target does not equal the political, military, or economic value to the sender—economic war could be waged when there is little or no benefit devolving upon the state(s) employing the techniques, while there is great punishment meted out to the target. For example, there was little benefit, other than moral, that accrued to the United States or other participating nations in the decades-long use of economic force against South Africa. However, the adverse impact upon South Africa was substantial. By the Brown-John standard, this would not constitute economic war. If the Brown-John formula conferred "substantial benefit upon the state(s)" or substantial punishment upon the target, it would.

Major trade wars start over such issues as those that separate the United States and the European Community. In 1993 President Clinton stated that the United States would impose trade "sanctions" against the twelve-nation EC over a dispute involving contract restrictions on the purchase of telephone equipment. The EC confirmed its position on the contract limits, termed the U.S. threat as "neither justified, wise nor necessary," and threatened to retaliate against U.S. companies.[46] Such disagreements could easily escalate into a trade war should they be given priority over the honest desire to promote global free trade.

The transition from economic competition to a more aggressive level of economic activity, be it a trade war or economic coercion, is critical. The trade war, by definition, is more dangerous by far and should be avoided.

A 1993 meeting between Japanese prime minister Kiichi Miyazawa and President Clinton produced the announcement of a "tough" policy toward Japan. Reportedly Clinton told the prime minister that Japan "must" open its markets to U.S. products, implying that absent such access, the United States would use economic force to encourage Japan to do so. In 1993 the Japanese did not signal a counterthreat that could have escalated to a trade war. By 1998 the circumstances might be quite different.

Either a trade war or a state of economic coercion could lead to an economic war, an escalation that will be addressed in the following pages. In general, however, economic war is a major use of economic force normally accompanied by the use of political and perhaps military force.

Figure 4 is not intended to imply that there is a routine progression from economic support to economic warfare. Economic war may be waged without going through a preliminary state of a trade war or economic coercion.

Economic coercion is the principal concern of this book, not trade war. Trade warfare is a different subject more given to analysis by the international economist. However, this is not to denigrate the impact and importance of trade wars. The specter of global trade wars is grim. In 1990 U.S. trade representative Carla Hills predicted dire consequences if the major nations did not reach an understanding on reform of the rules of world trade. She predicted increased protectionism, economic contraction, and job losses worldwide.[47]

While there are exceptions, economic conflict characteristically pits a powerful nation or coalition against a much weaker adversary.[48] Not often is the target state or entity capable of launching an economic counterattack. The defender is more likely to respond with a political instrument than a military one.

As defined here, the common element found in the categories of economic support, economic competition, economic coercion, and economic war is that each to some degree relies upon the use of the economic instrument to achieve an objective. However, only in economic competition is the objective purely economic. In economic support, coercion, and war, the objective routinely transcends economics and will include political, military, and possibly even social goals.

It is popular to equate economic conflict with economic sanctions and to define the term *sanctions* as being inclusive of all instruments of economic force. Such a generality deprives the policymaker of the capability to make distinctions among economic options or to rationalize a strategy that embraces the use of the economic instrument. Table 3 (chapter 6) offers a partial list of the instruments of economic force (including sanctions) that still require detailed definition and analysis.

When a nation joins a conflict, there is generally a mix of forces employed. Figure 5 is a graphic portrayal of some possible national force packages. The relative area of each force on each bar is intended to represent a gross estimate of the magnitude of the commitment. Under each lettered bar there is an example of the conflict that matches that force mix. The point to be made is that there are such force packages, not that they are exactly as represented in

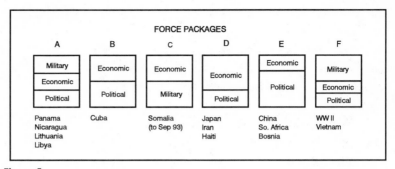

Figure 5
Possible Combinations of National Force

this figure. The single entry under force package C, Somalia, represents a snapshot of the situation in that country in September 1993, when some seven thousand U.S. and two thousand allied military forces were engaged in what was essentially a disaster-relief effort to deliver supplies to the starving Somalis. The lack of a measurable political component in this effort is an anomaly and probably due to the perception that the lack of a Somali political infrastructure inhibited political activity. As the operation developed through 1993, however, the military component of the effort took on increasing importance, with the principal aim becoming the capture and neutralization of Somali strongman General Muhammed Farah Aideed. That effort having failed, and with an abortive firefight on 3 October leaving eight Americans dead and seventy-five wounded, the military approach was abandoned in October 1993, and the objective of UN-U.S. forces in Somalia was reclassified as "political."

Chapter 4

The Threat

———————————————■———————

Girault! Initiate a thorough economic and military
analysis of the Czech and Slovak republics! I want to
know their weaknesses.

The villain Desaix in Larry Bond's novel *Cauldron*

n 1988 David Ignatius and Michael Getler wrote, "If military
conflict is receding, economic warfare seems to be on the rise."
Military historian T. N. Dupuy confirms the decline in the use
of military force to resolve international disputes as a function of an
evolving social maturity: "Increasingly reliable statistics since about
the beginning of the 17th Century demonstrate conclusively that
the incidence and lethality of [military] war has declined."[1]

The possibility that economic warfare may to some degree
supplant military war merits an appraisal of U.S. vulnerabilities to
the economic instrument. Ignatius and Getler elaborate: "From Asia,
the economic challenge to the United States from Japan and a half-
dozen neo–Japans seems to grow daily. Meanwhile, Western Europe

is organizing itself into a trading bloc that may prove as tough and unyielding a competitor as Japan. Indeed, some analysts worry that by the end of the century, the free world may be divided into three great trading blocs—Europe, the Americas and a Japan-dominated Asia—battling for the same limited markets." Friedman and Lebard have written, "It has become conventional wisdom that Japanese economic power and its future growth will outstrip and overwhelm the United States. The question no longer seems to be whether this will take place, but why is it happening?"[2]

Some, such as Edith Cresson, as a serving prime minister of France, see the world in perilous times and at the threshold of a global economic or trade war. Minister Cresson has been quoted as saying, "Japan is an adversary that doesn't play by the rules and has an absolute desire to conquer the world. You have to be naive or blind not to recognize that." Toby Roth of the U.S. House of Representatives has said, "We are on the brink. According to one poll, almost half of the American public believe that the United States is not doing enough to restrict the sale of Japan's goods in our country."[3] At present it appears that these warnings of Japanese commercial dominance have been overstated. Nevertheless, despite Japan's 1993–94 economic slump, it remains an economic giant with great influence and power in the world's marketplace that could have a negative impact on the U.S. economy.

Economic threats to the security and well-being of the United States can take place at several points along the spectrum of economic activity. We are concerned here with the threats that constitute economic coercion or economic warfare. (Trade warfare, as the reader will recall, is at the same level of aggression as economic coercion in the spectrum of economic activity but is not the focus of this effort.) For half a century the United States has been able to write the rules of the game of international economics. For half a century it has been the United States that has had a near monopoly on the aggressive use of the economic instrument to achieve its objectives. There is a consensus among international economic observers that the United States has either lost or is losing this near monopoly and is itself becoming vulnerable to the use of economic force. The consensus identifies the threat as emanating from two sources: a Japanese-dominated Asian bloc and a vitalized European Community.

Americans seem contemptuous of economic threats. Generally, military threats are taken seriously. Generally, economic threats are not. The lack of concern for the consequences of the economic threat may be due to a lack of appreciation of the magnitude or nature of the threat. It may be due to poor communications or the absence of spokesmen for the cause of economic preparedness. Whatever the reason, it has been consistently easier to circle the wagons to meet a military threat than to respond to an economic threat. This sensitivity to the military at the expense of the economic threat may be vanishing with the end of the cold war and with the increasing awareness on the part of the American public that national security has a significant economic component.

The scenarios commonly hypothesized for the use of economic force against the United States focus on three national vulnerabilities. The first is the national deficit (a financial vulnerability). The second is a dependence on other nations for critical resources. The third is a vulnerability to espionage. There is a fourth threat that is not routinely addressed. It is the threat of continued complacency and unwillingness of the United States to address the need to prepare for economic conflict. This fourth threat may be labeled incompetence and is self-imposed.

Financial Vulnerability

In the view of many analysts, U.S. payment imbalances and debt constitute a critical vulnerability. If either the Japanese or the Germans discouraged their investors from foreign lending in general or specifically discouraged the purchase of U.S. Treasury bills, the United States could not finance its debt from its own resources.[4] U.S. interest rates would skyrocket. Market growth would falter, generating an economic stalemate. The dollar would take a nose-dive, and national and international investors would lose confidence in the United States. In 1988 *Time* magazine presented this scenario:

> A local conflict has closed the Strait of Malacca, blockading Japanese tankers laden with Persian Gulf oil from entering the South China Sea. The Japanese Prime Minister places a call to the White House. "Good evening, Mr. President," he says. "Would you consider sending the U.S. Navy to escort my ships through the strait?" The President is well aware that the request is coming from America's biggest creditor. "Why of course," he replies. The Prime Minister thanks him, adding, "I am certain that your help will reassure our private investors enough so that they will buy their usual share of Treasury bills at next Tuesday's auction."[5]

In 1990 Steven Schlosstein presented a similar scenario.[6] He hypothesized that at a future date the Japanese, holding more than two-thirds of America's foreign debt, could refuse to accept any more IOUs, boycotting the purchase of Treasury bonds. Demonstrating the appreciation of the relationship among the three principal forms of national power, Schlosstein extends the scenario forward two years. In this sequence he conceives Mexico defaulting on its debt. The Japanese intercede and rescue the Mexican economy, creating a Mexican state dependent upon the Japanese (a benevolent use of ECONOMIC power to achieve a *diplomatic* objective). Japan subsequently foments a coup in the Philippines, establishing a government disposed to support a Japanese Pacific hegemony. Japan rearms as a nuclear power and dominates a "United States of Asia," hostile to U.S. interests (a use of *political-military* power). While Americans tend to find such scenarios outrageous, they are popular in Japan. Books such as *The Coming War with Japan,* which gain little recognition in the United States, become number one bestsellers in Japan.

The Japanese are aware that the United States and Japan are on a collision course. The current Japanese leadership appears to recognize that it is in Japan's best interests to foster a convergence, not divergence, of the economic policies of the two nations. Notwithstanding the best of intentions, the volatile nature of the economic competition between the two is an unchallenged fact. Opposing economic systems are intrinsic to the cultures of the two states. The fundamental changes necessary before the two systems can be considered compatible and mutually supporting often seem to be beyond the capabilities of either nation. At least in the short term, the best that can be hoped for are concessions and accommodations that will avoid the extremes of economic coercion, a trade war, or economic warfare.

The potential for an economic war brought about by world financial instability has become so ingrained in the public con- sciousness that it has been popularized in a pair of 1993 novels and Tom Clancy's 1994 thriller, *Debt of Honor.* If the public is so conditioned to such conflict, can the real thing be far behind? The dust jacket of one, *Cauldron* by Larry Bond, provides this synopsis:

> In a sequence of events startlingly fresh as tomorrow's headlines, Europe's financial markets plummet in a free-fall that gives way to rampant unemployment in major industrialized countries and famine throughout the Third World. A massive surge of economic refugees from poverty-stricken Eastern Europe and North Africa provokes a bloody reaction by nationalist extremists across Western Europe. A devastating trade war that nobody can win threatens to escalate into a shooting war that everyone will lose.

In columnist Jack Anderson's novel *The Japan Conspiracy,* the theme postulates a greater U.S.-Japanese trade imbalance leading to the organization of a cabal of powerful Japanese known as the Sonno Group (derived from the Japanese expression *Sonno joi,* translated as "Honor the emperor and expel the barbarians"). The Sonno Group rigs a major stock manipulation to bring down the stock market and bankrupt the United States. (The scheme is thwarted by a pair of patriotic U.S. lawyers.)[7]

Critical Resource Vulnerability

In October 1973, on the Jewish holy day Yom Kippur, Egypt and Syria launched an assault into Israel, catching the Israelis by surprise. The Israeli air force was badly punished by the unanticipated effectiveness of ground-to-air missiles supplied by the Soviets. The initial Egyptian assault carried them across the Israeli main battle positions on the Bar-Lev line. The Egyptians occupied and secured a portion of the Sinai. Eventually Israeli counterattacks soundly defeated both Syrian and Egyptian forces.

The capture of Cairo was averted only when American diplomatic pressure coerced the Israelis into a cease-fire on 24 October. The intensity of the American intercession was brought about, at least in part, by a surprise declaration on 20 October of an oil embargo by Arab oil-producing states. The Arab oil embargo employed two weapons. The first was a reduction in production that included a significant initial rollback followed by an additional 5 percent reduction each month. The second weapon consisted of a total ban on the export of oil. Initially the ban was limited to the Netherlands and the United States. It was later imposed upon South Africa, Rhodesia, and Portugal. It was the most dramatic and globally destabilizing act of economic coercion—particularly destabilizing for the United States and Great Britain, and to a lesser extent West Germany—since the 1967 Arab oil embargo against nations friendly to Israel.

The Yom Kippur oil embargo lasted for a period of five months. It had a great political and psychological impact upon the West and was a serious economic blow to the less developed, non-oil-producing nations. During the embargo period Japan lost 17 percent, the United States 18 percent, and Western Europe 16 percent of their normal allocation from the Arab oil producers.[8] However, the impact of this act of economic coercion—Daniel Yergin, in his sweeping history of oil, *The Prize,* describes it as "economic war"—was more than the hostile deprivation of an energy resource to punish and coerce supporters of Israel. The impact was to shape the geopolitical alignment of the globe and demonstrate the power of the economic weapon. It also demonstrated the vulnerability of even the resource-rich United States to a hostile withholding of a critical resource. The embargo set friendly Western nations against one another, with the West Europeans—who were more dependent than the United States upon Arab oil—being accused of being too compliant in their dealings with the Arab states. The United States—having substantial oil reserves, despite being the world's most profligate user of energy—was characterized as being too confrontational. Major U.S. oil companies found themselves on the horns of a dilemma. Could or should ARAMCO, for example, be an instrument in the imposition of an embargo against its own country, the United States? Did it have a choice?

The Arab use of the oil weapon—both the 1973–74 embargo and the subsequent inflation in the price of oil—was an act of economic coercion. It inflicted significant casualties. The U.S. gross national product dropped 6 percent between 1973 and 1975; unemployment doubled to 9 percent. In 1974 the Japanese GNP declined for the first time since the end of World War II. The panic in the global oil market led to a 400 percent increase in oil prices.[9] Less developed nations suffered the most.

The 1973–74 oil embargo demonstrated the economic vulnerability of the United States to limitations of vital resources. Oil is probably the most critical vulnerability. However, there are others. A 1988 Defense Science Board reported the United States to be "dangerously dependent" on foreign military supplies. The finding was independently confirmed by Congress's Office of Technology Assessment and by the General Accounting Office.[10] In 1991 the United States identified twenty-two technologies it classified as crucial to prosperity and security. The list included materials processing, manufacturing, computers, biotechnology, energy, and aeronautic technologies.[11]

The platinum group metals (PGMs), which include such

minerals as palladium, rhodium, and platinum, are critical to many industries in the United States. Their uses range from lasers (the defense industry) to catalytic converters (the automobile industry). The significance of these materials is magnified when one considers that 98.8 percent of the world's known resources are in either the former Soviet Union or in South Africa. No futurologist is so perceptive as to be able to forecast the future of either of these countries into the twenty-first century. However, a hostile Russian embargo of these minerals would be a serious concern. A hostile Russian and South African embargo would be a disaster.

Japan is acutely vulnerable to resource coercion, particularly so to the oil weapon. Some 70 percent of oil imported into Japan transits the Strait of Hormuz, 80 percent the Malacca Straits. Nobutoshi Akao, formerly the chief economic officer in the Japanese embassy in Washington, has told of a Japanese novel, *Yuddan,* that portrays disaster following the limitation of oil imports by virtue of a Gulf war. While wildly imaginative, the scenario portrays a 70 percent cut in oil imports over two hundred days, leading to the deaths of three million Japanese accompanied by catastrophic property losses.[12] It matters little that such a scenario defies analytical corroboration. What is important is that the scenario is sufficiently credible to the Japanese that they perceive their vulnerability to an oil embargo to be critical.[13]

It is quite possible, however, that George Gilder is right, that, "the central event of the twentieth century is the overthrow of matter. In technology, economics, and the politics of nations, wealth in the form of physical resources is steadily declining in value and significance. The powers of mind are everywhere ascendant over the brute force of things."[14] Given such a transition from the primacy of material to intellectual resources, the U.S. critical-resource vulnerability might appear to be diminished. However, there is also the possibility that U.S. dependence on foreign material resources could be replaced by a dependence on nonmaterial or intellectual resources. Gregor Peterson points out that in 1994 "the fully loaded cost for an MVS mainframe programmer is $80,000–$100,000 a year in the United States. The same programmer can be hired in Indonesia at $12,000 per year; in India at $2,000 per year; and in the People's Republic of China at $200 a year."[15] It is likely that in the twenty-first century, U.S. companies will choose to exploit these cheap intellectual resources, creating a dependence on a foreign resource that would foster a critical-intellectual-resource vulnerability as real as one regarding platinum, palladium, or rhodium.

Espionage Vulnerability

As international law specialist Joseph M. Sweeney and colleagues have written, "The conventional practice of states is not overtly to charge another state with espionage but to counter-attack in kind in what Dean Acheson once called 'the underworld of international relations'."[16] However, particularly within the U.S. political system, eco-nomic espionage is considered to be a violation of international trust.

A nation's vulnerability to economic espionage is a function, first, of the treasure it must protect; second, of the intensity of the hostile collection effort; and third, of the effectiveness of the nation's counterintelligence effort.

The U.S. Treasure

Notwithstanding the remarkable high-technology contributions made by the Japanese and the superior technical capabilities of members of the European Community, by every contemporary measure the United States is the world's leading producer of high-technology products and research.[17] The "tangible wealth" of the United States (excluding land) has been estimated at $24.7 trillion. Land values probably equal another $4 trillion. The U.S. GNP is about three times that of Japan and four times that of Germany. In 1993 the size of the U.S. economy, at market exchange rates, was nearly $6 trillion, while Japan's was about $3.6 trillion and

Germany's but $1.5 trillion. In terms of purchasing power the U.S. economy measures over $5 trillion, while China and Japan each are just over $2 trillion. In terms of inventive power the United States consistently granted twice the numbers of patents in the years 1989 through 1993 as did Japan.[18] The U.S. economy was growing at a rate of just under 3 percent in 1993, while growth in Japan was about half that and the Russian economy was predicted to shrink by 10 percent in 1993.[19] (Germany's growth at the halfway point in 1993 was a negative 1.3 percent.) The United States is the world's leader in productivity (output per worker-hour).[20] U.S. manufacturing output was 39 percent higher in 1992 than in 1980 and 95 percent higher than in 1970.

The United States is the world's largest exporter. In 1992 it represented 12.3 percent of global exports. Germany accounted for 11.8 percent and Japan 9.3 percent. According to a study by the management consultant firm McKinsey and Company, Japanese industry is nearly 83 percent as productive as that of the United States, and Germany is only 79 percent as productive.[21] In 1994 the United States had the world's most competitive economy, displacing Japan for the first time since 1985.

The United States controls a substantial share of the Japanese software market, about 55 percent. Some major U.S. companies have assets that exceed the assets of some nations. Microsoft, for example, has $2 billion in cash and no debt while spending $100 million a year on software development. The sheer magnitude and diversity of the treasure make it a rich target for economic aggressors.

The United States as a Target

The foreign economic intelligence effort directed against U.S. industry is forbidding. Senator David Boren, chairman of the Senate Select Committee on Intelligence, has warned that spying by foreign governments on American corporations is an increasingly serious threat: "There have been some instances where we felt we had some very strong evidence, certainly at least in one case, of a generally friendly country engaged in not just the theft of a private company's secrets, but using government intelligence services to steal secrets of American private companies."[22] In April 1990 Boren said, "As the arms race is winding down, the spy race is heating up." He added, "An increasing share of the espionage directed against the United States comes from spying by foreign governments against private American companies."[23] FBI Intelligence Division chief Thomas De Hardaway has said, "Economic information is highly sought after because it translates into economic power, and that's the name of the game in this day and age."[24]

The industrial spy can be innovative. Reports have it that in 1992 a class of U.S. first-grade students was used as cover to slip a spy into a high-technology industrial facility. The spy, who had a child enrolled in the school, encouraged a tour of the plant and then volunteered to accompany the class. The photos taken of the children by the spy included sensitive industrial secrets.[25]

With the end of the cold war, industrial espionage has been widely recognized, discussed, and addressed in the popular and professional journals. Books have been written on the subject not only because it is important but also because espionage makes good storytelling. Thomas N. Thompson, a confessed "spy for several U.S. law firms" traveling "throughout Asia, North and South America collecting information on basic industries in otherwise friendly countries," describes these operations as being conducted in the context of a "new Cold War battlefield."[26]

There is a consensus that U.S. industry—and inferentially U.S. national security—is vulnerable to, and has been victimized by, both allied and hostile nations. One report has cases of FBI-investigated "friendly spying" against U.S. industry increasing fiftyfold in nine months.[27] Nicholas Eftimiades has documented an extensive Chinese industrial espionage program targeting the United States. He predicts that the Chinese Ministry of State Security "will probably continue to penetrate and exploit the United States and other

Western nations' political, academic, industrial and technological institutions."[28]

Contemporary industrial espionage has many precedents. The pineapple was smuggled into Hawaii. Samuel Slater memorized and then smuggled the blueprints for cotton-spinning machinery out of England into the United States in 1789. In *Friendly Spies* Peter Schweizer tells of former IBM employee Raymond Cadet's 1980 theft of the company's "crown jewels": computer architecture plans called the Adirondack Workbooks. The proprietary, extremely valuable workbooks were delivered to Japan's Hitachi Corporation. Schweizer contends that the delivery of the materials cut the cost of Hitachi's research and development of some products by more than half.[29]

In 1990 Senator William S. Cohen encouraged the tightening of federal laws to combat espionage aimed at U.S. commercial and industrial targets. Senator Cohen stated that while in the past people betrayed their nation for ideological reasons, now they spy for profit: "Now our nation's secrets are sold at the espionage bazaar for the most generous buyer." According to journalist Bruce Nelson, "The successful nations are trying to steal high-tech secrets from one another. The Third World and former communist states do not have the money to buy or build themselves quickly to prosperity, so they are seeking a shortcut by stealing technical, scientific and commercial secrets from more advanced countries."[30]

Allies Germany, South Korea, Japan, Canada, and Israel have all been charged with waging industrial espionage against the United States. A Chicago firm, Recon/Optical, has charged that agents of the Israeli air force tried to steal the plans for an airborne spy camera. The Israelis agreed to settle the claim by paying $3 million in damages.[31]

As of 1990 William Sessions, then director of the FBI, believed that "the Soviet intelligence services are more active now than they have been at any time in the past 10 years." He added that their operations had been "systematically expanded" to target Western economic information and technologies. He also warned that Chinese intelligence officers were targeting Chinese American scientists who possessed useful economic and industrial information. Middle Eastern and Central Asian nations were also cited by Sessions as industrial spy threats.[32] In 1991 CIA director Robert Gates revealed that "moles" had been planted in American companies by foreign intelligence agencies. In 1992 he indicated that some twenty nations from every region of the world had targeted American business operations.[33]

U.S. intelligence agents have uncovered evidence that the French intelligence service, Direction Générale de la Sécurité Extérieure (DGSE), has recruited industrial spies in the European offices of IBM, Texas Instruments, and other U.S. electronics firms. The United States found that the intelligence gathered was being supplied to the French Compagnie des Machines Bull, a computer corporation.[34]

Robert Courtney, a U.S. consultant on industrial espionage, names Britain, West Germany, the Netherlands, and Belgium as having engaged in industrial espionage against the United States. Noel Machette, another U.S. counterespionage consultant, has said, "American businesses are not really up against some little competitor, they're up against the whole intelligence apparatus of other countries. And they're getting their clocks cleaned."[35] Ralph Laurello, director of the U.S. State Department's Overseas Security Advisory Council, describes economic spying as a growing problem.[36]

Henry Clements, head of the firm Technology Security Planning, Inc., has testified, "In the past three years, we've had three hostile buyout offers from the Japanese. They want to buy us and close us down."[37] In *Puppets of Nippon* Pat Choate alleges that Japan spends 80 percent of its espionage budget on U.S. operations. He charges that about another $500 million a year is spent on a U.S. public relations effort promoting Japanese programs. In 1980 a piece appeared in the *Japan Economic Journal* stating that "influence in Washington is just like in Indonesia. It's for sale."[38]

There is evidence that an anti-U.S. product disinformation campaign has been waged in Japan with the introduction of rumors that U.S.-made microchips were defective and that U.S. food products had produced deformed American babies. Boeing was wrongly accused of faulty maintenance causing the 1985 crash of a Japan Air Lines jet. It is estimated that 80 to 90 percent of Japan's intelligence effort is focused on economic activities.[39] Japan is also a target of industrial espionage. In 1992 Vladimir Davydov, a Russian trade representative serving in Tokyo, was charged with attempting illegally to export semiconductor and telecommunications equipment out of Japan.[40]

Russian spokesman Kobaladze maintains that economic intelligence has nothing to do with stealing secrets. It is the analysis of information.[41] The French are alleged to be masters of economic espionage. Former director of the French intelligence agency DGSE Pierre Marion defends the practice:

> I think that you have to separate very clearly what are the fields which are covered by an alliance and the fields which are not covered by an alliance. It's clear that when you are allies, you have certain sectors. I'm speaking of the armaments. I'm thinking of diplomatic matters where normally you should not try to gather intelligence. But in all of the other fields, being allied does not prevent the states from being competitors. Even during the Cold War, the economic competition existed. Now the competition between the states is moving from the political-military level to the economic and technological level. In economics, we are competitors and not allies. I think that even during the Cold War getting intelligence on economic, technological and industrial matters from a country with which you are allied is not incompatible with the fact that you are allies.[42]

Contrary to the Marion theory that industrial espionage is fair practice between allies, FBI deputy assistant for intelligence R. Patrick Watson has indicated that the United States has had private discussions with foreign intelligence officials to define "what is acceptable conduct and what is not." (It must be assumed that the limits of the understanding do not include spying on the scale of the alleged DGSE operations.)[43] Watson might well have quoted historian Will Durant, who wrote that international commerce must have a high moral standard and that "there are no morals in diplomacy, and *la politique n'a pas d'entrailles;* but there are morals in international trade, merely because such trade cannot go on without some degree of restraint, regulation and confidence. Trade began in piracy; it culminates in morality."[44]

Service 7 of the French DGSE is identified as the bureau responsible for economic espionage. According to U.S. newspaper accounts, the DGSE has extensive electronic eavesdropping capabilities to tap telephone lines and monitor conversations and electronic transactions.

It has long been an open secret in the aerospace industry that the annual Paris Air Show is an incubator for industrial intelligence operations. In April 1993 the CIA formally alerted the U.S. aerospace industry that French agents were targeting technical secrets.[45] Boeing Aircraft, in part for economy reasons but also in large measure because of French aggressiveness in engaging in economic espionage, decided not to participate in the June 1993 Paris Air Show. The CIA secured an official twenty-one-page document that substantiated its claim that the French government had organized an intelligence effort aimed at specific U.S. aerospace technologies. Allegedly the document identified forty-nine U.S. companies and twenty-four U.S. financial institutions as espionage targets. French officials did not deny the authenticity of the document but responded, "There is nothing in this document to indicate that it was released by French Government offices," a statement that can be interpreted in many ways other than as a positive denial. There was speculation as to whether or not the document was bona fide. In Peter Schweizer's view, "It's stretching it to say it's a spy target list." He speculated that it was written by a French technology agency (not the DGSE) to advise French diplomats (not espionage agents) on what to look for at the show.[46]

Reportedly the French were "hurt" by the allegation that they may have been involved in industrial espionage.[47] The French anguish reminds one of Captain Renault's outrage in Rick's Café Américain in the film *Casablanca:* "I'm shocked, shocked to find there's gambling going on here!" Some French speculated that the entire affair was a CIA plot to demonstrate the need for a CIA economic counterintelligence mission. Others speculated that it clothed a plot to embarrass the Europeans' Airbus Industrie. French reporters and officials asserted that in 1989 the French government made a commitment to put a stop to its economic espionage.

Industrial espionage against the United States may be greatly facilitated—or made passé—by the ease with which American companies may be purchased by foreign interests. Foreign purchases of high-technology companies have increased dramatically over the past decade. Absent an antitrust issue, there are few obstacles to such purchases. In July 1990, for example, computer giant Fujitsu bought 80 percent of Europe's fifth largest computer company, the British International Computers Limited (ICL). The purchase constituted a technological transfer that never could have been achieved through espionage. Eftimiades documents that the People's Republic of China "has attempted to purchase U.S. firms with access to high technology not authorized for release to foreign countries."[48] He cites the example of the China National Aero-Technology Import and Export Corporation (CATIC) purchasing MAMCO, a Seattle aircraft parts manufacturer. The Bush administration, citing CATIC's "checkered history," ordered the Chinese firm to divest itself of the Seattle high-technology industry. Administration officials were concerned not only about MAMCO's value as a source of in-flight refueling information but also about CATIC using MAMCO to penetrate other areas of restricted technology.

There is also so much information on global commerce in the public domain that it leaves slim pickings for industrial espionage. French counterintelligence officers estimate that 80 percent of today's economic intelligence data can be found in public records.[49]

The Clinton administration has promised that it would protest any allied economic intelligence activity aimed at U.S. industry and that there would be "no more Mr. Nice Guy" on the part of the Americans.[50] Clinton's Justice Department appeared to turn a dispute between Volkswagen AG and General Motors into a test case regarding industrial espionage by foreign nations against U.S. industry. In 1993 GM alleged that Jose Ignacio Lopez de Arriortua, formerly one of its most senior executives, stole sensitive records when he switched to the rolls of Volkswagen.[51]

FBI director William Sessions has confirmed that the FBI has targeted Russian industrial espionage operations being conducted in the United States.[52] Economist-columnist Robert Samuelson tells us that the Soviet Union has been stealing high-technology secrets from the United States for years.[53] In 1991 a Soviet KGB defector, Stanislaw Levchenko, addressing a conference on American international business security, predicted that Moscow, no longer committed to the cold war, would focus its substantial espionage apparatus on U.S. industry. He explained that the Russian economy has limited research of its own following the collapse of its economy. It would therefore concentrate its KGB resources on stealing American technology. The Levchenko scenario foresaw a subtle Russian intelligence effort that would take advantage of U.S. businesses capitalizing on the opportunities they found in a newly open Russian market, promoted by joint U.S.-Russian ventures. Levchenko, a former KGB major who defected in 1979, was joined by White House Office of Science and Technology official Michelle Van Cleave and former CIA director Richard Helms in alerting U.S. industry to its vulnerability to industrial espionage. They also warned of the limited protection U.S. industry could expect from the U.S. government.

To Spy or Not to Spy

Which brings us to the third function of a nation's vulnerability: the effort it is willing to make to protect its economic treasure. The

United States appears to be struggling with a decision to determine the appropriate intensity and scope of its activity in protecting its treasure against economic coercion or economic war. The U.S. intelligence community's interest in getting administration and congressional approval to engage in economic intelligence-gathering operations has waxed and waned. The requirement for and ethics of counterintelligence operations never seemed to be in doubt. However, the requirement and ethics of other—that is, offensive—economic intelligence operations have not been consistently or universally supported in the federal bureaucracy.

In 1989 CIA director William Webster did not eliminate active economic intelligence gathering when he noted that our political and military allies are also our economic competitors. He explained that "the intelligence community looks at...developments from a strategic perspective, examining what is occurring, the forces at play, and the ways that actions abroad can directly and indirectly affect our national security interests." He added, "Intelligence on economic developments and other issues has never been more important."[54]

In March 1990 President Bush formally endorsed economic intelligence and counterintelligence as a priority in a national strategy statement.[55] However, the action did not signal a comprehensive economic intelligence effort that included spying on allied nations.

During this 1990 period of searching for the proper role for the American intelligence community in economic espionage, Senator Arlen Specter was quoted as saying that such activity "is a bad practice. It's just going to encourage bad practices by competitors...but if it's a question of retaliation, that's different." CIA officials denied that they had targeted foreign countries for economic espionage. A senior official said, "Our problems in economics are not spy problems....We are an information-integrating-and-synthesizing agency."[56] (Which, by the way, is a partial definition of intelligence; all that is missing are the collection and dissemination functions.)

CIA officials confirmed that the vast worldwide network of electronic and human surveillance assets captured valuable economic data. They emphasized that dissemination of that information was not made to U.S. companies unless the companies were targets of illegal espionage. National Security Agency (NSA) director Vice Admiral William O. Studeman characterized such action as "helping out on the defensive side."[57]

In 1991 CIA director Robert M. Gates was adamant in opposing "commercial spying" by the U.S. intelligence community. In 1992 the director of the CIA reiterated his position: "I would like to state clearly that the U.S. intelligence community does not, should not, and will not engage in industrial espionage." In the same year the FBI's role in economic counterespionage was oriented to denying foreign spies access to U.S. core defense technologies and U.S. industry's proprietary and technical information.[58]

However, the debate over the propriety of the United States engaging in economic espionage was rejoined in 1993 when the Clinton administration's new CIA director, R. James Woolsey, was reported to be studying a plan to offer CIA intelligence to U.S. corporations. Woolsey's enthusiasm seems to have been moderated by more cautious administration officials and by resistance from the Congress. Not so moderate was Representative Dan Glickman, chairman of the House Permanent Committee on Intelligence. In March 1993 he said, "I'd like to be involved in determining sensibly and rationally, how we involve ourselves in economic issues...economic intelligence, economic espionage, trade and technology transfer issues." Glickman foresaw "a modern world of economic conflict."[59]

Director Woolsey and his Central Intelligence Agency seemed to have settled on an espionage policy by late 1993 when he was quoted as saying that the CIA would not engage in what is known as industrial espionage, or stealing business secrets from foreign countries. However, Woolsey did indicate that the agency would attempt to discover which intelligence services in other countries were so engaged, and that when found out, they would be exposed.[60]

There appears to be a consensus that the federal bureaucracy should share with industry its counterintelligence findings: the information it uncovers on espionage directed against U.S. industrial and commercial activities. Such counterintelligence information may be broadcast to the industry at large or, in special cases, to a sector or a single threatened U.S. enterprise. The dissemination of counterintelligence information itself can be a sticky wicket for the government. Congressman Matthew F. McHugh of New York expressed his concern: "If there's more than one American company interested in bidding, do you give the information just to one? And often there are coalitions of companies, a mixture of American and foreign. Should you share information with them?"[61] Inevitably, between the CIA's worldwide information-gathering system, the communication monitoring of the National Security Agency, and the Department of Defense's Acquisition Systems Protection Office, a wealth of economic intelligence falls into the laps of American operatives. Reportedly the U.S. intelligence community does not routinely share such information with U.S. corporations unless it discovers that a company is about to be victimized by an illegal act. (The illegality of the act may often be in doubt.) In 1989 William Webster, as director of the CIA, was quoted as saying that the U.S. intelligence agencies "will be looking to see if the Soviets compensate for cutbacks in defense research, development, and procurement by increasing their efforts to acquire Western defense information and technology."[62]

In 1990 a "knowledgeable official" was quoted as saying that upon the receipt of information of value, "We tell the [U.S.] government and they might tell the company to come talk to us. We wouldn't tell them the source of our information, but we would tell them they were about to be had. We provide only defensive information. And [at present] we don't look for it." Expanding on the defensive-use-only theme, Admiral Studeman, director of the NSA, has said that his agency will "definitely be helping out on the defensive side" especially "for those U.S. commercial operations engaged in sensitive kinds of economic enterprises."[63] Economic espionage aside, it must be assumed that the U.S. intelligence community does or would focus upon foreign activity that threatens the use of economic force against the United States. It must also be assumed that U.S. intelligence assets would be targeted on activities that support the United States in using economic force against another entity (nation, consortium, bloc, or corporation). There is, however, no consensus as to whether or not the United States itself should engage in other forms of economic espionage. The *New York Times* identified the controversy over the United States using economic espionage as "the hottest issue in intelligence circles."[64]

A government official is quoted as saying, "The real issue is do you want United States intelligence to steal the proprietary secrets of foreign nations. It's fundamentally anathema to our way of life. We can't do business this way." NSA director Studeman also raised the moral issue: "This country does not have, if you will, the business ethic and the arrangements that some of the other Western countries have that do engage in [gathering] economic intelligence information."[65]

In truth, the United States would have to embrace a new code of commercial ethics before institutionalizing a program of foreign industrial espionage. The U.S. legal system, the corporate culture, and reliance upon theories of how the market economy should operate—all conspire against the United States engaging in economic espionage against foreign countries except in times of economic, political, or military hostilities. But such contingencies should not be ignored. The U.S. intelligence community should be prepared, on a contingency basis, to engage in economic espionage when the circumstances demand it.

As this is being written, should economic espionage be waged against Iraq, Libya, North Korea, and other states considered to have hostile intentions? Within prudent limits, yes. Should economic espionage—as distinguished from economic counterintelligence—

be waged against France, England, Germany, Japan, or Korea? The answer is no, except under unusual circumstances, when there is an identifiable threat to the security of the United States. To some, this answer may seem to be as naive as Henry L. Stimson's famous statement on espionage: "Gentlemen do not read each other's mail." However, the former secretary of state's rejection of spying was unequivocal, whereas the answer given here on industrial espionage provides legitimacy contingent upon the presence of an identifiable security threat. There are questions that still beg study and answers. What are the prudent limits to economic espionage? When will it be effective? How covert must it be?

The Vulnerability of the Unprepared

The U.S. vulnerability due to a lack of preparedness is self-inflicted. If the United States continues to treat economic conflict as a mad aunt to be hidden in the attic, it will continue to be exposed to economic aggression. Its use of the economic instrument in the pursuit of national objectives will be mostly ineffectual and often counter-productive. Misuse of the economic instrument will soon deprive the United States of its overwhelming economic power to deter, coerce, end, or limit armed hostilities. It will devalue the synergism that comes with the competent orchestration of military, political, and economic power. Continued misuse will deprive the nation of a credible threat to encourage human rights, to influence trade, and to be responsive to the needs of its citizens and others.

Economic force improperly used can be counterproductive. It may actually strengthen a hostile regime (as when Mussolini used the League of Nations' use of economic force against him to rally Italian support for his personal rule). It may also encourage alliances among the user's adversaries (as was the case in the forming of the German-Italian Axis). The Soviet Union's employment of economic force against Yugoslavia in 1948 drove Tito into an informal alliance with the Western powers.

Economic force improperly used can invite military aggression (as may have been the case in the U.S. use of such force against the Japanese prior to World War II).

The improper use of economic force in lieu of military force may signal a timidity and unwillingness to risk a shooting war (as in the pre–World War II British and French preference for the economic instrument, which may have encouraged Hitler's confidence that his military adventures would not be challenged).

Continued abuse of the economic instrument will produce unintended collateral damage to both U.S. and target-nation industry, economy, and populations. The U.S. public will one day awake to the appalling consequences of the imprudent, amateurish, haphazard use of economic force that has been characteristic of the United States over many years, through many administrations and many congresses. The U.S. use of economic force against Panama provides one of many examples of the abuse of economic force that must be avoided.

Failure in Panama

Few countries in the world have been as vulnerable to the use of U.S. economic force as was Panama in the late 1980s. The Panamanian economy was (and remains) highly dependent upon the United States. In 1987 tiny Panama was the United States' fifty-sixth largest trading partner. The United States was the major importer of Panamanian goods. In 1985 U.S. merchandise and goods accounted for more than 30 percent of Panama's imports. More than 15 percent of U.S. commercial shipborne imports and exports pass through the canal. The 1977 Panama Canal treaties gave the United States the primary responsibility for defense and operation of the canal through the end of the century. In 1987 the United States provided substantial military and economic aid to the country even though it meant cooperation with an oppressive, corrupt Panamanian military. By that year Panama was suffering a severe financial and political crisis. The

Panamanians were fighting a critical liquidity problem. Because its currency was tied to the U.S. dollar, Panama could not rely on a central bank for an infusion of new money. The nation was fast coming to rely on a cash-only economy, having lost confidence in bank checks, credit cards, and traveler's checks.

The political crisis was fueled by the Panamanian strongman General Manuel Antonio Noriega, who became the raison d'être and focus of the U.S.-Panamanian crisis of the last years of President Reagan's and the first years of President Bush's administrations. Noriega assumed the role of commander of the Panamanian armed forces in March 1983. In the same year the Panamanian legislature passed a law that created the Panamanian Defense Forces, with control over all the armed and police forces. These military and paramilitary forces controlled the Panama Canal, immigration, and the regulation of civil aircraft. Noriega, now firmly in charge of the legislature, the armed forces, and key bureaucracy, installed his choice of president. By 1987 his drug activities, rigging of the 1984 elections, murder of at least one Panamanian official, corruption, electoral fraud, and despotism had become common knowledge. Public demonstrations against this de facto head of state were brutally crushed in that year.

In June 1987 the U.S. Senate, using the diplomatic weapon, passed a resolution urging Noriega to step aside until an investigation of his activities could be completed. The United States was pursuing a DIPLOMATIC campaign against Noriega/Panama. A few days later, Noriega supporters attacked the U.S. embassy in Panama, and the Panamanian government accused its historic benefactor of "interventionist aggression."

The Reagan administration was faced with a dilemma. The situation in Panama, and the drug crisis within the United States, dictated that more positive action would be needed to thwart Noriega's criminal and political thuggery. The nation's diplomatic weapon—manifest in the Senate's June resolution and the administration's closing of the consular section and the U.S. Information

Services Library at the U.S. embassy in Panama—was proving ineffectual in the redemption or removal of Noriega. The use of economic and military force was assessed.

While firming up contingency plans for the use of military force, on 11 March President Reagan launched an economic offensive against Panama. The effort evolved to an ECONOMIC-*diplomatic* campaign. Reagan ordered the withholding of canal toll payments to Panama. These payments, which amounted to between $6.5 million and $7 million per month, were critical to the Panamanian dollar-starved economy. Certain Panamanian trade advantages were also withdrawn. The remainder of March was a time of continued turmoil within the country, highlighted by civil riots by government employees who had not been paid by a government now strapped for cash; an unsuccessful coup against Noriega led by Panama's chief of police; power outages throughout the nation; and the brutal subjection of the populace by an armed force beholden and loyal to Noriega.

On 8 April President Reagan invoked the International Emergency Economic Powers Act (IEEPA). With the support of Congress the administration imposed economic pressure on the Panamanians by prohibiting American companies from making payments to the Panamanian government. In July 1987 the United States imposed a freeze on all economic and military aid.

In early 1988 Noriega was indicted by two U.S. federal grand juries, one in Miami and one in Tampa, on drug-trafficking charges. In February of the same year the president of Panama, Eric Delvalle, a Noriega protégé, exercised his constitutional prerogative and fired his patron Noriega from his position as head of the armed forces. The Panamanian National Assembly, controlled by Noriega, forced Delvalle from office and drove him into hiding. In August 1988, according to newspaper sources, an interagency planning group concluded that Noriega could not be toppled by any combination of economic, political, and psychological power.[66]

In an effort to demonstrate a political legitimacy, Noriega's clique agreed to hold presidential elections in early May 1989. Independent polling observers reported that the candidate in opposition to Noriega's choice was ahead by a three to one margin. Former U.S. president Jimmy Carter, one of the independent observers of the balloting, claimed that Noriega stole the election. The Noriega-dominated legislature ruled the election invalid before the final count of votes was made. The candidate in opposition to Noriega's man was beaten and his bodyguard killed by Noriega henchmen. Three months after the aborted election a provisional president, Francisco Rodriquez, assumed office, but Noriega remained in control of the country.

In September 1989 the U.S. Department of State extended its ban on sugar imports from Panama and increased the number of Panamanian companies Americans were not permitted to pay. A State Department spokesperson said the sugar limits would cost Panama $15 million in revenues. (This was cited as an advantage in achieving the U.S. objectives.)

On 3 October 1989 a U.S.-sponsored armed forces coup failed, and George Bush, now president of the United States, came under increasing pressure to do more to bring Noriega to justice. On 15 December Noriega confirmed the obvious and announced that the republic was in a "state of war" with the United States. (In fact the United States had been waging a classic economic war against the state of Panama since March 1987.) On 15 December the Panamanian legislature formally appointed Noriega "Chief of Government and Maximum Leader" to defend the nation against the U.S. economic aggression. The following day Panamanian sentries killed a U.S. Marine on a city street. On 19 December President Bush abandoned reliance upon the economic instrument to topple Noriega and committed U.S. ground, air, and naval forces against the Republic of Panama. On Christmas Eve Noriega came out of hiding and sought refuge in the Vatican embassy. On 3 January 1990 Noriega surrendered to U.S. military forces and was flown to the United States to stand trial on drug charges.

72

Analysis of the U.S. Failure in Panama

If the U.S. objective in the pre–19 December 1989 ECONOMIC-*diplomatic* campaign against Panama was to impoverish the Panamanian economy, it was an eminent success. As of June 1988 economic activity in Panama was reduced by about 45 percent, a level worse than the United States experienced at any point during the Great Depression of the 1930s. Unemployment doubled to more than 23 percent. (The highest unemployment figure in the United States during the Depression was 25 percent.) Retail sales fell off 70 percent. Sales of durable goods fell 90 percent. Industrial production sank to 60 percent of normal, while agricultural production was off 30 percent. Estimates were that nearly $1 billion had fled Panamanian banks to more secure harbors, and hopes of it returning were not high.[67] (The government was forced to impose a $100 ceiling on what could be withdrawn from savings accounts.) The country had no cash to pay its Honduran electric bill. (Honduras supplies about 4 percent of Panama's electricity.) More than forty thousand Panamanians, out of a population of only 2.2 million, fled the country during an eighteen-month period.

However, the objective of the U.S. economic offensive was not to destroy the Panamanian economy. It was to rid the country and the hemisphere of Noriega, which it did not do.

In warfare it is the norm that both sides take casualties. During the U.S.-Panamanian economic war the Panamanians suffered far worse, but the U.S. economic aggressor did take casualties. American businessmen in Panama complained that the U.S. economic coercion was driving them out of business. One source estimated that it would cost the United States $1 billion (war reparations?) to restore the Panamanian economy post-Noriega. The United States lost prestige and respect within the Latin American community and confirmed the opinion of many that the country was interventionist, paternalistic, and, worse, ineffectual. The U.S. economic weapon was devalued, as it failed to produce expected results. Panama's

Catholic bishops, no allies of Noriega, broadcast that the U.S. economic war was "unjust and immoral" and that it "had no noticeable success [while] impoverishing our people and...destroying the bases of our economy for years to come....The U.S. cannot justify this slow social repression against a whole nation."[68]

One pundit observed that the U.S. economic campaign had actually been counterproductive. It had been designed to generate popular support for a coup d'état against Noriega that never succeeded. Jesse Jackson was quoted as saying that the United States "had set the forest on fire to burn one tree."[69] Another observer called it the economic equivalent of "carpet bombing."[70]

The near-exclusive use of DIPLOMATIC force prior to 11 March 1987 failed to topple Noriega. By any measure the post–March 1987 use of ECONOMIC force, bolstered by the continued use of *political* force—plus the always present threat of the use of the *military* instrument—failed to bring Noriega to justice. It took but sixteen days for the U.S. military, as an instrument of last resort, to achieve the objective. (Military operations did benefit from prior and ongoing *economic-diplomatic* offensives.)

The basic truth to be garnered from this experience is that the United States failed to achieve its objective of ridding Panama of Manuel Noriega when it limited its efforts to the use of POLITICAL and ECONOMIC-*political* force. It was successful when it extended its efforts to the use of MILITARY-*economic-political* force.

Conclusions Regarding the U.S. Failure in Panama

Why did the United States fail to topple Noriega when it relied primarily upon the economic instrument? There are several possibilities worth examining. Perhaps the economic weapon was inappropriate and geostrategic conditions preordained failure. This was patently not the case. In the late 1980s there was probably no country more vulnerable to U.S. economic coercion than Panama. The country was in the midst of a debilitating financial crisis while its currency was tied to the U.S. dollar. Officials were confident that once economic pressures were exerted, Noriega's collapse was inevitable. Panama was uniquely dependent upon the United States as its principal source of revenue from canal toll receipts, trade, expenditures derived from a major U.S. military presence ($40 million a month), expenditures from U.S. industry resident in Panama (United Brands Company alone accounted for $2 million a month), and economic and military aid. The country was extremely susceptible to U.S. economic pressure.

In April 1987 Howard Baker, White House chief of staff, declared that Noriega was "much beleaguered" and called the use of the economic weapon "a remarkable success."[71] Did the economic instrument work—did it do its job while the administration failed to make the proper diplomatic moves to take advantage of the success? (That is, was the Panamanian economic war a success in the use of economic force that was done in by diplomatic failure?) Such a theory is espoused by Lally Weymouth, a regular contributor to the *Washington Post*. Weymouth claims that one month after the imposition of the economic penalties on Panama, a deal could have been struck for Noriega to step aside if the United States dropped its indictment of the Panamanian leader on drug-trafficking charges. Weymouth quotes Eliot Abrams, then assistant secretary of state for Latin America in the Reagan administration, as saying, "At the beginning of 1988, there were a lot of options, and we lost them month by month until the only one left was to invade."[72] Weymouth speculates that the diplomatic options were discarded because some administration officials believed they signaled weakness.

Another likely reason the political options were not pursued was the great confidence that the economic instrument was going to achieve the objective without any need to sacrifice advantages in a political compromise.

It may be that there were missed opportunities due to a failure to play the diplomatic card properly. However, it is beyond speculation that the economic instrument did not perform as administration officials believed it would and was therefore a failure judged against the expectations of those who used it.

An equally likely reason that the economic war against Panama was not a success was that it was poorly fought. Here was the United States going to war with a vastly inferior opponent, with almost all the indicators assuring an early, cost-effective victory. However, the intelligence concerning the ability of Noriega—as opposed to Panama—to withstand the process of economic strangulation was obviously faulty. The principle of the objective was violated in the confusion as to whether the United States was targeting Panama or Noriega.

The United States fought this war without assistance from its allies. In a fit of hubris the United States did not enlist the support of other Latin American countries in its campaign to assure them that it still had high regard for the sovereignty of its neighbors.

There were no contingency plans to wage economic war against the Panamanian Republic. The U.S. principals who made the decisions and the operatives who implemented them had no background to prepare them for this type of war. They had never read a text on the subject (there are none); they had never war-gamed such a conflict (there have been none); they were operating without a doctrine, a strategy, or tactics to engage in such warfare (there are none). If there were estimates of the time required to permit economic coercion to work, they were certainly well off the mark. While it is not a matter of public record, one must assume that the estimates of the casualties that were to be suffered and inflicted were far off the mark.

The economic instrument failed to work in the 1987–88 time frame against Panama in large part not because conditions were unfavorable or because it was the wrong instrument to use. The instrument was ineffectual because it was improperly employed by a leadership and bureaucracy that were and remain apathetic about the proper use of this weapon. (See chapters 11 and 12 for remedial prescriptions.)

Given the fruitless devastation of Panama by the United States in this economic assault, why was there not more protest from the American public, the Congress, and the media? We heard nothing from the American public because it was ill informed about the economic casualties the United States was inflicting upon Panama. It was ill informed because of a subtle, uncoordinated, in large part innocent conspiracy within both political parties, the legislative and executive branches of government, and the media. For many, the support for the use of the economic weapon—support that stifled criticism of U.S. activities—was generated by concern that military force might be used. Economic coercion was considered a less aggressive option. The political leadership, in both branches of both parties, shared somewhat equally in the blame for the failure, for the economic war was a bipartisan enterprise. Little was written or said about the failure because few of the electorate had a genuine appreciation for the nature of the conflict or the devastation it had imposed.

Economic wars will seldom be terminated without the successful employment of the diplomatic/political weapon. In the case of Panama, it is possible that the economic weapon succeeded only to be rendered futile by diplomatic blunder.

Finally, there were few U.S. economic body bags brought home. The American enterprises that took the most casualties were those operating in and out of Panama, with their plight generally ignored within the United States.

Summation

Four economic conflict threats have been identified in this chapter. All four are real. The finance threat is not immediate but could become more critical over time should the United States fail to put its domestic economy in order, an effort that would include reduction of the national debt and reversal of the trade imbalance.

The resource threat is more immediate and severe and will be so as long as the United States remains dependent upon Middle East oil and imported minerals. Such dependence can be and has been attenuated to a substantial degree by stockpiling resources.

The espionage threat is immediate, growing, and rife with ethical dilemmas. The role of the federal government in combating industrial espionage is limited. Should the threat increase to the point that U.S. national security is jeopardized, it is likely and appropriate that the federal government will become more active in industrial counterespionage. Until the threat reaches that magnitude, however, it appears that the responsibility for protecting U.S. industrial proprietary secrets will rest with U.S. private industry receiving help from the federal government only in exceptional circumstances.

The fourth threat, a lack of preparedness, is immediate, serious, and consequential. Fortunately it is the easiest to resolve, and solutions to the threat can be found entirely within the American system. All it takes is a commitment to provide a better-equipped, better-informed leadership and bureaucracy. Chapter 11 provides the rationale for an architecture to help resolve this threat.

Chapter 5

Legislation and the Morality Question

◼

Act only on that maxim through which you can at the
same time will that it should become a universal law.

Immanuel Kant

As Kant implies, the subjects of this chapter, law and morality, are intimately related. International and national laws
governing the use of economic force must reflect the mandates of our moral conscience. In the following passages on law
there is an emphasis on the practical aspects of bringing order to the
features of the U.S. legal system that govern the use of economic
force. Such reorganization cannot be done without recourse to the
dictates of our moral compass and reflections on what constitutes a
just use of economic force.

U.S. Legislation

Whatever one thinks of the United States employing economic sanctions, they are an unavoidable reality. Now is the time to bring order and wisdom to the underlying U.S. laws.

Barry Carter

There is one lone detailed, comprehensive analysis of the multiple U.S. laws that impinge upon the use of economic force. This important contribution is presented in a book written by Barry Carter, associate professor of law at Georgetown University and former member of the National Security Council staff.[1] (The appendix to the present work offers a table—derived from Carter's book, *inter alia*—of major U.S. legislation affecting authority to use the economic weapon.)

Carter concludes that the U.S. legal structure supporting the president's authority to use the economic power of the United States through "sanctions" is "haphazard." He writes, "Most of the statutes were passed primarily for other purposes and without any serious considerations of the best legal regime for economic sanctions."[2] On the one hand, the president has nearly unlimited authority for denying government programs or exports. On the other, the chief executive has very problematic authority in areas such as import regulation and financial transactions. In general the president has less freedom to use the economic instrument than leaders of many industrial powers (e.g. the United Kingdom, Germany, and Japan). Carter properly concludes that this haphazard arrangement tilts the president toward the employment of the very tools of economic power that may be the least effective. There are dangers in such an illogical structure of statutes, for the president may be forced to employ draconian measures with draconian consequences merely because they are the only measures permissible under the law, when lesser ones might have been as effective. At the other extreme, the legal parameters within which the president must operate may inhibit bringing the full economic power of the United States to bear on a target when required.

Carter's work provides some specific recommendations for introducing legislation to bring order out of the chaos. His recommendations are made in two broad categories of the president's non-emergency and emergency powers in the areas of exports, imports, and private financial transactions. The essence of the Carter recommendations is that legislation should be enacted that provides a new legal "framework" for authorizing and regulating the use of economic force for the purpose of achieving national security objectives. The legislation would provide the following fundamental changes. First, it would revise presidential nonemergency powers by:

—putting more stringent limits on the president's broad authority to control exports to target nations
—providing greater presidential authority to control imports from target nations
—providing greater presidential authority to limit target-nation access to the resources of private financial institutions

Second, such legislation would limit presidential emergency powers by:

—requiring mandatory prior consultation with Congress
—requiring periodic reporting to Congress on the ongoing use of economic force
—providing compensation to those exporters who are injured as a result of the imposition of economic force (absent a serious breach of the peace by the exporter)[3]
—discouraging the use of extraterritorial jurisdiction (i.e. the exercise of U.S. authority on U.S. commercial operations outside U.S. territory)

These recommendations merit serious consideration by the legislative and executive branches of the government. Carter's legislative reforms are integral to the concept proposed in these pages.

The U.S. chief executive is not subject to U.S. laws only, however. The United States is a signatory to a hodgepodge of agreements, treaties, and international laws that dictate both trade and environmental restraint. They often conflict, and interpretations and precedence of the laws make for a lawyer's nightmare or dream, whichever one's perspective. For example, one of the most potent weapons the United States has in its economic-coercion arsenal is Section 301 of the U.S. trade law, the Omnibus Trade and Competitiveness Act. Section 301—revised in 1944, having lapsed—authorizes the president to impose tariffs or quotas on the products of nations that violate a trade agreement with the United States. A Section 301 action may be initiated by either the United States or a U.S. company. American trading partners believe that Section 301 violates the spirit if not the provisions of the General Agreement on Tariffs and Trade. They would redraft the treaty to defang Section 301 and similar trade weapons.[4]

As the use of economic force becomes more prevalent and significant to the United States, there are those who believe that Congress should take a stronger hand in these affairs. This means that there should be a different reading of current legislation or that new laws should be passed. Congressman Richard Gephardt has written, "As our foreign policy becomes less based on military operations placed before the commander-in-chief and more focused on issues of economic and other areas in which Congress is equipped to participate, the role of Congress in the formulation of policy is bound to expand."[5]

International Law

The world is lacking a legal basis for imposing sanctions.

Sergey Oznobistchev

International law, or the law of nations, provides a set of legal rules that guide nations and other international bodies in their relations. The principal purposes of international law are to legitimatize the independence of states, guarantee self-defense, encourage access to economic markets and raw materials, and control the process of immigration.

There is no mandate that requires independent states to participate in a congress or conference or to be a signatory to a charter. However, it is expected that "civilized" nations will contribute to legitimate international cooperative efforts and, once agreeing to the provisions of a charter or treaty, abide by their commitment.

There are categories of international law pertaining to the use of economic force, retaliation, embargo, and navicerts.[6] Retaliation provisions establish boundaries for retribution of one state against another. Retorsion is similar and makes provisions for hostile acts, which acts may or may not be contrary to international law. Retorsion initiatives are acts short of military war and may include the severing of diplomatic relations, the designation of a diplomat as *persona non grata,* and the use of economic force. Embargo is defined elsewhere in these pages. Navicert law outlines the acceptable procedures to be followed by a belligerent naval vessel when making a search and investigation to determine if a merchant ship is subject to seizure.

Critical to our discussion here is the precedence in customary international law of the right of a nation to employ instruments short of war as acts of reprisal for an alleged breach of international law. Also central to our discussion is the dominant position of the United Nations as the font and arbiter of international codes and the Charter of the Organization of American States in hemispheric relations.

UN Charter

Article 2(4) of the UN Charter outlaws the use of force to settle international disputes, mandating that they be settled by peaceful means: "All members shall refrain in their international relations from the threat or use of force against the territorial integrity or political independence of any state or in any manner inconsistent with the Purposes of the United Nations." Exceptions to the provisions of Article 2(4) are provided for individual or collective self-defense against armed attack (Article 51); under the auspices of the United Nations (Articles 24 and 39); or subject to the invitation of the state where the force will be exercised (Article 2, paragraph 1).

However, questions about the intent of Article 2 abound. Does the article preclude only the use of physical, military force, or does it preclude the use of economic, political, psychological, and social force as well? Is it aggression when a powerful economic state employs economic force against a weaker state to change the behavior of the weaker state? What constitutes an action that is "inconsistent with the Purposes of the United Nations"?

While it does not have the legal status of the charter, an annex to the 1970 UN General Assembly Resolution 2625 addresses the subject of the legitimacy of the use of economic force in more specific terms. The annex provides that "no State may use or encourage the use of economic, political or any other type of measures to coerce another State in order to obtain from it the subordination of the exercise of its sovereign rights and to secure from it advantages of any kind." The annex also states that "armed intervention *and all other forms of interference* or attempted threats against the personality of the State or against its political, economic, and cultural elements are in violation of international law" (emphasis added).

The framers of the UN Charter envisioned an organization that would exercise far more power over the international community than has eventuated. Chapter VII of the UN Charter reserves to the Security Council the right to use mandatory economic, diplomatic, and cultural sanctions. The anticipation that the Security Council would have a monopoly on the use of military force has not been fulfilled. In practical terms this lack of UN predominance in the overall use of force has eroded confidence in the relevance of the charter in international conflicts. Further, the relevance of charter law may at times be suborned by considerations of customary or positive international law. A 1973 study of the use of nonviolent coercion and its legality under the provisions of UN Charter Article 2(4) concluded, "In the final analysis, relatively few types of conduct would constitute violations of article 2(4). Not only must such economic or political coercion be undertaken for impermissible purposes; it must also be of sufficient intensity to pose a genuine threat to the sovereignty of the target state. If not of that intensity, the coercion would best be dealt with, in the words of one author, 'not [as] an international crime, but [as] an international tort'."7

OAS Charter

Article 19 of the Charter of the Organization of American States (OAS) provides more of a conundrum for the United States in employing economic force within this hemisphere: "No State may use or encourage the use of coercive measures of an economic or political character in order to force the sovereign will of another State and obtain from it advantages of any kind."8

In 1971 it appeared that Article 19 of the OAS Charter would get a fair test on the use of economic force in a dispute between Ecuador and the United States. Over a two-week period Ecuador impounded eighteen U.S. home-ported tuna boats it claimed were poaching in its "territorial waters." The United States recognized a three-mile limit while Ecuador claimed territoriality to two hundred miles. Ecuador fined the U.S. boat owners $1 million. The OAS supported Ecuador's action. The United States retaliated using its economic muscle by suspending military sales to the South American nation invoking the U.S. Foreign Military Sales Act,

Section 3(b). Ecuador countered by accusing the United States of violating Article 19 of the OAS Charter and called for a Meeting of Consultation of OAS Foreign Ministers. The consultation resulted in sharp criticism of the U.S. laws that permit or mandate the imposition of economic force under certain conditions. The United States argued that it had the right to protect the legitimate pursuits of U.S. citizens operating in international waters.

The final outcome of the dispute shed no light on the interpretation or applicability of Article 19. Both Ecuador and the United States agreed to the consultative body's mandate to resolve their differences and "abstain from the use of any kind of measure that may affect the sovereignty" of another state.

Summary

Notwithstanding the provisions of the UN and OAS Charters or the UN General Assembly Resolution, the customary usage of economic force since the drafting of these documents and the weight of political and scholarly opinion validate the rights of the state to use the economic instrument coercively for the good of a single nation or the world in general.

When feasible, the United States will be on firmer legal ground bringing its economic force to bear through the United Nations. However, precedent legitimatizes a nation's unilateral use of economic force in its self-interest.

The Morality of Economic Conflict

In general, sanctions may create serious inconvenience for a population, but they may not impose grave harm on a population. The violation of basic rights as a result of sanctions may only be incidental, just as in war civilian casualties may only be incidental. For that reason, humanitarian provision, exemptions for sustaining basic needs of the population through sales or aid, will be a necessary provision of a just sanctions regime.

Drew Christiansen, S.J., and Gerard Powers

The morality or justness of economic conflict as an instrument of the state has seldom been debated in the abstract.[9] Columnist Peter Steinfels understated the dearth of scholarship on the subject when he wrote, "Most studies of sanctions, of which there are few, focus on their effectiveness, not on their morality." Steinfels continued, "So there is a need for a theory of just sanctions, like the historical theory of a 'just war'."[10] The morality issues have been discussed in real-world individual cases such as the Panamanian and Cuban affairs. However, as Drew Christiansen and Gerard Powers have found, there have been no standards against which to measure the moral propriety of economic coercion or war.[11]

The moral implications of the use of military force qua force, on the other hand, have been debated for centuries. The early Christian philosophers condemned all war. However, by the fourth century the ascendance of Christianity and its influence on statecraft demanded a legal and theological justification for the use of force. Philosophers such as Saint Augustine introduced the rationale for a just war (*bellum justum*). Saint Thomas Aquinas defined the terms more explicitly. What has since evolved from debates on the morality of the use of military force is a tradition of the concept of just war (or to be more precise, a justified war).

The tradition of military war identifies criteria to judge whether or not the use of military force is justified. The original debates on just war were grounded in religious theory. Today they are often discussed in secular terms. Nevertheless, they are still characteristically Christian.

Following is a discussion of the morality of economic force using the traditional, military just-war paradigm. Do the just-war questions we ask about military conflict apply to economic conflict?

Just Cause

The just-cause criterion requires that before a military war can be waged, it must be shown that war is necessary to repel an unjust aggression. The criterion has some relevance in considering the use of economic force. Clearly there was just cause in the use of economic force against Iraq in Desert Storm in 1990. Iraqi forces had invaded and systematically plundered a smaller neighbor and were poised to invade one or more others. It is less clear that the use of economic force could be justified under this norm in the 1988 Panamanian affair and the Cuban conflicts since 1960.

In the Panamanian conflict there was no indication that the Panamanian government or Noriega was intent upon aggression against another state. U.S. force was used to rid the Western Hemisphere of a criminal tyrant. The emplacement of Soviet offensive missiles in Cuba in 1962, Cuba's 1975 commitment of thirty-six thousand combat troops to Angola, and its deployment of twenty thousand troops to Ethiopia in 1978 constituted unjust aggression from the anticommunist U.S. viewpoint, and thus warranted use of the economic weapon by the United States. In each case, at least in part because of the use or threat of use of the U.S. economic weapon, the Cubans (or Soviets) terminated the aggression. Currently the Cuban capability for such aggression is slight. Nevertheless, economic pressures continue to be exercised against Cuba with devastating results.

Competent Authority

The competent-authority criterion provides that the appropriate legal authorities must authorize the use of military force. In the largest sense it is a norm that has little utility for measuring just economic force, since such force can be exercised at so many levels of social organization. When exercised at the national and multinational levels, however, it would require that heads of state or multinational organizations be the implementing authorities. It is barely relevant to measuring the morality of economic force.

Right Intention

The right-intention norm rejects punishment or the recovery of material possessions as sufficient justification for the use of military force. The protection of human rights and the defense against injury, however, are considered sufficient. This criterion is closely related to that of just cause, as both deal with objectives. In the just-cause case, however, the focus is on confirming the reality of the target's aggression. In the right-intention case, one must divine the intentions of the wielder of economic force: are they really as stated, or are there other, hidden, agendas?

The right-intention norm would have relevance to measuring a justification for the use of the economic instrument. For example, the Netherlands granted independence to Suriname in 1975. In 1982 there was ample evidence of Soviet and Cuban influence over the newly formed nation. In the same year Suriname's controlling faction brutally murdered fifteen of the most prominent opposition leaders. Both the United States and the Netherlands exerted economic force on Suriname by withholding substantial economic assistance and aid. The intent of the Dutch and the Americans, according to officials, was to force the Surinamese to take steps toward democracy and the recognition of human rights. In their discussion of this event Hufbauer and his colleagues express their view that the real intent of the United States was to "diminish Cuban, Libyan influence in Suriname."[12]

Although violating the norm for the use of military force, economic force has often been used to punish an adversary. For example, in 1983 the United States used economic force against the Soviet Union as punishment for the downing of a Korean airliner. In 1979 the Arab League imposed an economic embargo against Canada to punish the Canadians for their plan to move their embassy to Jerusalem from Tel Aviv.

Last Resort

Under the rubric of the just-war tradition, the use of military force is justified only when all peaceful alternatives have been exhausted. The economic instrument is clearly not a weapon of last resort. This principle could not apply to the use of the economic instrument. However, one might ask, Is economic force justified only after all political, psychological, and social alternatives to deter or reverse aggression have been exhausted?

Probability of Success

According to just-war criteria, there must be a sufficiently good prospect of success to justify the human and other costs associated with the use of military force. Clearly this norm would pose problems for the user of economic force. As stated elsewhere in these pages, the history of the successful use of the economic instrument is not impressive. Many times the economic weapon has been used merely to satisfy a domestic political objective. Many times the use of economic force has clearly violated this norm. The 1993–94 Haitian economic embargo is an example of good intentions, with a meager prospect of success, turning sour. A principal target of the embargo was the military regime's automotive fuel supplies. After months of the UN–U.S. embargo, the rogue military leadership was reportedly prospering by selling its surplus contraband fuel, imported from the neighboring Dominican Republic, for $10 a gallon.[13]

Proportionality of Goals

The human and collateral costs of employing the military weapon must be proportional to the benefits that are expected to be derived. (A well-known issue that is still debated is the proportionality of the use of the two atomic weapons dropped on Hiroshima and Nagasaki that brought an end to World War II.) The norm of proportionality appears to be a legitimate standard for testing the justness of the use of the economic weapon. Clouding the proportionality test, however, is the tendency to devalue the damage that can be inflicted in the use of economic force. Generally the use of military force will be more violent, more destructive, and as indiscriminate as the use of economic force—however, not always. Military force may be used in a peacekeeping role and inflict no damage. Economic force may promote famine, disease, and destruction.

In their November 1990 meeting the National Conference of Bishops encouraged the United States and its allies not to resort to "war" with Iraq but to "continue to pursue the course of peaceful pressure." Ironically, the "peaceful pressure" to which they referred was all-out economic war.[14] Senator George McGovern also described "economic sanctions" against Iraq as a method to achieve "a peaceful outcome." He clearly subscribed to the position that the use of military force implies war while the use of "economic sanctions" does not.[15]

During 1993 the United States had difficulty selling a worldwide trade embargo against Haiti, since many nations did not want to establish a precedent for the use of such potent force against a country that was not in a civil war and was not a threat to other nations.[16]

Discrimination

The military just-war criteria require that there be safeguards against inflicting undue collateral damage upon the target state. The discrimination norms for the use of military force specifically prohibit targeting civilian populations. There are serious problems in associating this norm with the use of economic force. While an economic embargo may not be targeted against the civil population directly, it will certainly have an impact upon that population. For example, a *New England Journal of Medicine* article identified a study that found that in Iraq, sanctions and the Gulf War had caused a threefold increase in infant mortality, largely from diarrhea, from January to August 1991.[17] In real numbers, a 1992 Harvard School of Public Health study concluded that tens of thousands more children were dying each year after the 1991 Persian Gulf War than before; the study attributed the deaths to military and economic warfare.[18]

While unusual, it is possible to target elites or heads of state rather than the general population. We have a 1993 example of such discrimination in the United States exercising immigration control over and freezing the assets of Haitian strongmen in an effort to restore the Aristide presidency. This selective use of economic force was not effective. To the contrary, indications were that the Haitian citizen was bearing the brunt of the punishment while the Haitian leaders were surviving or thriving. James Schlesinger, a former secretary of defense, has been particularly critical of the lack of discrimination in the use of the economic weapon in Haiti:

> Take…the political tool of starvation. We have regularly rebuked the Serbs for their ruthlessness in using starvation as a tool to achieve their political objectives. … Yet, examine the contrasting case of Haiti. There, we feel justified in employing starvation, even if it is inadvert, as a tool—for that is the effect of the American-inspired embargo directed against

Haiti. According to a recent Harvard study, 1,000 children a month are dying in Haiti as a result of the embargo. The elite, whom we seek to punish, suffer comparatively little.[19]

In September 1994 former president Jimmy Carter, serving as a presidential envoy to the Haitian military junta, professed that he was ashamed of his country for the damage inflicted upon the Haitian people by the U.S. embargo.[20]

Summation

Military just-war principles have some relevance for evaluating the moral issues associated with the use of economic force. However, the analogy is far from complete. It took centuries to codify the tradition of just war in military terms as it is known today. The debate has yet to be joined in codifying a tradition of a just war in terms of economic conflict. Nevertheless, the following preliminary conclusions can be drawn:

—While economic conflict can produce devastating damage to a state, generally it is a lesser form of violence and will inflict fewer casualties than military conflict.
—There must be just cause for the use of the economic instrument, but it need not be limited to deterring or repelling aggression.
—The just-war needs for authorization by competent authority and the right intention are applicable to the use of economic force.
—The last-resort requirement is not applicable. However, there is a need to demonstrate that political, social, or psychological efforts would not accomplish the objective.
—While it has often been violated in the wielding of economic force, the probability-of-success requirement does have application. The major problem in rationalizing the probability of success is the incomplete appreciation for the dynamics of economic force to make good judgments about what can succeed.

—The just-war "proportionality of goals and means" is applicable to the use of economic force.

—There are few historical instances of the use of economic force in which one might judge that the principle of discrimination has been exercised. Discriminate economic force has come to be an oxymoron.

A Code of Conduct

Absolute good faith with the enemy must be preserved as a rule of conduct. Without it war will degenerate into excesses and violences, ending only in the total destruction of one or both of the belligerents.

Rules of Land Warfare, U.S. Army, 1914

In this section we move from the question of morality to that of legality. As in the case of the morality of the use of economic force, the legality of waging economic conflict—in any form: coercion, trade war, or economic war—has seldom been debated in the abstract. Meaningful laws of military warfare date back to the Middle Ages, when they were promoted by ideals of chivalry and religion. Prior to the Middle Ages there were few restraints on the barbarism that characterized the battlefield. The first formal code of military conduct in war came in 1625 from Hugo Grotius in his "On the Law of War and Peace" (*De Jure Belli ac Pacis*).

Centuries of philosophical and practical debate have produced a series of laws of war. President Lincoln's General Order No. 100, "Instructions for the Government of Armies in the Field," of 1863, was one of the early codes of military conduct. In 1864 the first Geneva Convention, dealing with those wounded in war, was adopted. Conferences held at the Hague in the Netherlands in 1899 and 1907 and the Geneva Conventions of 1906, 1929, and 1949 consolidated many of the previous agreements. The nuclear age introduced special requirements, which promoted the codification of such laws as the 1967 law banning weapons of mass destruction in space.

In general these laws dealing with the use of military force are codified in treaties, conventions, and charters (such as the UN Charter and that of the Organization of American States). They prescribe that war must be waged only as an extension of authoritative, controlled political decisions and that it must not be indiscriminate. The laws promote peace and attempt to facilitate the termination of war. They define the basic rights of both combatants and noncombatants. Enforcement powers are limited, and reliance is placed on the punishment of war criminals (e.g. the Nuremburg Trials), the opinion of the family of nations, and, where possible, retribution against offending states.

There are no laws that could be considered a code of conduct for the prosecution of an economic conflict. There is a significant divergence between the conduct of military war and economic conflict. Such divergence makes it difficult to use the laws of military warfare to examine applicability to economic conflict (as we did with the just-war codicils). There are applicable edicts of freedom of commerce and navigation under customary international law. Usually such freedoms are codified in treaties and agreements. Most-favored-nation status, for example, is granted by treaty. There are other special trade relationships found in treaties such as preferential treatment, national treatment, open-door treatment, equitable treatment, and good-neighbor treatment. None of these edicts is easily enforced. The Permanent Court of International Justice and a number of other international courts have jurisdiction but little enforcement power.

The Organization for European Economic Cooperation—predecessor to the Organization for Economic Cooperation and Development (OECD)—to which the United States, Canada, and Japan became signatories in 1964, inhibits member nations from certain aggressive economic initiatives. (Finland, Australia, and New Zealand have also joined the organization, which includes all the major West European powers.) However, it is the General Agreement on Tariffs and Trade (GATT)—signed in 1947 by twenty-three countries, including the United States—that has had the greatest impact on the U.S. conduct of economic conflict. GATT mandates against discriminatory impediments to trade among the signatories. Such a prohibition would appear to preclude the use of most of the instruments of U.S. economic force against nations that collectively represent over 80 percent of world trade. However, as Barry Carter points out, the countries that are most likely to be targets of the U.S. use of economic force are not among the 110 signatories to GATT. In addition, the provisions of GATT are so broad that it is not difficult to find an exception to justify the use of economic force against a signer. Each use of economic force by one signatory of GATT against another substantially weakens the agreement, however, and could have a serious impact on the free flow of international commerce it is intended to promote.

The OECD, GATT, and similar international trade agreements may inhibit, to some small degree, the use of the economic instrument by the signatories. For example, in early 1991 the United States embargoed Mexican tuna because it was being caught using methods that slaughtered dolphins. Mexico charged that the U.S. embargo violated provisions of the GATT agreement, to which both countries are signatories. A panel of GATT judges ruled in favor of the Mexicans, and the United States was ordered to terminate the embargo.[21] Nevertheless, precedence and the frequent use of economic force would argue that there is little practical restraint upon the use of such force in international relations.

Thus far we have discussed the lack of any laws against the use of economic force, not how such force may be used. The distinction to be made here is between what the Germans call *Wehrwirstschaft* and *Kriegwirtschaft,* the first addressing the preparation and initiation of war and the second addressing the conduct of war. The combined laws of military warfare are explicit as to the treatment of prisoners and the inviolability of sanctuaries such as

THE DISMAL BATTLEFIELD

hospitals and educational, cultural, and religious structures. Pillage is outlawed, and the rights of neutral states are guaranteed. There are no such codified norms for the use of economic force. While compassion and a sense of responsibility may preclude the use of economic weapons that would lead to famine, foreclosure of medical treatment, long-term loss of natural resources, pillage of financial resources, pollution of the environment, or genocide, none of these objectives is specifically prohibited by law.

In sum, there is no international legislation that proscribes the initiation or conduct of economic force as is found in the many legalities prescribed for the initiation and conduct of military war.

Chapter 6

The Instruments of Economic Force

——————————————■———————

The instruments of battle are useful only if one knows how to use them.

Ardant du Picq

U.S. policymakers have a wide range of economic instruments at their disposal. Other nations may have fewer or different instruments in their economic armories. World bodies such as the United Nations, alliances such as NATO, corporations, and individuals all have different resources that may be used to achieve their objectives.

A list of the instruments of economic force is provided in table 3. Definitions are provided in the glossary. Following are examples and explanatory remarks. In a concession to the limits of our language, on occasion two terms may be used to describe the same activity. Blockade, quarantine, the stopping and searching of shipping, the physical denial of lines of communication, and the destruc-

99

tion of industrial or agricultural targets are not included in this list, as they are considered to be military, not economic, initiatives. However, they are initiatives that may be used in support of economic conflict.

The instruments of economic force may also be divided into two major categories, representing the carrot (a positive economic inducement) and the stick (an economic punishment). The carrot and stick instruments are discussed in chapter 8 under the principle of diversity.

In one of the essays in the Nincic and Wallenstein book on economic coercion, Johan Galtung identifies additional categories—or different dimensions—of "sanctions," including:

—individual versus collective targets
—intra- versus international changes sought
—unilateral versus multilateral
—general versus selective
—total versus partial[1]

Trade

Most-Favored-Nation Status

As is true with many of the instruments listed in table 3, most-favored-nation (MFN) status is not intrinsically an economic weapon. However, it may be used as such. Literally, it is a guarantee to a nation that it will have the right to trade equal to that of the most favored nation. MFN status provides significant rights and privileges but is rather broadly shared among nations. It serves international law in that it codifies the equality of states in commerce. It serves the international trade system by providing an instrument that may be used in treaty negotiations. It serves nations by providing the carrot and stick to influence relations with other nations. Prior to the collapse of the Soviet Union, the United States granted MFN status routinely and permanently to most noncommunist countries.

Table 3

The Instruments of Economic Force

Trade	Finance	Resource Management	Unconventional
Most-favored-nation status	Aid and loans	Stockpiling	Industrial espionage
Boycott	Indebtedness	Autarky	Bribery
Sanctions	Withholding payments	Limited extraction	Disinformation
Blacklist/graylist	Freezing accounts	Preclusive purchasing	Inciting work stoppages
Export/import licensing	Nationalizing assets	Technology transfer	Immigration control
Export credit guarantees and insurance	Impounding assets	Resource denial	Disrupting lines of communications
International law			Computer subversion
Export and import embargoes			Currency subversion
Arms sales			Smuggling
Tariffs			Currency theft
Travel limitations			Credit system subversion
Commodity dumping			Sabotage
Patent denial			Extortion
			Economic terrorism
			Economic propaganda
			Piracy

Note: For a detailed discussion of unconventional methods, see Shubik, "Unconventional Methods."

However, communist and some other nations' status was reconsidered every twelve months under the Jackson-Vanik Amendment. (For example, in 1983 the United States suspended Romania's MFN status to protest that country's immigration policies.)

When used as an instrument of coercion or in a trade war, MFN status can be most effective when there is the threat that it is to be withdrawn from a state that depends upon its privileges.

The extension of MFN status by the United States to China in 1993–94 was hotly debated. A 4 June 1989 massacre of students and workers in Tiananmen Square in Beijing had mobilized U.S. sentiment against the institutionalized repression in China. Given the deplorable state of human rights in China, there were U.S. advocates who favored withholding MFN status to force a guarantee from the Chinese that they would liberalize their oppressive domestic controls.

The debate was important. It was important to Americans who were offended by China's violation of human rights. It was important to American businessmen who favored extending MFN extension as they courted the Chinese market. (Pro-extension forces liked to cite the South African "Green Bay Tree" parable, which has it that this normally ugly tree will blossom and flower if only it is encouraged and watered.) It was extremely important to the Chinese, who had witnessed their position in the American market grow dramatically: China had risen from being the thirty-fifth largest trading partner of the United States in 1979 to the seventh in 1992, and it became the world's fastest-growing economy in 1993. President Clinton opted to extend MFN status to China—albeit for only one year—because, as he stated, he wanted "to support modernization in China."[2] He made it clear that the granting of MFN status to China was conditional and that the United States had not abandoned its position on China's human rights abuses. President Clinton also had to consider the economic benefits to be derived from an economically resurgent China, and he favored the Green Bay Tree approach in his decision to grant MFN status to that nation.

The Boycott

The source of the eponym *boycott,* both verb and noun, is Captain Charles Cunningham Boycott. An unyielding retired British army officer, Boycott managed extensive estates for the earl of Erne in County Mayo, Ireland. In 1880 impoverished Irish tenants, in a controversy over rents, refused to communicate with anyone—and particularly Boycott—who opposed their demands. Boycott was not merely given the silent treatment. His servants and workers abandoned him. Organized gangs destroyed the estate property and drove cattle through his fields. He was refused service in stores, he was hung in effigy, and his life was threatened. Boycott had been effectively excommunicated from Irish society. The protest came to be known as a boycott.

Since the perils of this stubborn British soldier, the boycott has been used often. A boycott of Israel by the Arab League—at one time including as many as nineteen states, among them Egypt and Saudi Arabia—preceded the creation of the Israeli state in 1948. The episode is instructive in its scope in terms of the number of states involved, the length of time enforced, and the levels of boycott. Its objective was to inhibit trade between Israel and the remainder of the world and lead to the demise of the Israeli state. The boycott was conducted at four levels:

—the primary boycott, in which the states of the Arab League refused to trade with the Israelis
—the secondary boycott, which provided for the Arab League blacklisting firms of any "third country" that might trade with Israel
—the tertiary boycott, which found firms not in the league refusing to trade with blacklisted companies out of fear that they also might be blacklisted
—the personal boycott, in which individuals, institutions, and other entities were blacklisted because they were seen to be friendly to Israel

Sanctions

The sanctions instrument is listed in table 3 only because the term is widely accepted in discussions of economic conflict. The term is employed so indiscriminately that it has limited utility in this effort. For example, Brown-John, in his treatise on "multilateral sanctions" in international law, identifies "four distinct but broad categories [of sanctions]: moral and political, economic, financial and physical." The sanction is defined in the *Encyclopaedia Britannica* as a "reaction…by members of a social group indicating approval or disapproval of a mode of conduct and to enforce behavioral standards of the group."[3] In one example of sanctions, the Eskimos may punish the man who steals another man's wife by ridiculing him in a nasty song composed by the injured party.

Blacklist/Graylist

A blacklisting is the process of including a trade figure on a roll of those that are to be boycotted. The target is made aware of the fact that it has been discriminated against, and the process is meant to influence the conduct of the target. A graylist is the same, except that the maker of the graylist finds that it is not politically or economically expedient to announce the fact that there is such a list or that the target has the distinction of being enrolled. The Arab League in its anti-Israeli economic campaigns used both the blacklist and the graylist extensively.

Export/Import Licensing

There are a number of U.S. laws that authorize and direct the licensing of the export and import of specific commodities from or into specific countries. One such is the Omnibus Trade and Competitiveness Act of 1988. The licensing mechanism is a procedure to implement restrictive trade activities. Licensing may control the import of such nonpolitical items as pornography or "fresh, chilled or frozen lamb meat," or the export of very political items such as arms and high-technology products to Iraq or the former Soviet Union and Warsaw Pact nations.

In 1966 and 1967 the United States became concerned about what appeared to be an obvious attempt by Taiwan to develop nuclear weapons. The United States did not stop the export of nuclear-weapon-building components and nuclear fuel to Taiwan, but export licenses were slowed. The slowdown in supply meant delays in Taiwan's production programs and a reduced output from its nuclear power plants. In 1988 the Taiwanese government forswore any attempt to produce a nuclear device.[4] The manipulation of export licensing scored a significant success for this use of economic force.

Export Credit Guarantees and Insurance

U.S export credit guarantees and insurance may be tendered as rewards, or they may be withheld as punishment or in coercion. These guarantees and insurance can be used as carrots when granted but as sticks when denied or withdrawn. Countries considered hostile to the United States, such as Cuba, North Korea, and Vietnam, have been deprived of these benefits.

International Law

The multiple provisions of international law can be invoked to justify or to encourage the use of the economic weapon. They can also be invoked to counter the use of economic force, as in 1982 when the United States, in an attempt to prevent the construction of the Soviet-European natural gas pipeline, sought to restrain the participation of U.S. corporations in the construction program. U.S. companies operating overseas were to be denied all exports from the United States should they assist in the program. A Dutch district court decided that a Dutch subsidiary of a U.S. company could not be constrained from performing under a sales contract made under Dutch law, because the United States had no such jurisdiction under international law. The United States did not contest the decision.[5]

Export and Import Embargoes

Export and import embargoes preclude the buying, selling, or bartering of certain or all commodities with respect to a target nation. They are blunt instruments and can cause great collateral damage to the implementing as well as the target nation.

Export embargoes may be limited to very specific items, as in the 1993 UN worldwide oil and military arms embargo against Haiti. Even in general embargoes, such as the UN embargo against Iraq in the early 1990s, it is routine to exempt such commodities as food and medical supplies. However, if the embargo against the export of the nation's products is successful—for example, oil from Iraq, which is worth $21 billion a year in hard currency—there will be little money available to import food and medical necessities.

The mere threat of an embargo can be an effective deterrent. The damage actually inflicted is most often a function of the time the embargo is enforced. As Richard Perle has pointed out, over the longer term, limits on the import of ideas and technology can be more effective than limits on products. (Perle's view must assume that the target country has the luxury of promoting ideas and technology and is not a subsistence economy.) Gunnar Adler-Karlsson has written that during the cold war, export embargo lists published by the United States and its allies were a valuable source of information for Eastern intelligence services. Not only did these lists provide them with the results of the West's appraisals of the Warsaw Pact's vulnerabilities, but they also alerted them as to the commodities they must produce or acquire from other sources.[6]

Like boycotts, embargoes often generate collateral damage that is comparable to military losses due to friendly fire. The United States imposed an embargo against Vietnam in 1975 when the communist forces of Hanoi overran the South. For almost two decades U.S. punitive economic measures against Vietnam inhibited that country's economic growth. However, in 1993 Hanoi began to recover and generated an embryonic bustling economy from which American business was barred by the United States. American businessmen complained that they, not the Vietnamese, were suffering economic casualties due to the U.S. embargo, which denied them a market of seventy-two million people.[7] On 3 February 1994 the Clinton administration announced the lifting of the embargo, permitting American businessmen to conduct business openly with the Vietnamese (some business was already being conducted covertly).[8]

Arms Sales

Arms sale restrictions are a form of embargo. The United States has often limited the sale of arms to countries that have demonstrated that they would employ the weapons in opposition to the best interests of the United States or in violation of human rights. In those countries that have been dependent on U.S. weapon systems, the abrupt halt of replacements, spare parts, and new compatible systems is extremely disruptive. It may not be enough, however, to dissuade the target from opposing U.S. policies (post-1979 Iran being an example). The embargo of arms to South Africa had an unanticipated result in that it encouraged the South Africans to develop a domestic defense industry, which became successful enough to find export markets of its own. Some support the theory that the arms embargo placed upon the warring factions of the original state of Yugoslavia worked to the benefit of the Serbs in their systematic destruction of the Bosnian minority. Nevertheless, the embargo of the sales of arms can be a useful tool of economic coercion.

In several instances arms sales were offered as carrots to Pakistan to encourage the Pakistanis to abandon a nuclear weapon construction program. In August 1976 Henry Kissinger offered the sale of one hundred A7 fighter aircraft. In April 1979 Jimmy Carter also offered the sale of jet aircraft. Despite the blandishments of France and the United States, in February 1982 the Pakistani foreign minister announced that Pakistan had the elements of a nuclear device, which if assembled would become a nuclear weapon.

Tariffs

There are several dimensions of the tariff instrument. While we think of tariffs as a levy made by an importing country upon goods of a foreign nation at the port of entry, Barry Carter has proposed a punitive tariff assessed at the point of export. He has proposed that such a tariff could be imposed upon Iraqi oil exports by the United Nations as a reparation to countries that suffered losses by virtue of the Iraqi occupation and savaging of Kuwait.[9]

As with the use of most of these instruments, there is a price associated with the levy of tariffs in either economic competition or conflict. The following are GATT statistics that demonstrate what it might cost a nation's consumer when a tariff is imposed with the purpose of protecting jobs.[10]

Industry	Cost of Tariff (per job saved)
Specialty steel	$1 million
Color TVs	420,000
Ceramic tiles	135,000
Clothing	36,000–82,000
Agriculture	20,000 (per farmer)
Dairy	18,000 (per cow)

Travel Limitations

The most common use of travel restrictions as an economic instrument is the limiting of access to airports of a target nation's air carriers to punish, persuade, or dissuade. In 1983 Korean Air Lines

Flight 007 traveling from New York to Seoul, Korea, was shot down by Soviet fighter aircraft. In retaliation, the United States closed down the two Aeroflot ticket offices still allowed to operate in this country. (The Reagan administration had already suspended all flights by the Soviet state airline to the United States in response to a Polish crisis of 1981.) In addition, the administration expelled three Aeroflot officials and was instrumental in getting allied nations (West Germany, Japan, Spain, and the United Kingdom) to boycott Aeroflot flights.

In 1993 the United States denied entry visas to seventy-nine Libyan athletes scheduled to participate in the World University Games in Buffalo, New York. The denial was part of a larger embargo against Libya following Libyan implication in the 1988 bombing of Pan Am flight 103 over Lockerbie, Scotland.

Access to the United States is being limited to impede illegal entries of Mexican nationals across the border. There is a major economic aspect to Operation Blockade, which is being conducted across a twenty-mile stretch of the Rio Grande at the El Paso–Juarez crossing. An underground economy, fed by illegal workers, provides cheap labor but also poses a personal security threat to the citizens of El Paso. Along with the nannies, maids, and shoeshine entrepreneurs who work illegally in this border city, there are also car thieves, house robbers, and muggers. The Border Patrol's campaign is a reverse blockade that is not designed to inhibit an economic commodity from entering another nation (e.g. petroleum to Haiti or arms to South Africa) but rather an effort to prevent an economic commodity (labor) from entering the United States illegally.[11]

There is a difference between limiting access for purposes of routine security—protecting commercial, technological, or industrial secrets—and the use of travel limitations as an economic weapon. Access limitations for security purposes is routinely accomplished within industry and academia to protect assets that could give competitors valuable leverage in the marketplace or scientific community. Travel limitations for security purposes have been routinely imposed by the United States within its borders to protect valuable information on military posture and force readiness. Travel limitations imposed as an economic weapon are most often a deterrent or a punitive action with an objective other than security. (However, with the ubiquity of the Soviet intelligence apparatus in Cuba from the 1960s to the early 1990s, U.S. restrictions on travel to Cuba obviously had security implications.)

Commodity Dumping

Both in legal and in economic terms, dumping is defined as international price discrimination: the practice of charging a higher price at home than for export, not necessarily below cost. In routine economic competition, commodity dumping is considered "unfair trade" that gives the purveyor an undue advantage in the international marketplace. When used as an economic instrument, the objective is not merely to seek an advantage in the marketplace but to coerce the target country to comply with the wishes of the country doing the dumping.

Currently the conventional wisdom is that commodity dumping has been perpetrated with greatest skill and effect by the Japanese. In 1991 the United States took defensive action against the Japanese, who were dumping flat-panel display screens for laptop and notebook computers in the U.S. market at more than 60 percent below their manufacturing costs. The U.S. response was to impose tariff penalties on the screens equal to the discount. Similar complaints were made in the same year about the dumping of Japanese minivans. The United States brought its complaint on minivan dumping to the International Trade Commission for a ruling.

But these are examples of commodity dumping in the arena of economic competition, not economic coercion. To demonstrate commodity dumping in a hypothetical case of coercion, imagine that a wheat-exporting nation and the United States were involved in a serious disagreement that warranted the United States using its economic power to persuade its adversary to take a certain course of action. Under this commodity-dumping option, the United States could first threaten to dump its huge wheat reserves onto the world market. This dumping could depress the value of wheat worldwide, inflicting substantial damage upon the economy of the target wheat exporter. Should the deterrent threat fail, the United Sates could use this economic trade weapon and bring pressure on its adversary until it acquiesced.

Patent Denial

A classic case of the use of patent denial as an instrument of economic competition, if not conflict, was the Japanese government's delay in granting a computer chip patent to Texas Instruments (TI) for almost thirty years. The Japanese use of the technology in the interim gave a substantial advantage to companies such as Toshiba, NEC, Mitsubishi, Hitachi, Fujitsu, Matushita, and Yamaha. The patent, finally granted in 1989, will earn for TI some $200 million to $800 million annually. However, no compensation was granted for the thirty years of misuse of the TI technology.[12]

In early 1994 the Japanese considered revising their patent laws in a manner that would make it legal for their national companies to produce and sell pirated U.S. software through reverse engineering. The damage that could be inflicted upon American software producers is manifest when it is recognized that such programs as Microsoft's Word for Windows, which retails for about $400, is sold in pirated form for less than $10 in Asian bazaars. Proving that nothing is simple in international commerce, and that the loyalties of multinational corporations are divided, there were major American software companies—including Sun Microsystems, Storage Technology, Broderbund Software, and others—that supported such a Japanese initiative. The Clinton administration and major software developers such as IBM, Microsoft, and Lotus Development opposed this change in Japanese law.[13] This U.S.-Japanese debate over the protection of software patents is not an economic-conflict skirmish. However, it does demonstrate the potential utility of patent administration as an instrument of economic force.

India has also been guilty of formulating and administering national patent laws in such a way as to permit, if not encourage, commercial piracy. India's abuse of pharmaceutical patent rights has been particularly troublesome. Gerald J. Mossinghoff, president of the Pharmaceutical Manufacturer's Association, has said, "There is no country in the world where patent piracy of valuable patented medicines has been more rampant...than in India."[14] In 1993 Brazil was close to having U.S. economic weapons used against it for failing to protect U.S. patents, trademarks, and trade secrets as had been promised. However, in each of these examples the violation of the international patent code was done within the venue of economic competition. Using patent denial as a weapon in economic conflict merely involves changing the motivation and the objective. Should one industrialized nation, one that possesses many high-technology patents of great value, become engaged in a long-term controversy with an equally advanced nation, both would be vulnerable to coercive patent denial initiatives.

Finance

Brown-John has written that "the variety of potential financial sanctions is almost unlimited."[15] The finance instrument of economic force includes many options that under the proper circumstances could have more utility than those classified as trade weapons.

An interesting sidelight to the 1990 invasion and occupation of Kuwait was the economic war waged by the Kuwaitis using finance instruments as their principal weapons. While the Iraqis won the initial phase of the military operation, it was the Kuwaitis who scored big gains in their economic counterattack. The battles were fought in the world's banks and finance centers. The objectives were money rather than real estate or military forces. When Saddam

Hussein invaded Kuwait, Iraq was insolvent. It had a foreign debt of over $70 billion and a debilitating annual shortfall of hard currency. It is estimated that Iraq plundered Kuwait of about $800 million in foreign reserves, $32 million in gold bars, and $1 billion from commercial banks[16] (a classic case of currency theft under the unconventional-instrument category). The Kuwaitis retaliated from London with their overseas assets to encourage Turkish-Pakistani cooperation against the Iraqis and to punish Jordan for its complicity with Saddam Hussein. Using all of the instruments in the finance category, Kuwait did much to limit Iraq's sources of cash and credit.

Aid and Loans

Aid and loans can be both a carrot and a stick. U.S. aid has been provided to secure cooperation from nations on every continent. Withholding of that aid can have a serious impact on a recipient nation's economy. The carrot/stick dichotomy may be illustrated in the U.S. concern for human rights in South Africa. The Green Bay Tree become a metaphor for South Africa for the Nixon and Reagan administrations when they proposed that relations with that country required nurturing to encourage the blossoming of human rights. The opposing school of thought was that the Green Bay Tree was a metaphor for apartheid, which must be starved and eradicated.[17]

In a second example, the United States terminated aid and loans to Jordan in an effort to induce Jordan to refrain from supporting Iraq.

A third example is the U.S. practice of blocking new loans to Vietnam from the International Monetary Fund.

Finally, in its 1980s economic offensive against the USSR, the Reagan administration exerted pressure on Western allies to discourage giving short-term credits that would permit the Kremlin to meet its payments to its creditors. It was a ploy that Schweizer characterizes as a "deft manipulation of the credit market for national security ends."[18]

Indebtedness

The creditor to a nation that has a large debt has an advantage. There are opportunities to coerce or negotiate from a position of strength. At the current level of sophistication in the use of the economic weapon, it will be rare that any nation would deliberately put another nation in debt for the purpose of generating a dependency that could be exploited. However, whether deliberately or not, the Middle East oil magnates have created such dependencies and are not reluctant to use their advantage. In 1978 debtor nation Egypt felt the economic lash of the Arab League creditors who were punishing Egypt for Anwar Sadat's compromise with Israel in the Camp David accord.

Withholding Payments

When there is a close relationship and dependence between nations, withholding payments of routine, periodic obligations is often possible. On 11 March 1988 President Reagan announced that in furtherance of the economic war being conducted against Panama in an effort to oust strongman Manuel Noriega, he was withholding payments to Panama that had been collected as tolls for commerce going through the canal. On 8 April the administration invoked the provisions of the International Emergency Economic Powers Act to order American firms dealing with Panama to withhold all payments to the republic (to include taxes).

Freezing Accounts

On 8 November 1980, during the Iranian hostage crisis, President Carter froze all Iranian assets in American banks within and outside the United States. The president was using the finance weapon both to defang the Iranians to keep them from using their petrodollars as leverage against the United States, and to hold their assets hostage in the economic war that ensued. The freezing of financial assets can be a potent weapon when used against states that trade extensively in the international market and have substantial reserves in foreign banks.

The freezing of accounts can pose serious extraterritoriality problems—that is, the authority a country such as the United States has over the financial enterprises it operates outside its borders. As a practical matter, however, freezing an adversary's financial assets works, at least over the short term, until the weighty matters of extraterritoriality can be resolved in the international and foreign courts.

Freezing U.S. citizens' accounts by issuing a "Notice of Blocking" to a financial institution can be an effective means of enforcing embargoes and travel bans. During June 1994 the United States took such action against a group of two hundred Americans who traveled to Havana for a one-week visit in defiance of a U.S. ban on travel to Cuba.[19]

Nationalizing Assets

Modern industrial states, including the United States, recognize the sovereign right of all states to nationalize property held by foreign entities. There is a provision, however, that the foreign owner of the property must be fairly compensated. Nationalization with fair compensation is a legal procedure that could nonetheless be a useful economic instrument of coercion. Nationalism without compensation is considered illegal and may be a more useful tool over the short run. Nationalizing assets may be one of the few effective economic instruments available to poorer nations dealing with major economic powers.

Impounding Assets

Impounding differs from freezing in that in the former the user actually takes control of the assets. An example of the impounding of assets is the September 1992 UN takeover of Iraqi deposits in banks around the world as punishment for Iraq's failure to agree on compensation for the destruction it caused during the Gulf War.

Resource Management

Stockpiling

Stockpiling is a defensive instrument used to reduce a nation's vulnerability to shortages of critical commodities imposed by a belligerent or for other reasons. The classic examples of stockpiling are found in the strategic petroleum reserves maintained by the United States, Germany, and Japan.

The decision to stockpile petroleum in the United States has a long, interesting history. It was President Eisenhower who in 1956, following the Suez crisis, originally proposed the concept of stockpiling petroleum to be used in emergencies. It was the shah of Iran who in 1967, following the Six-Day War, suggested that the excess Iranian oil stocks should be imported by the United States, to be stored in salt mines as a strategic reserve. The United States currently stocks sufficient petroleum reserves in special facilities to provide emergency supplies for an extended period at reduced consumption rates.

Autarky

Autarky—the process of achieving economic self-sufficiency—is, like stockpiling, a defensive economic instrument. The best possible circumstance of autarky provides "aggregate equilibrium," which eventuates when the national demand for goods and services equals the national supply. Complete autarky is impossible for an industrial nation in the twentieth century and will probably remain so in the twenty-first. Partial autarky can be achieved by either developing a nation's own resources or finding alternatives within its national capabilities.

116

In 1940 Japan's Ichizo Kobayashi, minister of commerce and industry, laid out that country's plan for achieving autarky within its economic sphere through conquest:

> With Japan, Manchoukuo and China as the nucleus and embracing Great Eastern Asia, a common economic sphere should be created. The sphere ought to be able to adopt and carry out an economic policy of self-sufficiency without the assistance of Britain or America forthwith and in the future that of any other country. The proposed common economic sphere could be made independent and to rest on a secure basis so that it might push with vigor the policy of self-sufficiency in the truest sense of the word.[20]

Limited Extraction

Limiting extraction of a critical resource is a relative of the embargo. In the embargo there is a refusal to supply a commodity to one or more entities when there is the presumption that there is an abundant supply. In limited extraction there is a de facto embargo because the supplier has chosen not to extract the commodity, creating a shortfall in supply. The prime examples of limited extraction were the periodic slowdowns of OPEC producers to control the price of oil.

Preclusive Purchasing

Preclusive purchasing is the process of an economic power "cornering the market" to prevent a target of economic coercion from having access to the commodity. It is an instrument that has limited application, since it is extremely difficult to find or create a market for a valuable commodity that can be controlled by one party. Nevertheless, the potential does exist for, say, the preclusive purchasing of an advanced computer chip, for the purpose of economic coercion of a target. The chip would have to be difficult to duplicate and be of unique value to the target of the coercion. It has been reported that in 1982 a top secret Department of Defense five-year planning directive made provisions for "preemptive buying" to limit Soviet access to critical technologies.[21]

Technology Transfer

The United States is exercising control over its technology in a number of ways under several laws for security purposes. It also used the limitation of transfer of its technology, military and otherwise, as an economic weapon during the cold war. From 1949, with the birth of NATO's Coordinating Committee (COCOM), the lists of embargoed materials that were not to be furnished to the Soviet Union and its Council for Mutual Economic Assistance (COME-CON) countries mainly included technologies.

Resource Denial

In 1990 it was reported that the United States was considering interrupting the water supply into Iraq to force Saddam Hussein to withdraw from Kuwait. Iraq relies upon the Tigris and Euphrates for over 90 percent of its agricultural and industrial water. The headwaters of both rivers lie in Turkey, which has the capability to interrupt that supply. The impact on Iraq would have been immediate, devastating, and indiscriminate. The water-weapon option was too drastic for Washington strategists, who feared the creation of a dangerous precedent in an area where water is such a precious resource.

Unconventional

The unconventional instruments listed in table 3 are generally thought of as being "illegal, dishonest or unethical."[22] Most of these instruments would be used only for economic war, but they could conceivably be used as weapons in trade wars or economic coercion.

Industrial Espionage

See chapter 4, "The Threat."

Bribery

A cynic might hold that in many cases what we describe here as bribery is in reality just the carrot approach (as in the granting of most-favored-nation status). There is a difference, however, in that bribery, as we use it here, is the inducement to do something wrong. The carrot approach is the inducement to do something right (right, at least, in the eyes of the offerer). There have been serious proposals that industrial nations could solve the arms proliferation problem by offering financial support to less developed nations in exchange for their guarantee not to develop or import armaments. The financial quid pro quo by the major powers was described by one observer as a blatant bribe.[23] James Woolsey, director of the CIA, has been quoted as saying that economic discrimination against the United States has been promoted by "bribing foreign governments to give contracts to their countries' companies" rather than to American firms.[24]

Disinformation

There are many opportunities for a belligerent to use disinformation during economic conflict. The planting of a rumor that a high-value computer chip was defective, infected with a virus, or programmed to self-destruct could make it worthless on the international market. The planting of a rumor that certain agricultural or packaged-food exports were contaminated or violated local social taboos could make them unmarketable. Fictitious claims that a firm had ties to the Israelis could make their product anathema in some Arab states.

An interesting example of disinformation was uncovered in August 1993 when the *New York Times* published reports that the Pentagon had misled when it claimed that a 1984 test ICBM had been intercepted and destroyed in flight by an experimental infrared–sensing rocket produced in the Strategic Defense Initiative (SDI) program.[25] This technological coup was compared by an administration spokesman to the feat of "hitting a bullet with a bullet." In fact, the 1993 *Times* report contended, the intercept and ICBM destruction never actually occurred as claimed. Rather, the ICBM carried an explosive charge in the warhead that was designed to detonate in the event of a near miss. In part, the article alleged, this was a carefully crafted piece of disinformation designed to deceive the Soviets. The speculation is that the objective of the ploy was economic, to cause the Soviets to spend their limited resources to counter a successful SDI program. The Russian ambassador to the United States, Vladimer Lukin, claimed that such disinformation ploys "accelerated the Gorbachev revolution by five years."[26]

Inciting Work Stoppages

For decades during the height of the cold war there were rumors and suspicions that some labor disputes in the United States and other Western nations had been inspired by the international communist movement. While there may have been truth in some of the allegations, as Stephen P. Gibert has pointed out, the American trade union movement was in large measure capitalist and anticommunist. Nevertheless, Richard Pipes makes the point that there were trade unions in the West that were manipulated by Moscow.[27] There were many plausible reports that the head of the Central Soviet Trade Union Organization, A. N. Shelepin, having at one time been head of the KGB, influenced activities within the communist-controlled trade unions that inspired work stoppages.

Immigration Control

Immigration and border controls have a long history. Given the efficiency and ease of international transport, the disparity of living standards between have and have-not nations, the flight from political and military war, ethnic violence, the growth of international commerce, and a host of other reasons, people are crossing international boundaries and homesteading in greater numbers every year. A UN report estimates that there are more than one hundred million migrants residing in host countries—about 2 percent of the world's population—and that the migratory pressures are increasing.[28]

Nations may exercise immigration control in a campaign of economic coercion or war or a trade war against entire populations, elements of a population, or individuals. In the simplest form of immigration control, these human targets are not permitted to enter or take up residence or qualify for citizenship in the enforcing state. There are many examples of states imposing such restraints against the entire population of an adversary during major war—World Wars I and II, for example. There are examples of the selective imposition of such restrictions when Arab states denied access to any person arriving from an Israeli port of embarkation without reference to that person's nationality or religion. In June 1993 the United States forbade access to about a hundred Haitian military, business, and political leaders in conjunction with the campaign of economic coercion to restore ousted president Aristide.

Disrupting Lines of Communication

We most often think of disrupting lines of communication (LOCs) in terms of maritime operations. In fact overland routes may be just as vulnerable as sea lines, and land operations may be just as effective as naval. There are other tools that may be used to shut down communication paths. Legal and toll measures may be taken by a user of economic force to inhibit the free movement of commerce. In 1988 South Africa was charged with waging "economic warfare by rail" against its landlocked neighbors, particularly Zimbabwe but also Zaire and Zambia. The charge was that the South Africans had sabotaged rail lines from these countries to sea ports in Mozambique.

Cutting LOCs that carry a nation's trade may have the same effect as a port blockade. Absent an overt military war, cutting LOCs is considered an unconventional operation. During open armed conflict it is usually a component of military strategy and tactics.

Computer Subversion

Nations have become dependent upon computer technology to manage data, to design, manufacture, control, and inspect industrial products, to control systems, and to perform many other critical functions. Such dependence generates a substantial vulnerability. An example of subversion of a computer system as a component of an economic war occurred during the prelude to the military war Desert Storm. In 1990 the French claimed that after the 2 August invasion of Kuwait, some French-made computerized systems used by the Iraqi military were brought down by computer viruses that had been implanted for just such a contingency.[29]

A globalization of the consumer market has been made possible by the computer. Berliners can order clothes from the Orvis catalogue using the on-line computer network CompuServe. This growing electronic global market is vulnerable to very simple subversion techniques.

Currency Subversion

In contemporary history there are few examples of successful currency subversion. The effective use of such a weapon would be so destructive to a nation's economy that it must be considered one of the ultimate economic weapons (the equivalent of an economic-conflict nuclear weapon). There is the fear that its use could invite retaliation and so it is best left on the shelf of the armory (a parallel to the use of nuclear, biological, and chemical weapons). The Germans attempted to subvert British currency during World War II by dropping counterfeit pound notes over England. However, the counterfeits were of such poor quality that the program failed. In 1940 the British retaliated by dropping facsimiles of Nazi ration stamps on Germany.[30]

The German World War II counterfeit effort was crude, but contemporary technologies have made counterfeiting much easier. In 1994 a team of counterfeiters operating from Lebanon's Bekka Valley, under Iranian and Syrian protection, reportedly produced $1 billion of the most nearly perfect $100 bills the Secret Service has ever detected.[31]

In 1992 the Estonians threatened to replace the ruble with its own currency, the kroon, in an effort to gain control of its own economy and to further sever its relations with Moscow.

The United States was the target of a Soviet attempt to subvert its currency in 1979. A KGB section was instructed to drive up the price of gold, which it was assumed would undermine world confidence in the U.S. dollar. The ploy to manipulate the gold market failed.

Smuggling

Smuggling for profit and to avoid tariffs or other restraints, even on a national level, should not normally be considered an economic weapon. However, smuggling on a national scale as a defensive measure to compensate for an effective embargo is an economic weapon. The Iraqis benefited from extensive state-encouraged and state-sponsored smuggling across its land borders during the UN-sponsored economic embargo of the early 1990s.

Currency Theft

The theft of currency is a possible but unlikely tool in economic conflict. Particularly for industrial nations, the theft would have to be of such great magnitude that it strains credulity to imagine that it would be possible. However, terrorists waging an economic war could benefit greatly by currency theft. The Russian revolution was supported in part by revenues derived from bank robberies directed by Joseph Stalin, who operated under the pseudonym Koba.

Credit System Subversion

There is the hypothesis that as the world's credit system becomes more sophisticated and more centralized, it also becomes more vulnerable.[32] There are many likely targets for a belligerent during an economic conflict. One vulnerability is the automated data processing of the Federal Reserve System, defended by redundancies but nevertheless vulnerable. Flooding a country with false credit cards would be more effective today than counterfeiting currency.

Sabotage

The term *sabotage* was coined when workers threw their wooden shoes (*sabots*) into the new machinery introduced during the Industrial Revolution to replace workers.

A key element of the plot of Larry Bond's novel *Cauldron* is the sabotage of a Polish helicopter rotor fabrication plant during a 1997 economic war. The sabotage, inflicted to create a cause célèbre to escalate an economic conflict, does just that. It is difficult to imagine a major industrial power being controlled by the villains portrayed by Bond. However, it seems more likely should the sabotage be perpetrated by a rogue state led by a Qaddafi, a Noriega, or a Saddam Hussein to promote a larger economic scheme.

Extortion

Extortion is the flip side of bribery, with the threat of pain rather than the promise of reward being the distinguishing characteristic. Extortion is so commonplace in international relations that it assumes a mantle of diplomatic dignity. Most extortion in the international arena is economic. One of the great fears of an Iraqi takeover of Kuwait, and the leverage Iraq could then exert on Saudi Arabia, was that Saddam Hussein would control so much of the oil production capacity of the world that he could extort a position as leader of the Arab world and dominate the oil markets.

Economic Terrorism

Economic terrorism has been waged by the Irish Republican Army in Northern Ireland for decades. On 6 January 1992 a terrorist act occurred that the authorities classified as an "economic warfare" event. The detonation of two massive car bombs in Belfast produced panic and chaos that brought the city's commerce to a halt. The terrorist act succeeded in disrupting the country's economy at its capital and nerve center. Such terrorism can deal both an immediate and a long-term blow to the commerce and industry of a state.

Economic Propaganda

Since the days of Joseph Goebbels's outrageous manipulation of the truth, the term *propaganda* has had a bad name. In popular parlance propaganda has come to mean lying. In fact propaganda can be either fact or fiction; it does not have to be disinformation. We define *economic propaganda* as the dissemination of information to influence the economic attitudes or behavior of a target group in order to achieve the user's economic objectives.

President Clinton directed economic propaganda against the Japanese government when he made an appeal directly to the Japanese people petitioning their help in righting Japan's long-term trade imbalance with the United States. In what was described as having been "choreographed to win the hearts and minds of the Japanese," Clinton told his hosts that the trade imbalance was not to their benefit, and that they would profit if their leaders took actions to balance the scales.

Clinton's economic propaganda end run followed by a day the Japanese rejection of his basic approach to reduce Japan's trade surplus. The president's ploy for reaching past the Japanese government to win the Japanese public over to his position had, according to a *Los Angeles Times* account, "mixed results."[33]

Piracy

Our concepts of piracy have changed dramatically since the buccaneering days of Henry Morgan. While pirates who prey on shipping or small craft may still operate in waters such as the South China Sea, the contemporary pirate is more likely to be a brigand who infringes upon patents or copyrights on software, literature, film, or music. While state-sponsored piracy is uncommon and limited to rogue states such as North Korea, nations such as China, Taiwan, and South Korea are exceedingly tolerant of national entrepreneurs who violate international and copyright codicils.

Chapter 7

The Utility of Economic Force

Sanctions have a place in international law, providing we do not burden their use with excessive overexpectations.

C. Lloyd Brown-John

Does economic force work when it is used to achieve national (or multinational) objectives? The answer is, It depends. Hufbauer, Schott, and Elliot have conducted the most thorough analysis of the effectiveness of what they term "economic sanctions." Based on their review of 116 cases in which "sanctions" have been employed—mostly by the United States—they conclude, "In designing foreign policy strategy, policy makers need to take a close look at both the cost and the effectiveness of sanctions. Although it is not true that sanctions 'never work' they are of limited utility in achieving foreign policy goals that depend on compelling the target country to take actions it stoutly resists."[1] The authors then present their analysis of "success" by (1) type of policy goal, (2) international cooperation achieved, (3) international assistance to the target country, (4) stability of the target country, (5) the relative size of the country employing and the country that is the target of sanctions, (6) the duration of the sanctions, (7) costs to the target country, (8) costs to the sender, (9) the type of sanction employed, (10) the other forms of force employed to achieve the objective, and (11) sanctions initiated prior to 1973 and those initiated between 1973 and 1989.

Hufbauer, Schott, and Elliot do not measure the impact of the use of economic force on one nation in terms of its impact on others. The U.S. trade limits placed on Japan in April 1987 pressured other Asian nations to make trade concessions to the United States out of fear that they might receive the same treatment as the Japanese. Taiwan responded by sending a delegation to Washington to contract for $450 million of U.S. goods. South Korea promised to freeze its $7.3 billion trade surplus with the Americans.

Nor do Hufbauer and his colleagues measure the effectiveness of the use of economic force as a function of the competence of the user of that force. This is obviously a critical variable. A central postulate of this work is that a major reason the economic instrument fails is because it is neither understood nor properly employed. It fails because users have neither organized, planned, educated, nor trained to employ economic force. Neither has any user rationalized the use of economic force to permit the generation of a policy, doctrine, strategy, or tactics of economic conflict. Neither Nelson Mandela nor Frederick W. de Clerk would disagree that economic force worked in South Africa and made a meaningful contribution to breaking down the barriers of apartheid. The Comprehensive Anti-Apartheid Act of 1986 is credited with being an important component in exerting pressure on South Africa to permit universal elections in that country. Not only did the embargo cost South Africa an estimated $32–40 billion between 1985 and 1989, but it also was a major reason that the South Africans were forced to quit their Angolan war. Jennifer Davis, who monitored the impact of economic force on South Africa for over twenty-five years, observed, "Although … [sanctions] have been a potent force in the struggle for South African liberation, I cannot claim they have been either swift or overwhelmingly effective. Nevertheless, sanctions did play an important role in bringing down apartheid and opening the government to black South Africans."[2] The leading South African financial publication, the *Financial Mail,* editorialized on 28 November 1985, "Don't kid yourself. Effective sanctions do work."

Nincic and Wallenstein relate the effectiveness of economic force to the objective sought: "On the whole then, the effectiveness of economic sanctions seems rather doubtful—at least if the purpose is to force a significant policy change or to cause the removal of an unpalatable government. Their overall usefulness has not, however, been refuted since these objectives do not exhaust the functions that can be served by economic coercion." For example, David Reuther, a foreign service officer of the U.S. Department of State, has been quoted as saying, "In the case of Iraq, there is unprecedented international consensus to hold Iraq accountable and hence extensive cooperation in the application of sanctions. Sanctions contribute significantly to preventing Iraq from rebuilding its war industries and replacing its material losses to its military machine." Congressman Robert G. Torricelli, chairman of the Foreign Affairs Subcommittee on Western Hemisphere Affairs, encouraging the continuation of the U.S. embargo of Cuba, states categorically, "An economic embargo is an effective tool in leveraging governments to accept international standards of conduct."[3]

It is too early to determine reliably the extent to which the use of Western economic force contributed to the collapse of the Soviet Union. Many former officials of the Soviet state believe that the Western "trade weapon," employed within the overall strategy of containment, had a direct and consequential impact on their system that led to its collapse.[4] Margaret Thatcher credited Ronald Reagan with imposing "an economic strain on the Soviet Union" through a vigorous and perhaps deceptive pursuit of the Strategic Defense Initiative.[5]

In the book *Victory* Peter Schweizer persuasively argues that the Reagan administration waged a secret war "that hastened the collapse of the Soviet Union." He quotes former secretary of defense Caspar Weinberger as saying, "We adopted a comprehensive strategy that included economic warfare to attack Soviet weaknesses." According to Schweizer the strategy included, *inter alia,* "a campaign to reduce dramatically Soviet hard currency earnings by driving down the price of oil with Saudi cooperation and limiting natural gas exports to the West" and "a widespread technological disinformation campaign, designed to disrupt the Soviet economy."[6]

An opposite view is argued by Raymond Garthoff of the Brookings Institution in his book *The Great Transition.*[7] Garthoff, while recognizing the contribution of the Reagan military buildup, contends that the principal cause of the Soviet collapse was the impact of Mikhail Gorbachev's *perestroika* and *glasnost.* This embryonic Reagan-strategy-versus-forty-five-year-containment-strategy argument promises to mirror the sociologist's nature-versus-nurture controversy. As in the nature-versus-nurture debate, the Reagan-versus-containment-strategy argument must ultimately come to the truth that they both are important.

In 1993, after thirty-three years of the use of economic force against Cuba, reinforced by the 1992 Cuban Democracy Act and the collapse of the Soviet empire, Fidel Castro finally proffered several olive branches to the Americans. He indicated that he was willing to give up political power; he agreed to permit Cuban exiles returning on visits to bring more assets back into Cuba; he legalized the use of the dollar in local Cuban trade; and he showed a willingness to negotiate compensation for American assets seized and nationalized in the 1960s. As of this writing, it is unrevealed how much of Castro's offering is real and how much of it is a political smokescreen.

The United States has relied heavily on the use of economic

force against rogue states or regimes. The embargo against the Haitian regime led by General Raoul Cedras, in an effort to return duly elected Jean-Bertrand Aristide to the presidency, proved to be a roller-coaster ride. On 3 July 1993, following months of an economically debilitating UN embargo, Cedras signed an agreement on Governor's Island, New York, to turn the reins of government over to Aristide by 15 October. The use of economic force was hailed by many as a spectacular success, and the embargo was lifted on 27 August. However, by 13 October it was a certainty that Cedras was not going to keep his bargain. On that day the UN Security Council voted unanimously to reimpose an oil embargo on Haiti and freeze the financial assets of Haitian military leaders. The United States sent six naval ships to enforce the embargo around the island.

Up to September 1994 the United States and the United Nations were reluctant to use military force against the Haitians. Political force did not convince Cedras and his supporters that they should step aside for the return of Aristide. Many thought economic force represented the best potential for achieving U.S. and UN aims. In the words of Haiti's prime minister, Robert Malval, an Aristide supporter, "Sanctions are the best way to appeal to what is left of reason among the people who have led this country into chaos for the past two years."[8] Haitian military leaders denigrated the impact of U.S. and UN economic force upon their control of the island nation of 6.3 million people. Up until September 1994 they were consolidating their political base for the long term. A U.S. official was quoted as saying, "Everyone is just thrashing around—the military has us boxed in a corner, and no one has any idea of what to do except let the situation ride for a while and hope something breaks our way."[9]

The economic instrument was not wielded vigorously or effectively against Haiti. The Dominican border was open to an almost unlimited importation of goods into neighboring Haiti. The Balaguer government—which probably would have been cooperative in implementing the embargo if adequate pressure had been applied by the United Nations and the United States—admits that it permitted such trade "for humanitarian reasons." European countries were not confined by the terms of the embargo, and craft flying the Nigerian flag were free to enter Haitian ports with a wide variety of goods.[10] To some extent the targets for the U.S.-UN application of economic force, the Haitian army leaders, profited from the embargo.

If this use of economic force against Haiti had been a military operation, the media and the public would have called for the resignation of generals and secretaries of defense for failure to prosecute the engagement with sufficient vigor. Memories of the irresolute General George McClellan would have been revived. If it had been principally a political effort, the media and public would have charged that the directors of our foreign policy were inept and naive.

The early-1990s economic campaign against Iraq is also instructive. Following the end of the Desert Storm war in 1991, the U.S. strategy was to bring sufficient economic force against Iraq to promote a domestic instability that would make Saddam Hussein vulnerable to a coup. A UN Security Council embargo was imposed that, *inter alia*, prevented Iraq from selling its oil, a principal source of its revenue. The UN-mandated embargo was not to be lifted until Iraq complied with UN demands for an international monitoring of its production facilities for weapons of mass destruction. Also included in the Security Council conditions was the demand that Baghdad cease its military attacks against Iraqi Kurds and the Shiite Muslims. The UN mandate was being reviewed every sixty days to determine if there was justification for termination. As this is being written, U.S. officials report that while the economic damage to Iraq is substantial, Saddam Hussein still has complete control of the country.[11]

How should one evaluate the results achieved? If the objective was to bring about the collapse of Saddam Hussein's regime—and the wisdom of that was debatable, given the countervailing threat of a dominant Iran—then economic force proved no more efficacious than military and political force. If the expectations were that economic force alone was going to topple the dictator within two or three years, obviously the expectations were unreasonable and violated the principle of the objective, which requires that goals be achievable. (See chapter 8.) If the use of economic force was only one component of a broader strategy that included political and military ingredients, both overt and covert, could it be that the economic component was successful while the political and military components were not? The question is important. With singular exceptions, economic conflicts will be terminated through a political process. We speculated in chapter 4 that the failure of economic force to achieve U.S. objectives in Panama in 1989 may have been due to a failure in political negotiations—not that economic force failed to achieve conditions that would lead to the satisfying of U.S. objectives. If Hufbauer, Schott, and Elliot found that economic force did not achieve stated objectives in some 66 percent of the cases studied, how many of those failures can be attributed to the failure of the diplomatic process?

Richard Pipes, Harvard Russian historian and former presidential adviser, has been quoted as saying that sanctions have utility to "communicate a sense of moral outrage." He is further quoted, "One only has to consider what happens when aggression is not followed by some kind of punitive measures; not to react in such instances is silently to condone it." Michael Kramer contends that "sanctions are an important step of the ladder to war."[12]

General Douglas MacArthur claimed that the economic war waged against Japan by the Allies following World War II was proving to be more devastating than the atomic bombs had been.[13] In 1947 the Allies reversed their policies and encouraged the growth of Japanese industry and commerce, which produced one of history's most remarkable economic recoveries. The economic isolation of Japan was effectively destructive. The support of the Japanese economy was miraculously productive.

The question of utility may be phrased other ways. Is the use of economic force in itself counterproductive in that it tends to do long-term damage to the global economy? Former chairman of the Joint Chiefs of Staff General David C. Jones and former army chief of staff General Edward C. Meyer believe that the answer to the first question is yes. In a 1990 study report they stated, "Today, national economies are inextricably interlinked with each other. The collapse of a few major financial institutions would injure not only their owners and clients, but the financial stability of much of the world, including the United States." They concluded that "trade wars among nations could lower everyone's standard of living."[14] (One should emphasize that trade wars are a very specific, and probably the most counterproductive, type of economic conflict.)

Might the use of economic force backfire on the user? Ramon Cernuda, a prominent Miami Cuban activist, has called the economic offensive against Castro "the biggest mistake the United States has made since supporting the Bay of Pigs." Pierre Salinger, one-time press secretary to John F. Kennedy, has written, "Embargoes and sanctions beef up leaders and ruin the populations. ... The only embargo that worked was against South Africa."[15] The U.S. resistance to the construction of the Soviet Union's Siberia-to-Europe gas pipeline was initially believed to be counterproductive. Under pressure from its allies the United States abandoned many aspects of its economic coercion to stop the construction of the pipeline. It was built without U.S. help, which demonstrated European-Soviet capabilities independent of U.S. technology and soured U.S.-European relations. With the passage of time the effectiveness of the U.S. campaign against the pipeline was reexamined, and at least one analyst evaluates it as a resounding success.[16]

The automatic imposition of economic penalties written into economic treaties such as the North American Free Trade Agreement can be an invitation to special interest groups to "make mischief with international trade for their own narrow protectionist interests."[17]

THE DISMAL BATTLEFIELD

An example of how one statesman found economic force to be counterproductive appears in Anthony Eden's diary entry of 1943, "We built Mussolini into a great power." Eden was referring to the use of economic force against Mussolini in an effort to encourage conciliation on his part. Mussolini used the multinational initiative to intensify his militancy and to consolidate his grip on the Italian state.[18] There are those who contend that the U.S. economic coercion of Japan led to the attack on Pearl Harbor.[19] There are also those who contend that Fidel Castro's longevity is due in part to the Cuban fight against the American devil that is responsible for Cuba's economic plight.

U.S. business has problems with the use of the economic weapon, with some contending that it inflicts undue casualties on U.S. industry. In 1983 the president of the National Association of Manufacturers, Alexander Trowbridge, wrote to Commerce Secretary Malcolm Baldridge, urging that the administration refrain from using economic force. He pointed out that American industry suffered "more than short-term inconveniences" when export restrictions were imposed. Trowbridge contended that American industry also suffered the loss of longer-term commercial opportunities.[20] Big business reservations have a historical precedent. In 1814 Thomas Jefferson wrote in a letter, "Merchants have no country. The mere spot they stand on does not constitute so strong an attachment as that from which they draw their gains."[21]

Roland D. Pampel, president and CEO of Bull HN Information Systems, has said, "If the government decides it's going to control importing and exporting by imposing duties it can really mess up companies—because the major companies don't operate on the national level anymore."[22]

The economic weapon may also inflict undue casualties (collateral damage) on a target nation. In 1993, after months of suffering through a UN–U.S. embargo, Haiti was on the brink of a complete economic collapse that punished the Haitian people terribly while its military leadership survived. One diplomat was quoted as saying, "I thought after Vietnam we had heard the last of destroying a nation in order to save it. But that is what we are doing here."[23]

Certainly the modern-day use of economic force has not lived up to the expectations of President Woodrow Wilson, who declared in his post–World War I campaign for the League of Nations, "Apply this economic, peaceful, silent, deadly remedy and there will be no need for force.... It does not cost a life outside the nations boycotted, but it brings pressure upon the nation which, in my judgment, no modern nation could resist." Nor does it appear that it will ever meet the expectations of Howard S. Brembeck, chairman of the Fourth Freedom Forum, who stated, "Once we accept the fact that economic power, not military power, is our strongest weapon, we can settle international disputes without war."[24]

Nevertheless, the question as to whether or not economic force "works" is nearly moot. Notwithstanding ratios of success to failure, all indications are that economic force is being used and will be used with greater frequency. Often, following an abortive use of political coercion, it is the only alternative to military force. All indications are that it will continue to be the weapon of choice used by the United States and other powerful nations and international bodies to achieve their objectives. As a test, pick up any major newspaper published in the United States on any given day, and chances are good that there will be more than one article that discusses the U.S. use of economic force. U.S. policymakers perceive economic force as being useful as an alternative to military force. They perceive it as a demonstration of resolve to a target or a domestic constituency. Scholars Lopez and Cortwright write, "The debate [over the utility of economic force] continues. Meanwhile, sanctions have become an international fact of life. They may not always be an effective alternative to war, but they *are* an alternative."[25]

Some observers anticipate economic war between the world's great economic powers in the near future. In his book *Head to Head* economist Lester Thurow implies the inevitability of what could be

THE DISMAL BATTLEFIELD

defined as economic war involving the European Community, Japan, and the United States. And he does not lament the prospect: "From everyone's perspective, replacing a military confrontation with an economic contest is a step forward. No one gets killed; vast resources don't have to be devoted to negative-sum activities.... Relative to the military confrontations of the past century, both the winners and the losers are winners in the economic game ahead." In economic terms Thurow refers to the Japanese objective as being "strategic conquest."[26]

Columnist Charles Krauthammer warns of a Japanese drive for market dominance and calls for an economic NATO to combat the threat. Friedman and Lebard, in their book *The Coming War with Japan*—a bestseller in that country—speculate on the potential for a military conflict between the United States and Japan that is preceded by intense economic competition that fits our definition of economic war.[27]

Is economic force effective? According to the investigations and methodology of Hufbauer, Schott, and Elliot, it is in 34 percent of the cases. Hufbauer and his colleagues do not purport that their methodology and results are irrefutable. Nevertheless, let us accept the 34 percent figure for success as the best available in a neglected area of scholarship. Considering the moderate investment the user country generally makes in exercising its economic muscle, 34 percent appears to be a good return. The figure 34 percent, garnered on the cheap, also appears good when compared with the costs that might be incurred in the exercise of expensive military power. (When we witness Vietnam, Korea, and Lebanon, we must acknowledge that military force does not guarantee even a superpower a 100 percent success probability.) The success figure looks good when one considers the deterrent value achieved when a country has demonstrated its willingness to use the economic weapon.

Could success statistics be improved with the proper rationalization of the use of the economic instrument, with adequate organization, education, and training of employing forces? Logic dictates that it could. Could it be increased to 50 percent or to 68 percent, and at what cost? When compared with what is expended in preparing for the use of military force, the cost to improve on the operational effectiveness in the use of economic force would be minuscule. It is more difficult to make comparisons with the expense in the exercise of political force, but again, the relative cost would be minor.

Chapter 8

Principles of
Economic Conflict

———————————■———————————

War acknowledges principles, and even rules, but these
are not so much fetters, or bars, which compel its
movement aright, as guides which warn us when it is
going wrong.

A. T. Mahan

The value of a set of principles is not that it prescribes an inflexible menu for the practitioner. Rather, it provides a framework and definition that facilitates discussion, analyses, education, and training. As a practical matter, principles such as those proposed here can provide a checklist for the educator, trainer, planner, and operator. Principles of economic conflict should be universal, having application to large as well as small, rich as well as poor, and status quo as well as expansionist nations. However, they will not apply equally or uniformly to all nations. For example, Japan, the United States, Russia, Germany, and an economically integrated Europe have very different economic weapons and economic vulnerabilities than do Bolivia, Cambodia, Thailand, and the Philippines.

The rationalization of these principles must focus on that end of the spectrum of economic activities we have described as economic coercion/trade war and economic warfare. They would probably not relate to the more benign relationships such as economic support or economic competition (although the international businessman may find some applications for these principles when engaging in serious economic competition). The principles should be stated in terms of national, not commercial or individual, conflict. As previously acknowledged, nations are not the only users of economic force, and nations may use the economic instrument intra- as well as internationally. Consortia of nations, cartels, and perhaps multinational corporations may use economic force to achieve their objectives. Nevertheless, the principles needed in this context should focus on the use of the economic instrument by one nation (or more) to exert sufficient force to modify the behavior of another.

The following are candidate principles of economic conflict.[1]

1. The Principle of Diversity

There are many diverse facets of economic conflict. The use of the term *sanctions* to describe all types of economic coercion tends to oversimplify a diverse, complex dynamic.

There are multiple objectives a nation may have when defending against, deterring, or using economic force. In an offensive use of economic force, the objectives may range from the total disintegration of the target state to the symbolic communication of tension and hostility. In defensive economic war, the objectives may extend from the protection of competitive markets through the limiting of technology transfer to the stockpiling of strategic materials to achieving a state of autarky. A nation's objectives in the use of economic force may also be domestic and political, to demonstrate leadership and resolve to a constituency. One scholar contends that "international sanctions are imposed for acts of wrongdoing;...

they are punitive in intent."[2] James M. Lindsay identifies five objectives that are sought when "imposing trade sanctions: compliance, subversion, deterrence, international symbolism or domestic symbolism."[3] (Lindsay's "symbolism" refers to the making of international or domestic political statements.) To these we might add objectives that relate to promoting humanitarian/civil rights, facilitating a larger war, protecting or subverting patents, achieving political goals, changing trade policies, ideological suasion, deterrence, inhibiting nuclear and conventional arms buildups, ending military conflicts, toppling a regime, and many others.

The United States has used its economic might to combat nuclear proliferation (North Korea and Iraq); to deter commodity dumping (the Soviet Union's unfair uranium-trade practices); to open foreign markets to U.S. products (South Korea, Taiwan, and Japan); and to punish aggression (Iraq in 1990–93). In 1993 the new state of Ukraine organized what the Russians termed an "economic blockade" of the Black Sea to pressure some seventy thousand sailors to swear allegiance to Kiev, an act that represented the use of the economic instrument for a purely political objective.

As demonstrated in table 3, there are also many diverse instruments for this form of conflict.

There is diversity as well with regard to the users and targets of economic force, which may range from individuals to states and multinational corporations. Among the many possible combinations of those employing and those who are targets of economic force, we have extreme examples of nations targeting corporations and corporations targeting nations. In 1979 nongovernmental embargoes of Iran were instituted by U.S. bankers, exporters, and longshoremen in protest against that country's seizure of U.S. hostages. The Japanese government banned Japan Aviation Electronics Industry, Ltd., from exporting for eighteen months as punishment for that company illegally shipping components for Iranian missiles and jet fighters. The reverse of this exercise of economic power was the American corporation, Levi Strauss and Company—the world's

largest maker of brand-name apparel—closing its Chinese operations because of that country's "pervasive violations of human
rights."

We have at least one example of a superpower using economic
force against individuals. In June 1993 the Clinton administration
imposed economic pressure on some one hundred senior Haitian
government officials, business leaders, and their families. This selective, personal use of economic power was an effort to reinforce the
campaign of economic coercion against the Haitian leadership
while, to the extent possible, sparing the Haitian people more suffering.[4]

Economic force may be used by a single nation, against a single nation, by a consortium of nations, against one or several nations,
and many combinations of such possibilities.

As James Barber has reported, economic force may vary in
terms of whether it is applied universally, comprehensively, and as a
mandate. He points out that "Rhodesia is the only case in which an
effort has been made to maximize sanctions on each of these three
scales—universal, comprehensive and mandatory."[5]

There is a diversity in the role economic force may play in a
major confrontation where all forms of force may be used. There
are the possibilities of MILITARY-*economic-political,* ECONOMIC-
political-military, and other combinations of conflict. There may also
be a synergism in the effectiveness of the ECONOMIC-*military-
political* campaign where the whole would be more effective than
the sum of the parts.

There is a diversity of approaches to bringing economic force
to bear. The positive, or carrot, approach involves the awarding of
economic benefits. The negative, or stick, approach uses the denial
of economic benefits. The 1982 controversy over economic measures to be taken against Poland provides an example of the carrot-
stick approach. Reportedly some members of the Reagan
administration were in favor of using a big stick by declaring Poland
in default on the $3 billion it owed the United States and the $10.6

billion it owed West Germany, France, and Austria. Others, who favored using the carrot, won out. The United States, with great generosity, paid $71 million to the U.S. banks in lieu of Poland's interest payments on loans guaranteed by the United States. The rationale behind the U.S. decision was complex, for it involved concern not merely for Poland but for the stability of key West European banks, which would have been badly shaken by a Polish default.

The 1993 debate over whether to extend most-favored-nation status to China was based on whether to use the carrot (extend MFN to reward and entice China) or the stick (withhold MFN as punishment for the Tiananmen Square bloodshed). It appears that the Clinton administration preferred the carrot approach, which included the removal of bans on an array of high-technology sales in exchange for the Chinese guarantee not to sell medium-range missiles abroad. In 1994 the United States arranged for construction inside North Korea of two light-water nuclear reactors valued at $4 billion to encourage the North Koreans to discontinue their nuclear arms manufacturing program. David Cortwright, president of the Fourth Freedom Forum, assesses the economic carrot approach thus: "Positive reinforcements may be more effective than punitive measures in convincing government decision makers to alter objectionable policies."[6]

There is diversity in the manner in which economic force may be initiated. It may come as the result of support of the United Nations, a confederation of states, or another nation. It may be brought to bear because legislation requires its use under a certain set of circumstances. In the United States it may be initiated by either the legislative or the executive branch of government.

2. The Principle of the Objective

A clearly defined objective is a prerequisite for coordinating economic initiatives with allies and within the national security establishment. It must be clearly defined to the adversary. And in the United States it must be clearly defined to the electorate. The manner of enforcement must be identified, and the conditions under which the measures will be lifted must be announced. Sergey Oznobistchev warns that before economic force is used there must be a clear definition of the mandate, when force is to start, and when it is to be terminated.[7]

The objective must be tenaciously pursued with capabilities consistent with other national security objectives and supportive of the application of other forms of force.

During a June 1982 visit to Europe President Reagan proposed to NATO allies that they coordinate efforts to use trade and financial measures to undermine Soviet determination and strength. The administration did not appear to have clearly defined objectives that were compatible with and in support of the NATO strategy. Notwithstanding the ultimate success of the Reagan economic war, the lack of clear objectives cost the United States the support of its NATO allies in structuring a comprehensive strategy for the use of economic force against its principal adversary.

More often than not, governments and the media, evaluating the effectiveness of economic coercion or war, confuse the damage inflicted by the instrument with the objective. In the 1990 embargo against Iraq, for example, the *London Times* editorialized, "So far, UN sanctions have been remarkably successful."[8] However, denying Iraq the opportunity to import and export goods through its ports was not the objective of the economic coercion; withdrawal from Kuwait was, and there were absolutely no indications that the Iraqis were inclined to withdraw from their conquest.

By late 1994, in the post–Desert Storm use of UN economic force against Iraq, the Arab nation was destitute. The Iraqi dinar, once valued at $3.10, was worth 450 to the dollar. Government employees were working for the equivalent of one or two dollars per month. The publishing, health care, and transportation systems had collapsed. Yet the target of the UN economic offensive, the

Saddam Hussein regime, remained firmly entrenched. Two lessons may be drawn from this event. First, one should never underestimate the staying power of the absolute tyrant. Second, damage to a nation's economy does not guarantee that the objective of the use of economic force has been achieved.

There is a second example in the United Nations' 1993 use of economic force against Serbia. The use of economic force did not force Serbia's president to seek peace in Bosnia, even though it did create hyperinflation that produced economic and social chaos. Nevertheless, an Associated Press dispatch by Dusan Stojanovic characterized the economic offensive as enjoying success, citing the fact that inflation had reduced the average monthly pay of the Yugoslav citizen from $500 to $30, that black market dealings represented 50 percent of the economy, and that gasoline was selling for $8 per gallon.[9] Notwithstanding the economic impact, the Serbs persisted in their systematic genocide of their historic rivals, the Muslim Bosnians.

The objective in offensive economic coercion or war must be attainable. If it is not, the results of the exercise of economic power will undoubtedly be a failure attended by unwarranted economic and human casualties, the loss of the user's prestige, and the denigration of the credibility of the user's economic power. For example, in the case of Panama the objective, while well defined, was not attainable. The evaluation of the resiliency and vulnerability of the target was apparently couched in terms of the state—that is, how much economic punishment Panama could stand—rather than in terms of the real target, Noriega. There was a significant difference.

In 1991 the U.S. Air Force chief of staff, General Merrill A. McPeak, described the naval blockade of Iraq prior to the initiation of the ground war as being "spectacularly successful."[10] There is no doubt that the blockade imposed great hardship on Iraq and was a tactical success. However, if the objective of the blockade and McPeak's aerial campaign was to force the Iraqis to withdraw from Kuwait, as advertised, neither was "spectacularly successful." Rather, from a strategic point of view they were failures. The Iraqis were driven from Kuwait by a combined force in the MILITARY-*economic-political* formula, not by military or economic or political force alone.

There are those who claim that the most significant success in the use of economic force in the twentieth century was the U.S.-directed Western Alliance economic war waged for fifty years against the Soviet Union. There was never any doubt as to the objective, which according to a member of the U.S. Congress was "to bring the U.S.S.R. and the Soviet Bloc to their knees."[11]

Not only must the objective be clearly defined, it must also be clearly enunciated. Jack Roney, a career Agriculture Department employee, while on a year's leave of absence at Johns Hopkins University, published a report on President Jimmy Carter's grain embargo that condemned Carter for not clearly articulating the objective of restricting grain sales to the Soviets. The embargo—described by Roney as a "damning mistake"—failed, he asserted, because Carter did not articulate "the objectives and expected impacts" of this use of economic force. As a result, Carter lost both U.S. domestic support and the cooperation of major grain-producing allies such as Canada and Australia.

We must not be naive. Often the pronounced national objective is not the same as the actual political objective. When national leaders believe they must act forcefully in an international affair, economic force may be employed symbolically, as an alternative to a more drastic military action. In such an event the leadership and the students of economic force must measure its utility against the genuine, political, objective, not the artifact.

3. The Principle of Concentration

The application of economic force should be focused on a specific, vital area or areas of an adversary's economic vulnerabilities. Failure to do so will not only create the risk of wasting assets but also diminish the user nation's credibility and the perception of the utility of its economic power. This requirement assumes that there is an effective intelligence operation in place that is capable of identifying such vulnerabilities.

A nation, or other economic entity, need not have overwhelming economic superiority over a target nation to exercise economic force successfully. However, results are more likely to be achieved in a timely fashion if overwhelming force is focused on a specific, high-order vulnerability. Note that the principle of time is cited in this statement. One could describe the exercise of economic force as covering the range from the swift thrust of the stiletto to the slow strangulation of the bear hug. The economic war conducted against Panama is an example of death by dozens of quick thrusts of the stiletto. (Recall that it did destroy the Panamanian economy, even though it did not lead to the destruction of Noriega.)

The principle of concentration requires that the players focus upon the capabilities of the user and the vulnerabilities of the target. The half-century economic war against the Soviet Union did not permit a meaningful degree of concentration. The Soviet target was too big, too diverse for the stiletto. The USSR did not demonstrate many exploitable vulnerabilities over the short term. The USSR collapsed, in part, because of the application of DIPLOMATIC-*economic-military* pressure over a broad range of long-term vulnerabilities.

4. The Principle of Flexibility

Adopting a plan that is so rigid that it cannot be changed could squander unforeseen opportunities. The Reagan administration argued that withholding the use of economic coercion is one form of retaining flexibility. On the question of declaring Poland's debts in default, R. T. McNamara, deputy secretary of the treasury, wrote, "By not declaring a default we preserve our options.... Not declaring default now...preserves the flexibility to lighten credit and foreign exchange pressure if future Polish and Soviet responses warrant."[12]

Flexibility implies a strong leadership and competent bureaucracy that employs the economic weapon with much of the attention that is given to a military or diplomatic campaign. Real-time information must be gathered, intelligence produced, opportunities identified, and forces mobilized, concentrated, redirected, committed, suspended, and recommitted against the target as circumstances dictate. The U.S. bureaucracy is not currently structured to engage in economic conflict with this competence.

5. The Principle of the Magnitude of the Effort

The magnitude of the force employed must be sufficient to accomplish the objective yet proportionate to the value of the goals. The nation that is to exert economic pressure must have good intelligence and understanding of the strength of the target nation's capabilities. It requires an appreciation of the target nation's compressibility, or the enemy's vulnerability may be grossly overestimated. The magnitude of the effort required must be estimated in terms of time as well as resources. A careful estimate of cost must be balanced against advantages expected. If the effort required to achieve the objective is disproportionately costly, other alternatives or objectives should be considered. For example, John R. Block, secretary of agriculture during the Reagan administration, estimated that every $1 billion in farm export sales that the United States withheld from the Soviet Union cost the nation thirty-five thousand jobs plus another $1.5 billion in other transactions. Collateral damage is also a consideration determining the appropriate magnitude of economic force to be applied against an adversary. In the case of the measures employed against the Panamanians in an effort to oust Noriega from his position of power, the collateral damage to the Panamanian economy was devastating, crippling the nation's economy while Noriega weathered the storm.

6. The Principle of Security

Measures must be taken to ensure the protection of the nation's economic system from an adversary's use of economic force. However, he who tries to protect everything ultimately protects nothing. Chapter 4 identifies and elaborates on the threat that coercive foreign economic initiatives can pose to the United States. Economic security measures include stockpiling, securing lines of communication for trade, international alliances and agreements, and tariff regulation. The most important security measure, however, is a well-organized, well-trained, and legally equipped bureaucracy that is prepared to defend against economic force.

A classic contemporary problem of security of economic interests is the West's oil lifeline from the Middle East. In the pre-Gorbachev years the Soviet threat to the economic well-being of the United States and its partners was properly believed to be not merely military but political and psychological as well. The U.S. counters to the Soviet threat prior to the Gorbachev era were to use all three instruments of national power: the economic, through loans, guarantees, and arms sales; the military, principally with the Sixth Fleet and the Rapid Deployment Force; and the political, through diplomatic initiatives.

7. The Principle of Time

Time impacts on the application of economic force in several ways. Short-range tactical economic measures are less likely to be effective than long-term strategies, although effectiveness is also a function of the magnitude of the force brought to bear and the vulnerability of the target. A major use of economic force applied immediately is more effective than the gradual ratcheting up of such force over time. Gradualism permits the target to accommodate, become inured, and find solutions to economic pressures.

The timing of the application of economic force is important.

Good timing is often dependent upon the cyclic nature of an adversary's vulnerability (e.g. the cyclic periods of harvest and weather). Responsiveness to the conditions that are eliciting the use of economic force is a function of good timing. Early use of economic force in an adversarial situation is often critical. Some believe that the difficulty in achieving objectives in the 1992–94 U.S. use of economic force against Haiti was due to the delay in the U.S. commitment, which permitted the Haitian military leadership to "dig in and develop means to survive the sanctions."[13]

In times of crisis there is a tendency to overvalue economic force. In quiescent times it is undervalued as a component of long-term strategy.

Both the long- and the short-term effects of applying economic force—effects pertaining both to the target and to the using nation—must be considered.

The value of economic force changes over time and is a function of such varying things as the nature of the state, international relations, the state of the world economy, environments, and technology.

Richard Stolz, a former CIA deputy director for operations, provided an example of the importance of timing in the use of the economic instrument. In mid-1993 there were those who were encouraging the suspension of the arms embargo that had been levied on the Bosnian Muslims in May 1992 to assist them in winning back the lands stolen by the Serbs and Croats. As Stolz pointed out, the timing was all wrong to lift the embargo of weapons. It would be too late to help and would be a "cruel joke" that would only compound the misery of the Bosnian people.[14]

8. The Principle of Unity

If there is to be a successful use of economic force, the use of national resources must be effectively coordinated, controlled, and concentrated upon the objective. Based on her work with the

Institute for International Economics, Kimberly Elliot has found that there is a greater emphasis on multilateral as opposed to unilateral use of economic force. She notes that since 1990, unilateral "sanctions" by the United States have been imposed only once. Christopher Joyner, director of an American Society of International Law project on this subject, maintains that the political efficacy of economic force is contingent upon the cooperation of implementing states.[15]

States that have centralized, controlled economies may more easily employ their economic strength against decentralized, less controlled economies (although centralized economies, by their nature, may have proportionally less economic force to employ). Alliances that are directed by the strongest power may reach decisions more easily than those that are collegial.

Interdependence of national economies requires unity of action among nation-states that are allied or have common purposes. World economies are so integrated that exercises of economic force will usually impinge upon one's own economy, the economy of one's allies, and the economy of nations other than the target nation.

The effectiveness of an initiative in the application of economic force is often contingent upon the cooperation of other parties to achieve some unanimity. Most obvious are initiatives that involve embargoes, sanctions, and boycotts. Reagan's June 1983 proposal to use economic force against the Soviet Union was set back when French president François Mitterand stated, "We are not going to wage any kind of war against the Russians. . . . You have to be very serious about such a course. It could lead to real war. If economic embargo is a first act of war, it risks being caught up by a second. No it is not the right move." The 1992–93 embargo of most goods to and from Yugoslavia took sixteen months to receive universal support from bordering states.[16]

Representative Diaz Balart, encouraging an international rather than the U.S. national embargo against Cuba, said, "No unilateral embargo can by itself overthrow a government....[My] resolution asks for our allies to side with us to end foreign financing of what is a brutal dictatorship."[17]

Unity of purpose cannot ignore the existence of powerful forces in the private sector that may either support or subvert a national policy or initiative for the application of economic force. Two European companies, John Brown (in England) and Atlantique (of France), significantly subverted the U.S. economic offensive against the construction of the Soviet natural gas pipeline by supplying critical technologies to the Soviet engineers.[18]

Responsibility for developing a national strategy for the application of economic force should be shared by government and private enterprise. In the final analysis it is the government that must set national policy, mobilize resources, organize, develop the requisite intelligence, and exercise leadership if the United States is to make use of its economic power. The private sector must be prepared to cooperate and to participate in the formulation of policy and the prosecution of strategies. As indicated in chapter 4, the private sector must to a very large extent provide for its own security against economic espionage and other forms of economic aggression.

The effectiveness of a coercive economic initiative is often contingent upon the coordinated application of other forms of national power (i.e. the military, political, psychological, technological, and cultural).

9. The Principle of Stability

Long-term stability is required for long-term economic programs. States with stable ideological concepts and infrequent changes in their leadership are well equipped to form and prosecute long-term strategies and mobilization of resources. States that are ideologically polymorphous, and are subject to periodic changes in leadership and in concepts of the nation's role in the international order, are not as well equipped.

THE DISMAL BATTLEFIELD

10. The Principle of Resilience

Almost three years after the overwhelming military defeat in the Gulf War and an extremely effective embargo in tactical terms, Saddam Hussein, the Iraqi dictator, remains in complete control. This demonstrates two verities. One is the staying power of the absolute tyrant. The other is the resiliency of a state-dominated populace to survive under extreme hardships.

Nations have distinct characteristics and degrees of compressibility within their economies. Resilience provides stamina to the target nation to withstand the economic pressure brought to bear. Resilience may also permit the nation employing economic force to minimize the cost of its initiatives. The resilience of a nation's economy may result as much from sociological, psychological, geographic, and situational idiosyncrasies as from those that are economic. When measuring resilience it is important to identify the objective properly. Initial appraisals of the resilience of the target in the Panamanian war identified the nation as the target; the nation lacked resilience and therefore was highly vulnerable. The true objective, however, was Noriega, who had a very high order of resilience and was personally secure from U.S. economic attacks.

In 1989 President George Bush renounced an economic weapon when he promised U.S. farmers that food would never be used as a "diplomatic tool." The fear of the economic casualties they could suffer had prompted the farmers to lobby against the use of the food embargo. Resilience means that a nation is willing to accept economic and associated casualties in this form of conflict. Nations expect casualties in conventional military operations, and the loss of thousands of young men in military warfare is the norm. However, there often seems to be a reluctance to accept casualties in economic war. This unwillingness to pay the price for the use of economic force is a principal source of the vacillation, the lack of stamina, and the controversy that surround the use of economic force by the United States.

Chapter 9

The Dynamics of Economic Force

With many calculations one can win; with few one cannot. How much less chance of victory has one who makes none at all!

Sun Tzu

A t this point, some verities about the nature of economic conflict bear repeating.

First, it seems obvious that rarely would the economic instrument be employed without the concurrent use of diplomatic force of some nature.

The nation is not the only entity that may use the economic instrument to gain an objective. Individuals have done so (e.g. the individual boycotting of firms engaged in commerce with South Africa). Multinational organizations have done so (e.g. the League of Nations' economic proscriptions against Italy after its pre–World War II invasion of Ethiopia or the United Nations authorizing the blockade of Iraqi ports in 1990). Multinational corporations have done so, as have international cartels. However, in 1995 the nation-state is the most important player in the use of economic force, with the United Nations running second.

Economic force is characteristically used by a more powerful nation against a weaker adversary. But not always. A nation that is weaker politically, militarily, and economically may have economic resources—oil, military bases—vital to a more powerful nation and may be capable of extracting concessions through the threat of withholding those resources.

In this chapter we examine the U.S. framework that is needed to support effective engagement in economic conflict, both offensive and defensive. The outer surface of this framework is national policy. It shapes the core of the dynamic. The bureaucracy must be organized and equipped to satisfy this policy. The next layer is doctrine, which provides a commitment as to how economic force shall be used to achieve U.S. national objectives. As one peels the layers of economic conflict, the next level is the national strategy, while at the core are tactics, intelligence operations, legal authorities, rules of engagement, moral codes, and so on.

National policies emanate from the chief executive. They are influenced by the legislature and are sometimes interpreted by the judiciary. National policies identify broad goals and objectives and may identify restraints and resources. They may be stated in routine government publications, in separate pronouncements, or in conjunction with other policies. They may be written or oral. The overriding requirements for such an international declaration is that it emanate from the chief executive and that it be within that official's jurisdiction. There is currently no national policy either for managing economic force or for engaging in economic conflict.

It is unlikely that any other nation has formulated or adopted a policy for employing economic force. In 1993 Alexander Oznobistchev and Dmitri Evstafiev, fellows at the Institute for U.S.A. and Canada Studies in Moscow, wrote, "Russian policy on sanctions should be defined—both legislatively and by regulation.

The articulation of Russian policy should be independent of the position of the 'world community' or of any international organization."[1] As these Russian scholars point out, the same need exists at the level of multinational organizations such as the United Nations and the Organization of American States.

Following is a straw-man U.S. national policy for economic conflict:

—Economic force has utility and will be used to achieve U.S. humanitarian, democratic, and national objectives whenever it has been established that less forceful means have been ineffectual.

—Trade wars—that is, absent an armed conflict, an economic confrontation in which the economic resources of two or more belligerents are heavily engaged and the economic integrity of one, both, or all adversaries is at stake—are inherently counterproductive and shall be avoided short of responding to a threat that seriously endangers the national welfare.

—The U.S. use of economic coercion will be selective and focused to avoid collateral damage to a target nation or third parties.

—The magnitude of the U.S. economic force exercised will be proportionate to the response to be elicited to ensure that it is sufficient to accomplish the objective, yet not so great that it inflicts unwarranted damage.

—Careful consideration will be given to the timing of the U.S. application of economic force, recognizing that the time of the initiation of such force and the duration of its exercise could be critical.

—No application of U.S. economic force will be undertaken without an assessment of its impact upon the U.S. economy.

—Whenever practical, the cooperation of U.S. allies and other nations and international organizations will be sought in the application of economic force.

—The U.S. objectives in defending against and employing coercive economic force are to ensure that the nation is organized to recognize, evaluate, manage, and mobilize its resources to (1) defend against other national economic initiatives that are designed to coerce the United States into taking actions it determines not to be in its best interests; (2) defend against those who would gain an economic, political, military, psychological, or sociological advantage over the United States through aggressive means; and (3) use U.S. economic force to modify the behavior of a nation whose conduct is sufficiently detrimental to the best interests of the United States to warrant such a response.

To paraphrase Morris Janowitz, doctrine is the "logic" of professional behavior. It is a synthesis of scientific knowledge and professional expertise on the one hand and of traditions and political assumptions on the other.[2] Doctrine includes many fundamental precepts and principles that may be documented and included in a single source. Doctrine is less stable and durable than policy but more stable than strategy or tactics. Doctrine must be capable of change, however, and must serve the contemporary users of economic force. The U.S. doctrine for economic conflict could include principles such as those cited in chapter 12. The doctrine would define terms and establish a comprehensive and universal language for the use of this force. The doctrine should serve as a basis for generating strategies and tactics for the employment of economic force. The work of such scholars and analysts as Klaus Knorr, Gary Clyde Hufbauer and his colleagues, and Barry Carter should be reflected in such doctrine. This book has been written to make a contribution to the generation of a U.S. doctrine for economic conflict.

The national strategy for the use of economic force is the accretion of all the art and science of the use of the economic instrument under all conditions, from economic tranquility to economic war, to achieve national objectives. It is the total of the national competence to wage economic conflict, captured in a single plan of action. It includes the actual use of economic force, the threat of its use, and its relationship to other forms of national power—that is, the military, political, social, and psychological—in achieving these objectives. The strategy of economic force is broad-brush and includes the entire theater of operations, which for the United States is global.

A strategy for the use of economic force is specific to a nation or a coalition and would have but limited application to another nation or coalition. It includes considerations of time, strengths, vulnerabilities, policies, and objectives. The most effective strategy for the use of economic force is the one that renders the use of that force unnecessary.

The strategy for the use of this force must recognize that a period of peaceful reconstruction of the adversary's economy may be the responsibility of the nation or coalition that inflicted the damage and must therefore be taken into consideration when assessing the costs of the strategy.

This strategy must satisfy national policies and complement parallel strategies.

Tactics are operational details that prescribe the optimum methods for the employment of economic force. Tactics are the "how" of the equation. They are the instruments with which a belligerent achieves its strategy. Economic-conflict tactics involve the employment of the instruments identified in table 3 under the categories of trade, finance, resource management, and unconventional. Economic-conflict tactics must rely upon established principles, although innovative tactics may circumvent such principles when better judgment dictates.

The tactics of economic conflict will prescribe guidelines such as favored methods for improving the conduct of export and import embargoes; the benefits versus the liabilities of a total versus a partial embargo; preferred methods for attacking specific targets within the adversary's complex; the best time to impose or lift an embargo; and how to anticipate potential responses. Tactics identify the best methods of freezing assets, withholding payments, and terminating aid and loans. Tactics tell us which kinds of disinformation work with what types of targets in which kinds of scenarios. A sound body of tactics evolves more from lessons learned than from esoteric rationalizing. Tactics change to accommodate new weapons and new adversaries. Defensive tactics differ from offensive tactics. There are extemporaneous as well as codified tactics. Extemporaneous tactics are often intuitive rather than cognitive. Tactics, however, must be routinely practiced, tested, and documented.

What remains is operations, to include all those functions that contribute to the effective conduct of an enterprise of economic force. These functions include planning, intelligence, counterintelligence, training, educating, resource allocations, communications, security, and so on. These functions cannot be effectively managed without an adequate infrastructure. Today the United States has no such infrastructure. Worse, there is no federal organization that is responsible.

Chapter 10

The Role of Seapower in Economic Conflict

———————————————————■——————

[Blockade] is a belligerent measure which touches every member of the hostile community, and, by thus distributing the evils of war, as insurance distributes the burden of other losses, it brings them home to every man.

A. T. Mahan

Military air, ground, and naval forces all may play significant roles in an ECONOMIC-*military-political* conflict. Naval forces, however, have historically been the most supportive military tool in the exercise of economic coercion or economic war. Naval forces continue to be the military weapon of choice for enforcing economic mandates or defending against the use of the economic instrument. Maritime forces have great utility in economic conflict because the bulk of the world's commerce travels over sea lines of communications (LOCs), and states that rely on commerce conducted through seaports become vulnerable to naval blockade. The U.S. naval establishment sponsored one of the most serious scholarly attempts to collect and discuss

161

the dynamics of economic conflict in its 1976 workshop on the subject.[1]

Maritime forces do not have a monopoly on the control of sea LOCs. In some operating environments air forces may also be used to interdict or monitor seaborne traffic. Ground forces may be used to control land areas that dominate critical choke points such as straits and approaches to ports and harbors. However, it is the modern-day fleet that has the best potential for enforcing a nation's mandates in economic conflict.

U.S. fleets have potent air, surface, subsurface, and amphibious force capabilities that have great range and flexibility. They have sophisticated command and control systems that make them immediately responsive to the instructions of the National Command Authorities when political control is essential. Naval task forces composed of surface ships, high-performance aircraft, helicopters, trained landing parties, small boarding craft, and specially trained search teams provide a potent tool to the nation engaged in economic conflict. Friedman and Lebard have concluded, "The most successful embargoes by the U.S. occurred when it could physically control a nation's access to the sea. For most countries, this goal can never be achieved. For the United States it is attainable worldwide and at will. The blockade of Cuba is a case in point." They add, "Dominating the oceans can be used for economic gain."[2]

Naval forces may play one or more of the following roles in an ECONOMIC-*military* or MILITARY-*economic* conflict:

—They may be used to enforce a blockade[3] of commercial shipping through target ports of entry or exit by (1) intercepting all or designated commercial shipping, inspecting cargo, and turning away, returning, or destroying all vessels transporting materials determined to be contraband (selective embargo); (2) intercepting all commercial shipping and turning it away from, or returning it to, designated ports (total embargo); (3) mining the entrances to selected or all ports to deny access or exit to selected shipping (discriminate denial; mines, of course, may also be laid by land-based and naval aircraft as well as by ships).

—They may be used to break a blockade of commercial shipping through target ports of entry by mine clearance operations or by combating the armed forces of a blockading operation.

—They may be used along sea lines of communications far distant from target ports to interdict and destroy or reroute commercial shipping.

—They may be used along sea lines of communications to escort and protect commercial shipping.

—They may be used to destroy or protect, or to blockade or prohibit a blockade of, oil platforms, sea mining or fishing grounds, and similar ocean assets.

—They may be used to destroy or protect sea surface or subsurface supply or communication channels (pipelines and cables).

Blockade of an adversary's commercial shipping is the principal contribution of the maritime force engaged in economic conflict. (Blockade of combat ships, as in the U.S. Civil War and the two world wars, is not an act of economic conflict.) The naval blockade is one of the oldest forms of naval warfare, and blockade strategies and tactics have changed little over the centuries. During the 1990 blockade of Iraqi ports, Coast Guard law enforcement detachments (LEDETS), U.S. Marines, and navy Seals were used in boarding operations reminiscent of the Viking boardings prior to the time ships acquired heavy guns and became floating batteries and aircraft platforms.

Blockades have played a significant role in the history of international conflict. One such was the British blockade of France in 1775 that immediately preceded the Seven Years' War. Napoleon Bonaparte's defeat by the English was greatly facilitated by the British total blockade of French ports imposed in 1806 (a blockade that led to the War of 1812 between the United States and Britain, which in turn led to the British blockade of all the ports and sea-coasts of the United States). During the Civil War President Lincoln imposed a total blockade against the Confederacy. The British established the "Economic Warfare Division" within the admiralty in 1939 specifically to control the use of seapower in economic conflict during World War II.

U.S. Navy Rear Admiral E. W. Carter has written that "the naval campaign of the First World War was primarily a struggle between the British and German blockades." He also identified a World War II Pacific "submarine blockade," citing the fact that the Japanese started out the war with six million tons of shipping. By the end of 1944, despite a major shipbuilding replacement program, Japan had only two million tons of commercial shipping, causing severe shortages of oil, rubber, and other raw materials.[4]

The term *naval blockade* has a specific meaning in the rubric of international law, which describes it as an act of war against a belligerent nation.[5] Therefore the term is often avoided, and U.S. spokesmen have referred to blockades as quarantines (the 1962 Cuban missile crisis) or as interceptions or interdictions (the 1990 Iraqi conflict). The rules for a blockade were agreed to by the major sea powers at the London Naval Conference of 1908–9.

In international law the term *blockade* is defined as "a naval operation carried out by belligerents in time of war, designed to prevent vessels of any and all states from entering or leaving specified coastal areas."[6] International law requires that a blockade be maintained by sufficient force for it to be recognized, and that it be formally declared and notified to neutrals.

The term *embargo* also has a specific meaning in international law and is defined as "an act of economic reprisal sometimes differentiated from a wartime blockade by being referred to as a 'peace-time' blockade, i.e., it does not entail the right to stop and to seize neutral shipping that may be contravening the embargo."[7] In that sense an embargo is less formidable than a blockade. Unlike blockades, embargoes can be imposed without military force (e.g. by refusing to trade with certain nations). During wartime a blockade may be imposed to enforce an embargo.

As discussed in chapter 2, for sound, legal expedience, euphemisms abound in describing the closure of ports to commercial shipping. Favorite substitutes for the term *blockade*—which connotes an act of war against a belligerent nation—are *quarantine* and *interdiction*, neither of which is defined in international law. The term *quarantine,* used in the naval restrictions imposed on Cuba in 1962, was appropriate because there was no declaration of war or belligerency. The purpose of the "quarantine," nevertheless, was to halt Soviet deliveries of offensive military arms to Cuba. The use of the term *interdiction* vice *blockade* in the closure of Iraqi ports in 1990 was favored because of an interpretation of Article 51 of the UN Charter, which recognizes the customary right of an individual and collective self-defense.

Abraham Lincoln faced a conundrum in the early days of the Civil War when he wanted to proclaim a blockade against the South. Gideon Welles, the U.S. secretary of the navy, advised against a blockade since under international law it would imply that the Confederacy was a nation with all the privileges attendant thereto. The English had a vested interest in his decision and advised Lincoln that he would be creating commerce problems for them if he did not declare a blockade. The president opted to favor the English position over Welles's advice and declared a blockade against the Confederacy.

In more specific and traditional naval terms, a blockade has been described as follows:

> Generally, a naval blockade, interdicting and penalizing all sea traffic between the world at large and a specific state, is a belligerent right and only a belligerent right. It is, in customary international law, considered a legitimate interference with the freedom of the seas enjoyed by third states only when a war condition exists. Once legally established, a blockade imposes upon all who use the seas a duty to avoid an effec-

tively blockaded port or area upon pain of condemnation. As an operation of war, this lawful restraint upon the freedom of the high seas is acquiesced to by all maritime nations so that shippers are not in a position to appeal to the flag state in avoiding penalties for conscious breaks into the locked-off sea areas. Such a naval action may be initiated, however, only after notification to the maritime world; must be accomplished with sufficient force; be undertaken in earnest; and be applied impartially to ships of all nations. A right to visit and search foreign ships is then, and only then, uniquely granted the blockading belligerent. Merchantmen in proximity of [an] area of operations are required upon signal to lie to. They resist search and ignore signals upon jeopardy of damage or destruction without liability to the belligerent for the consequences.[8]

Note that in terms of international law a blockade is a purely naval operation. There does not appear to be equivalent specific terminology for describing the act of denying air space or access to air terminals or ground lines of communications.

During periods of armed conflict, the blockading force may destroy an adversary's commercial shipping. During periods short of armed hostility, naval forces may redirect shipping to alternative ports for impounding or inspection. They may also stop, board, search, seize, or destroy contraband or merely deny ships access to one or more ports.

The strategy behind a naval blockade may be complex. It may involve the recruitment of allied naval vessels to enforce the closure of ports. It may involve the recruitment or coercion of neighboring states to close their overland border points of access to the target state. There may be a requirement to justify and validate the naval blockade in international courts. There may be a need to identify nations, ships, or materials that are exempt from the blockade. There may be requirements to provide for humanitarian relief for the populace of a target state.

The tactics of the naval blockade are rather primitive but have stood the test of time. There have been advances in the technologies of detection and tracking intelligence. Photoreconnaissance aircraft and satellites, with quick-response distribution of intelligence, are great facilitators in identifying and monitoring commercial shipping in target waters. Man-portable sensors have proven useful in identifying the presence of some types of contraband. Rules of engagement are more complex than they were in the days of Lord Nelson. The inspection, processing, recording, and reporting of commercial shipping documents may be more demanding than they were decades ago. Nevertheless, the basic tactics of intercepting, inspecting, and turning away shipping from target ports have not changed dramatically.

Well-trained modern naval forces such as those of the United States have the skills to adapt quickly to the demands of the blockade. Ship-handling and gunnery techniques for the interception, channeling, warning, or destruction of commercial shipping are routine. Within the U.S. naval forces, the Coast Guard brings the most valuable experience for operations and for training other forces to act as boarding, inspection, and seizure teams. The Coast Guard's LEDETS proved invaluable in the Iraqi blockade. MEUSOCs (marine expeditionary units, special operations capable) are trained for operations that are compatible with such boarding operations. Navy Seal teams are extremely flexible and proficient and have little trouble making the transition to provide boarding teams for naval blockade operations.

U.S. naval forces are capable of responding rapidly to provide well-trained fleets, ships, and teams to conduct blockade operations. Special courses of instruction in the fundamentals of visit, board, search, and seizure operations are conducted by such units as San Diego's fleet training group. Tactical sweep procedures—that is, the techniques of searching for contraband aboard a commercial vessel—and the inspection and processing of merchant vessel documentation are also taught. There is a wealth of tactical detail documented in the U.S. Coast Guard Maritime Law Enforcement Program archives.

The effectiveness of a naval blockade will depend upon, *inter alia,* the ocean and terrestrial geography. The interdiction and protection of merchant shipping at sea, in international waters, is generally more difficult to accomplish than the enforcement of a blockade. However, interdiction and protection may be facilitated if the target sea lanes of communications pass through straits such as Hormuz, Gibraltar, or Malacca. During the 1990 blockade of Iraq the Strait of Hormuz afforded a valuable choke point to the allied naval forces monitoring the traffic going into and leaving the Persian Gulf.

If the blockade takes place under conditions of armed hostility, under international law commercial shipping can be attacked and sunk, making interdiction procedures less complex. Armed hostility, of course, poses special problems for the defense of naval fleets, however.

Fleets may also contribute valuable information on commercial shipping as inputs to the overall economic intelligence assessments made by a nation.

The mining of harbors and ports is an effective, often total, way to blockade, as was demonstrated in the Vietnam War at Haiphong. However, the U.S. minelaying and -sweeping capabilities have been sorely neglected. Mining is a relatively inexpensive, safe, quick, effective means to blockade that can be accomplished with relatively unsophisticated technologies.[9] There seems to be great opportunity here, however, to capitalize on technology to produce even more efficient minelaying and -sweeping capabilities. Minesweeping, on the other hand, is a relatively expensive, dangerous, slow, and ineffective operation that requires the dedication of specialized forces.

The shibboleth that the military always fights the last war seems to have been disproved in the last sixty years of the twentieth century. In the context of naval power, World War II produced innovations such as amphibious warfare, naval aviation, an array of revolutionary missiles, and responsive command, control, reporting, and intelligence systems. Since World War II there have been a series of reevaluations of the utility of seapower to support U.S. national strategy. These evaluations have ultimately led to new naval doctrine based on the latest national security strategy, which is routinely released into the public domain.

One such pronouncement is called "From the Sea," a U.S. Navy and Marine Corps White Paper signed on 29 September 1992 (and updated in 1994).[10] The paper provides the basis for the generation of naval doctrine for the twenty-first century. In this document there is a shift in focus to littoral operations and maneuver from the sea. However, nowhere in "From the Sea" is there a reference to how the navy will support economic-conflict operations in the remainder of the twentieth century and into the twenty-first.[11] (It does refer to the art of managing crises by "precisely tailored diplomatic, economic and military signals" but fails to indicate the role naval forces will play in such activity. There is a reference to interdicting "the adversary's movement of supplies by sea" and the requirement for "open sea lanes of communication," but this is thin gruel for the significant role naval forces will play in ECONOMIC-*military* operations in the twenty-first century.) It is hoped that the reason for this omission was that this White Paper was not presented at a level of detail that would include citations such as blockades and mining.

Commander James Stavridis, writing in the Naval Institute's *Proceedings,* describes a military strategy for the post–cold war era that is supported by a joint military structure capable of, *inter alia,* imposing a complete blockade of all target ports and coastal areas.[12]

Naval strategist Roger Barnett highlights the effectiveness of the naval blockade in his argument that contemporary and twenty-first-century regional conflict will impose a requirement for effective naval forces:

> Even though blockades take a long time to work, are difficult to implement with high effectiveness, are blunt rather than sharp policy instruments, and frequently cause unin-

tended harm to innocent parties, they offer a less dramatic and less politically polarizing alternative to combat. Trade embargoes have been used frequently by the United States; blockades are the enforcement phase of embargoes. Accordingly, blockades will continue to be a serious option for the United States in the future security environment, and the Navy (with possible assistance from the Coast Guard) will be the at-sea instrument of any blockade.[13]

Barnett's words would have been appropriate for inclusion in the 1992 White Paper.

Chapter 11

Organizing the U.S. Bureaucracy for Economic Conflict

The primary object of organization is to shield people from unexpected calls upon their powers of adaptability, judgment and decision.

Sir Ian Hamilton

enator Daniel Moynihan captured the essence of the organization of the U.S. bureaucracy to manage economic conflict when he wrote, "There is no organization in our national government that is responsible." He then identified the de facto if not the de jure principle in the organization for economic conflict: "The State Department has the 'lead' responsibility but is always preoccupied with something else. The Treasury Department collects customs and worries about the balance of payments....The Commerce Department keeps statistics and promotes exports—sort of....There is a...rule: when everyone is responsible, no one is."[1]

The principal organizational failure of the U.S. bureaucracy in the management of the use of economic force is just as Senator

Moynihan puts it: there is no one in charge. This is not to say that there are no activities that are working effectively in this arena. There are, although their capabilities are severely limited by the laissez-faire environment in which they function. The Treasury Department's Office of Foreign Asset Control (FAC) is making a substantial contribution as "America's watchdog of economic sanctions." While its rather loosely defined authority appears to be chiefly operational, the FAC is one of the few organizations in the bureaucracy where there appears to be a concern for the rationalization of the dynamics of economic force. The FAC is a small office that has performed with uncelebrated distinction in contemporary U.S. economic conflicts.

The FAC, with a staff of about seventy and an annual budget of about $2.5 million, administers the use of economic force against foreign countries in furtherance of foreign policy and national security objectives. It has no responsibility for the administration of defensive measures, for the generation of policy, or for training and education (other than the training of its own staff). FAC authorities are not spelled out in law—as are those, for example, of the Department of Defense in the National Defense Act—but are delegated by the president. The principal source of the FAC's derived powers are found in the Trading with the Enemy Act and the International Emergency Economic Powers Act. There are six divisions within the FAC and a chief counsel. The divisions are broken down into functional categories of licensing, compliance monitoring, enforcement, international liaison, management of foreign assets that have been blocked, and planning and programming.[2]

Despite CIA director Gates's contention that the economic intelligence situation in the United States is "bureaucratically tangled,"[3] the CIA's Office of Economic Research reportedly has more relevant economic statistical data than there are opportunities to use them. However, when there is no one in charge, the FAC, CIA, and Commerce Department foot soldiers are committed to conflict without essential direction, policy, or control.

Other major players in the administration of economic force are the State Department (strategy and policy guidance), the National Security Council staff, the Customs Service, the Commerce Department, and the Federal Bureau of Investigation. The State Department and the NSC seem to share responsibility for the generation of what strategy exists for the use of economic force.

The U.S. approach to organizing for economic conflict is often that of interagency cooperation organized within an interagency policy-coordinating committee. The White House staff may participate as well as the Department of Justice (other than the FBI). The arrangement lacks stability. It does not foster the formulation of essential policy. It has no continuity. It diffuses responsibility and wastes resources. It provides little institutional memory. It is poorly suited to provide the quality of advice required by decision makers. What America needs more than anything else in preparing for economic conflict into the twenty-first century is the designation of a department or agency to oversee, direct, and coordinate all activities relevant to the use of and defense against economic force. It needs to assign authority and responsibility for the generation of policy, doctrine, strategy, tactics, intelligence, legislation, and education and training agendas. Responsibility, authority, and resources must be assigned to practice, game, and evaluate the art of economic conflict.

Admittedly there are serious international-relations problems associated with a nation's organizing for the conduct of economic conflict. Imagine the misgivings of the United States' Pacific and European allies should they discover that the U.S. bureaucracy has been reorganized to facilitate the waging of economic war or coercion. They would certainly be interested in knowing which nations had been identified as potential targets. Or imagine the U.S. public's misgivings should it learn that Japan had created a Bureau for Economic War.

Clearly, in today's international environment any initiative to create a mechanism to manage economic conflict by any economic power would be regarded with suspicion. It could invite retaliation or countermeasures and set in motion entirely new perspectives on national security and international trade. In the worst case it could incite trade wars and be devastating to the world economy. It would be difficult for a nation to explain that its economic weapon had been mobilized for the purpose of bringing economic pressure to bear only on the Idi Amins and Hitlers of the world. It would be difficult to convince allies who were economic competitors that they would be safe from the use of such force.

Likewise, institutionalizing economic conflict could stimulate acrimonious debate in the United States over the effectiveness and morality of the economic weapon (not a bad thing in itself, since the leadership has seldom been challenged by the electorate on the propriety of the use of economic force as it has been on the use of military force). In a real-world crisis many who strongly support the use of economic force do so because they consider it a less violent form of coercion/warfare than would prevail if the military option were exercised. However, when the effectiveness and morality of economic force are debated in the abstract, these proponents quickly abandon ship.

In a U.S. domestic debate on the utility and morality of the use of economic force, it comes down to this:

—Almost universally, economic force is considered to be nonviolent and is preferred to the use of military force.
—The public appears to be more willing to accept both friendly and enemy, both combat and collateral, casualties in economic conflict than in military conflict.
—However, to serious students of the international scene it remains a tool of aggression.
—As a tool of aggression, it is unlikely to be supported by those in the United States who abhor any form of international conflict.

So should the United States let sleeping dogs lie and continue to ignore the need to organize for this form of conflict? It appears that the United States has several options that are not mutually exclusive.

First, it could stay the course, continuing to do what it already does:

—conduct a fairly extensive counterintelligence effort, diverting cold war assets to economic information gathering and intelligence processing
—disseminate counterintelligence alerts and warnings only when it is clearly perceived as a threat to U.S. industry
—avoid collecting and processing economic information to produce intelligence that might be used against allied or friendly nations in an economic conflict
—avoid any manifest centralization of authority for the purpose of planning, training, and exercising or for waging economic conflict
—rely upon the informal charters of departments and agencies such as the Treasury Department's Office of Foreign Assets Control, the Department of State, and the staff of the National Security Council

Second, the United States could clandestinely organize the bureaucracy to manage economic-conflict resources. That is:

—assign responsibility for managing the use, and the preparation for the use, of economic force—to include studying, planning, training, exercising, and coercing and warfighting—which could be placed in a single or several departments or agencies
—codify the organization with legislation or executive orders
—charge the U.S. intelligence community to collect information and process intelligence for both offensive and defensive economic conflict

Third, the United States could maintain the status quo, as in the first alternative, but contract with activities outside the bureaucracy to study, plan, train, and exercise for the use of and defense against economic force. The operations and products of the private sector could be made public and have limited (classified) distribution within the government.

Any of these alternatives that rely upon the clandestine organization of the bureaucracy for economic conflict is doomed to fail. Matters of this magnitude, in this era, in the open society of the United States, simply cannot be kept secret. Any option that is perceived as endorsing, promoting, or merely authorizing an aggressive use of economic force against contemporary political allies will generate such fierce international opposition that it would be counterproductive.

It is possible to delineate responsibilities within the federal bureaucracy more clearly, without a manifest centralization of authority and without the creation of an economic conflict czar. The Department of State could be given formal responsibility for the generation of policy, doctrine, and strategy. The academic/private sectors could produce plans (which need not be specific as to national targets); conduct training and exercises (to provide legislative and executive branch staff and principals a better appreciation for the use of economic force); and provide augmentation teams to assist and advise during operations. For activities other than operations the State Department's Foreign Policy Institute could well be the focus for contracting and oversight service; for operational activities, the Treasury Department's FAC could well be the focus. The military's Industrial College for the Armed Forces could make a substantial contribution in educating and training policy- and decision makers. Allied-nation access to and participation in such activities would be encouraged. Special economic intelligence could still be limited and in some cases would be restricted from foreign distribution.

There is no novelty in this proposal to use the private/academic sector in this fashion. There are many private/academic service organizations that have performed such services on a major scale for the United States. Nor is there novelty in having allied participation in the education process on how to plan, train for, and use economic force. Each of the nation's military war colleges has done so for generations.

What are the benefits of contracting the study, planning, exercising, and advising for economic conflict while inviting allies to participate?

First, it should bring order to the process, put a department or agency in charge, and delineate responsibilities for specific activities.

Second, contracting to manage the process removes much of the perception of the U.S. government preparing for economic war.

Third, inviting allies to participate in the study, training, and exercise aspects of the program would reassure them that the program was dedicated to the study of and preparation for this form of conflict in a general sense, and not focused upon friendly nations.

The focus of this effort is upon the U.S. organization for the use of the economic instrument. Nevertheless, the organization of the United Nations for the use of economic force is also relevant. Scholars Lopez and Cortwright have pointed out that since the 1990 end of the cold war, nations have relied more upon the United Nations to resolve international disputes. They see a momentum that encourages UN-sanctioned use of economic force to deter aggression and terrorism, to defend human rights, and to prevent the proliferation of weapons of mass destruction: "After more than four decades on the sidelines, the United Nations has become a major player in the sanctions game."[4]

While the United Nations has sanctions committees, they are rudimentary mechanisms, not capable of coping within the extent of their jurisdiction. Their meagerly staffed committees are bereft of the essential tools to engage in this form of conflict. Lloyd Dumas has called for the organization of a UN Council on Economic Sanctions and Peacekeeping that would include the five members of the Security Council (Great Britain, France, Russia, China, and the United States) plus other major players (one assumes Japan, Canada, and other major economic powers).[5]

Chapter 12

Conclusions

———————————————————————■—————

Life is the art of drawing sufficient conclusions from insufficient premises.

Samuel Butler

I t has not been intended here to promote or to discourage the use of the economic instrument to achieve U.S. national objectives. Rather, the purpose of this book is to encourage a more intelligent use of economic force by a United States that is better informed and better organized to administer the instrument. A better appreciation for the dynamics of economic conflict could either promote or discourage broader use. However, it is most likely that a better appreciation will inhibit the application of such force under circumstances when its success is questionable or its use promises to be counterproductive.

By any measure—whether it is the number of conflicts, the focus, the intensity, or the scope—economic conflict has become more significant and prevalent in the intercourse between nations. The erosion of confidence in the utility of military force has promoted the use of economic force. This does not mean that military force no longer has utility. It does mean that in this post-Vietnam, post–cold war era there is a tendency to use military power with more discrimination.

It is difficult to predict what the twenty-first century will bring. However, if trends continue, economic force will be used with greater frequency until such time as it reaches a threshold where wise statesmen will seek less disruptive instruments of statecraft. Does economic force work? The answer is that the utility of economic force depends upon many related factors. Among the more important are the objective that is to be achieved, the degree of competence in the use of the instrument, and the effectiveness of political endeavors to terminate the conflict on favorable terms.

As in the application of any form of national force, the objective must be realistic. The objective must be worthy of the cost to be suffered by both sender and target. It must be achievable with the instruments of economic force available. A degree of competence to engage in economic conflict is required that in 1994 is not to be found in the arsenal of any nation or coalition of nations. Political initiatives to terminate the conflict on terms favorable to the user of economic force must be timely and effective.

The United States is as well prepared to wield and defend against the use of economic force as any nation or coalition of nations in the world. However, this capability is a function of the overall competence of its bureaucracy and its political, military, and economic strength. It is not due to competence in wielding the economic instrument. In an absolute rather than relative sense, the United States is incompetent to use or defend against the use of economic force effectively. Those who make decisions on, or are implementers in, the use of or defense against economic force do so without a national policy or doctrine; without concepts of employment or an adequate legislative or organizational framework; without strategy, tactics, or historical perspective; without a language, library, data bank, complete intelligence, experience, knowledge, or training.

The process for achieving operational competence in the use of and defense against economic force is neither complex nor difficult. The costs would be nominal compared with the investments currently made in preparations to engage in political or military conflict. Four classes of threat were identified in these pages. The first three, stemming from financial, resource, and espionage vulnerabilities, are not as serious as the fourth: the current lack of preparedness. The most serious abuses or misuses of U.S. economic power—characterized in such calamities as the 1987–88 economic campaign against Panama—are due in large part to an ignorance of the dynamics of economic conflict.

The United States must mobilize its resources to engage better in economic conflict. Such mobilization will require an approach that includes the support and cooperation of American industry. U.S. industry must not be positioned so that it is compelled to ignore or resist government programs to use economic force. The subject of the legal and political implications of mobilizing U.S. industry, absent general war, requires another book. The growth in the numbers, magnitude, and power of multinational corporations is relentless. The extent to which the United States will want or be able to influence their operations in an economic conflict is problematical. The extent of the problem is evidenced in this 1989 statement by the president of the NCR Corporation: "I was asked the other day about United States competitiveness and I replied that I don't think about it at all. We at NCR think of ourselves as a globally competitive company that happens to be headquartered in the United States."[1]

Other nations would undoubtedly perceive a U.S. mobilization of its economic weapons as a threat. Such a perception could produce benefits as well as penalties. The perception would reinforce the deterrent potential of the U.S. economic instrument in the view of target nations. However, there is the danger that allied economic competitors would perceive that the United States was mobilizing for an aggressive use of economic force against them. Such perceptions could escalate relations from the level of routine economic competition to the more dangerous one of economic conflict (to include a trade war). This threat of escalation could be diminished by maximizing academic and private sector participation; being as open as possible about U.S. activities; and permitting allies to participate in the process short of having access to the most sensitive of U.S. intelligence and planning.

Economic force is not a panacea for the resolution of international problems. However, it is now and it will remain a useful tool for the United States. When wielded by another power, it could someday be a threat to this country. For these very basic reasons the U.S. leadership must prepare now for this form of conflict.

Appendix: U.S. Legislation and Agreements Affecting Authority to Use the Economic Weapon

Legislation or Agreement (Year/Emergency Powers?)	Summary	Comment
International Emergency Economic Powers Act (1977/yes)	Gives president authority to declare national emergency with nearly unlimited options to control exports/imports and finance transactions.	Provisions are vague, and congressional review has been limited by Supreme Court. Intended to replace the Trading with the Enemy Act (which is still effective).
Export Administration Act Amendments (amended in 1985/yes)	Limits presidential control over exports. Section 14 authorizes president to control U.S. private credit transactions. Section generally prohibits secondary boycotts.	All U.S. exports must be licensed by Department of Commerce. Certain circumstances require congressional consultation and authority.
Comprehensive Anti-Apartheid Act (1986/no)	Provides broad mandatory limits on commerce with South Africa. Significant and unique limits on financial transactions.	Strengthens congressional controls on presidential powers for South Africa.
Miscellaneous bilateral foreign assistance (military assistance, arms sales, loans, insurance, food, seaport/airport access) (various/no)	Many legal authorities to provide foreign assistance or access to be proffered as carrot or denied as stick.	Executive branch has broad authority to grant or deny assistance or privilege.
Magnusen Fishery Conservation and Management Act (1976/no)	Conditionally authorizes fishing rights in U.S. waters (200 nautical miles from coast).	Rights may be expanded by executive branch.

Legislation or Agreement (Year/Emergency Powers?)	Summary	Comment
Atomic Energy Act (1954/no)	Grants president extensive authority to limit exports of nuclear materials, equipment, and technology.	Amended by Nuclear Nonproliferation Act of 1978. Presidential authority to limit export of nuclear commodities is extensive. Executive branch authority to authorize is limited.
Arms Export Control Act (1976/no)	Governs foreign military sales.	Presidential authority to limit export of military arms is extensive. Authority to authorize is limited.
General Agreement on Tariffs and Trade (1948/no)	U.S. is signatory to agreement that guarantees nondiscrimination in trade relations among signers.	Since most signatories are unlikely targets for U.S. use of economic weapon, and since verbiage of agreement is vague on subject, it has had little impact.
Section 232 of Trade Expansion Act (1962/no)	Authorizes president to adjust imports to U.S. if they endanger U.S. security.	The definition of what constitutes "national security" is the principal issue in this legislation.
Specific country import limits (various/no)	Imports to U.S. from Cuba, Libya, and Uganda are limited by statutes.	U.S. code authorizes president to impose a total embargo on all trade with Cuba. U.S. law authorizes similar discretion relative to Libya. With 1979 departure of Idi Amin, Uganda restraints were lifted.

Legislation or Agreement (Year/Emergency Powers?)	Summary	Comment
Specific commodity import limits (various/no)	Various U.S. code provisions limit import of specific commodities into U.S.	Examples of import quota systems imposed by U.S. law are for sugar, meat, copper, coffee, textiles, furs, cotton, peanuts, and certain dairy products.
Specific policy issues (various/no)	Various statutes require/authorize extension or withdrawal of trade relations or benefits based on a nation's policies such as emigration and human rights.	Relevant statutes include Title IV of the Trade Act of 1974 and Trade Agreements Act of 1951.
Johnson Act (1934/no)	Can be used to prosecute those who violate prohibition against extension of private credit to nation in default to payment of debt to U.S.	The many exceptions to the provisions of the act make it difficult to invoke.
Section 187c of UN Participation Act (1945/no)	Grants president broad powers to use economic weapons whenever they are mandated by UN Security Council.	Requires a mandate by UN Security Council before president can act.
Trading with the Enemy Act (1917, revised 1982/yes)	Intended to be superseded by the International Emergency Economic Powers Act, but it includes a grandfather provision to permit president to exercise wartime economic controls.	Applicable in wartime but currently used against Cuba, North Korea, and Cambodia.

Appendix *continued*

Legislation or Agreement (Year/Emergency Powers?)	Summary	Comment
Cuban Democracy Act (1992/no)	Reinforces a 30-year trade embargo against Cuba, encouraging a secondary embargo by nations friendly to the U.S.	A politically volatile bill with opponents charging that it is an attempt to curry favor of Cuban American community while making it impossible for U.S. business to operate in Cuba.
Omnibus Trade and Competitiveness Act (1988/no)	Reforms export controls with emphasis on high-technology products. Has a 1994 revived Section 301, which provides for labeling countries unfair in their trade practices.	There was speculation in April–May 1993 that a revived Section 301 (Super 301) would be imposed to thwart Japanese trade practices that promote imbalances in trade.

Sources: Carter, *International Economic Sanctions;* Harris and Bialos, "Strange New World of United States Export Controls"; Moyer and Mabry, "Export Controls as Instruments of Foreign Policy."

Notes

Preface

1. While they are few, there are some extremely worthy publications on the subject of economic conflict. One that is notable is the pioneer work done by Hufbauer, Schott, and Elliot (*Economic Sanctions Reconsidered*), and another is that provided by Barry Carter (*International Economic Sanctions*). Both of these sources are referenced extensively in the following pages.

2. For example, see Scharfen, "Military Power," and Scharfen, "Efficacy of Economics"; Scharfen and Ball, "Principles of Economic War," 59–69.

Chapter 1: Introduction

1. There are those who believe that speaking of trade in "war metaphors" increases the likelihood that there will be a "trade war." A countervailing opinion, subscribed to here, is that identification of the problem, in realistic terms, is necessary before the problem can be solved or ameliorated. See McGurn, "I Hear Asia Calling."

2. One may argue that there are five, not merely three, elements of national power if psychological and cultural components are included. For our purposes, however, it is sufficient to consider just the three principal elements of military, political, and economic power, as these are the elements of power most likely to be converted to force.

3. See, for example, Robert Kettner, "The Tyranny of the Economically Correct," *Washington Post,* 18 April 1991, A17.

4. Hufbauer, Schott, and Elliot, *Economic Sanctions Reconsidered.*

5. The single exception is found in Scharfen and Ball, "Principles of Economic War." In 1985 and 1990 Hufbauer, Schott, and Elliot—referenced extensively in the following pages—did offer a list of nine "do's and don'ts" and nine "commandments" for the use of "economic sanctions," such as

"Don't bite off more than you can chew" and "Do pick on the weak and helpless." However, these helpful hints do not qualify as principles.

Chapter 2: The Language of Economic Conflict

1. Passell, "Economics," 1.

2. Loring, *Soviet Economic Warfare*, 1; C. Pass, B. Lowes, L. Davis, and S. J. Kronish, *Harper Collins Dictionary, Economics* (New York: Harper Perennial, 1991).

3. Roger Barnett properly comments that the term *aggression* is troublesome and has no broadly agreed-upon definition. In contemporary usage it is used pejoratively. It is a cousin to the political term *destabilizing*, which means "I don't like it." The term *aggression* is used frequently in this work without joining the controversy of attempting to provide a definition that may enjoy universal support. When used here, *aggression* is meant to connote a forceful violation by one party of the basic rights of another. That is, it is used in the pejorative sense.

4. Hoke quoted in James K. Glassman, "A Bit of Creative Accounting Makes the Budget a Fraud," *Washington Post*, 30 July 1993, D1; George Orwell, "Politics and the English Language" (1946), in *A Baker's Dozen*, ed. Richard H. Haswell and John W. Ehrstine (Dubuque, Iowa: Hunt, 1974), 39.

5. W. Lutz, *Doublespeak* (New York: Harper Perennial, 1990), 2–7.

6. Adler-Karlsson, *Western Economic Warfare*, xii.

7. Minckler and Rebh, "Economic Conflict and National Security Research."

8. Nincic and Wallenstein, *Dilemmas of Economic Coercion*.

9. Morita and Ishihara, *The Japan That Can Say No*.

10. Steven R. Weisman, "From the U.S. Envoy, Salvos of 'Friendly Advice,'" *New York Times*, 10 November 1989, A4.

11. ABC, *Frontline*, "Losing the War with Japan."

12. W. Branigin, "Noriega Appointed Maximum Leader," *Washington Post*, 16 December 1989, A21.

13. M. Dobbs, "Soviet Reform Requires New Urgency," *Washington Post*, 4 December 1989, A1.

14. "Soviet Says Sanctions Must End," D1.

15. Schweizer, *Victory*, 40, 168.

16. *New Encyclopaedia Britannica*, 15th ed.; Richard Perle, "The Eastward Technology Flow: A Plan of Common Action," *Strategic Review*, Spring 1984, 24–32.

17. Schweizer, *Victory,* 72, 126.

18. Friedman and Lebard, *Coming War with Japan,* 394.

19. Lissakers, "Money and Manipulation," 111.

20. Stephen Glazier, *Word Menu* (New York: Random House, 1992).

21. Kennedy, *Preparing for the Twenty-first Century,* 127.

22. For example, see Bienin, *Power, Economics, and Security.*

23. Nincic and Wallenstein, *Dilemmas of Economic Coercion,* 3.

Chapter 3: The Problem

1. Jim Hoagland, "So They Talked a Lot about Money," *Washington Post,* 6 April 1993, A21.

2. Hufbauer, Schott, and Elliot, *Economic Sanctions Reconsidered,* 7; Verity quoted in Wines, "Security Agency Debates New Role"; Les Aspin, "Four Scenarios—Choose One," *Washington Post,* 9 March 1990, A23.

3. Christiansen and Powers, "Unintended Consequences"; Luttwak, "America's Setting Sun."

4. Weinberger quoted in Bruce I. Gudmundsson, "Understanding the Master," *Marine Corps Gazette,* October 1993, 79.

5. Stavridis, "To Begin Again."

6. James Carville, "Help Those Whom NAFTA Will Hurt," *Washington Post,* 25 July 1993, C7; Kennedy, *Preparing for the Twenty-first Century,* 127; Mike Moore, "Messy, but Useful," *Bulletin of the Atomic Scientists,* November 1993, 2.

7. Jim Hoagland, "More Donald Trump Than John Wayne," *Washington Post,* 13 January 1994, A27.

8. John Glenn, "China's Dangerous Arms Exports," *Washington Post,* 3 December 1993, A29.

9. Blustein, "Japanese Fear New Trade Disputes."

10. Bond, *Cauldron;* Crichton, *Rising Sun;* Anderson, *Japan Conspiracy;* Clancy, *Debt of Honor.*

11. Boren quoted in Wines, "U.S. Urged to Emphasize Economic Strength"; Hoagland, "World Cop?"

12. Levin quoted in *Washington Post,* 26 November 1989, 36; "Helms Urges U.S. to Use Food Exports for Foreign Policy Leverage," *Washington Post,* 2 March 1981, A3; Nelan, "How the World Will Look."

13. There are those such as Max Singer who demur. Singer, while accepting the importance of economic power in the future, visualizes a "Real World Order" that rejects economic conflict while encouraging

cooperation. Such a world will expend its resources on making its economy flourish (with a growth in GNP). The rationale is that cooperation is a much sounder investment than conflict. In the best of worlds this may be true. However, realistically, nations still seem to be disposed to engage in all forms of unproductive conflict, including economic.

14. McGovern, "Elements of 'McGovernism.'"

15. Robinson, "Progress toward Commercial Disarmament." (Also advocating economic disarmament is E. N. Luttwak in "America's Setting Sun.")

16. Waterman, "Introduction to Economic Warfare."

17. Milner and Baldwin, *Political Economy of National Security;* Tyson, *Trade Conflict in High-Technology Industries.*

18. Shubik, "Unconventional Methods."

19. *The Reader's Catalog* (1989); Adler-Karlsson, *Western Economic Warfare.*

20. Samuelson, "Books I Didn't Read"; Schelling, *International Economics,* 487–533; Galtung, "Effects of International Economic Sanctions."

21. Hufbauer, Schott, and Elliot, *Economic Sanctions Reconsidered;* Carter, *International Economic Sanctions;* Bienen, *Power, Economics, and Security;* Wu, *Economic Warfare;* Knorr, *Power of Nations;* Schelling, *International Economics.*

22. This judgment is in no way intended to detract from the fine efforts of impressive scholars such as Hufbauer, Schott, Elliot, Carter, and others. It is simply that they have addressed concerns other than the organization for and use of the economic instrument in conflict.

23. Zoellick quoted in Hobart Rowen, "Missing an Economic Strategy," *Washington Post,* 18 April 1991, A21; Kissinger, "International Trade."

24. Jim Hoagland, "The Sanctions Bromide," *Washington Post,* 12 November 1993, A25.

25. Smith, *On Political War.*

26. Klaus Knorr came closest to providing a complete and detailed analysis of the use of economic force, but his interests were broader, including the entire spectrum of aggressive statecraft.

27. Raspberry, "Fly on the Wall."

28. Morgan, *Merchants of Grain,* 245.

29. Schweizer, *Victory,* 21.

30. *Insight,* 11 December 1989, 36.

31. "Getting in on the Action," *Journal of Commerce.*

32. Safire, "Staying a Superpower."

33. Gertz, "World Economy New Focus."

34. Wines, "U.S. Urged to Emphasize Economic Strength."

35. Gregor Peterson, letter to author, 20 January 1994.

36. Pyatt, "No Way to Win."

37. Some prominent economists, such as Horst Schulmann, former West German finance secretary, also speak of "finance wars." See *Journal of Commerce,* 28 December 1982, 23B.

38. See, for example, Michael E. Porter's "The Competitive Advantage of Nations" and Christopher Bartlett and Sumantra Ghoskal's "Managing across Borders," both sponsored and produced by Harvard University Graduate School of Business Administration, 1993.

39. Some would argue that the alleged U.S. loss of its competitive edge to the Japanese is a fiction. Businessman Gregor Peterson writes that the "economic star" of the Japanese "is falling as their cost of capital increases, as their labor costs become uncompetitive, and as technology leapfrogs their high-cost infrastructure." Peterson, letter to author.

40. Blustein, "Japanese Seek to Clip Wings."

41. John Mintz and Ruth Marcus, "Saudis Switch Jetliner Order to U.S.," *Washington Post,* 20 August 1993, B1.

42. Samuelson, "Why Are We Fighting with Japan?"

43. Not to be confused with the three "cod wars" between Iceland and Great Britain during the mid-1970s.

44. Schrage, "High Technology"; Peterson, letter to author.

45. Brown-John, *Multilateral Sanctions,* 7.

46. "U.S. to Impose Trade Sanctions against EC," *Winston-Salem Journal,* 28 May 1993, A21.

47. Hills quoted in Stuart Auerbach, "Prophet of Failure Haunts Trade Talks," *Washington Post,* 22 July 1990, H1.

48. An example of a weaker nation imposing "sanctions" on a more powerful target is the June 1990 action of Zaire against Belgium in retaliation for an alleged interference in Zaire's internal affairs by the former colonial ruler.

Chapter 4: The Threat

1. David Ignatius and Michael Getler, "The Great Non-debate on American Foreign Policy," *Washington Post,* 23 October 1988, C1; Dupuy, "We Are Less Warlike."

2. Ignatius and Getler, "Great Non-debate," C1; Friedman and Lebard, *Coming War with Japan,* 135.

3. Cresson quoted in Thurow, *Head to Head,* 81; Roth quoted in Friedman and Lebard, *Coming War with Japan,* 271.

4. Jeffrey E. Garten, "Japan and Germany: American Concerns," *Foreign Affairs,* Winter 1989/90, 93.

5. *Time,* 4 July 1988.

6. Steven Schlosstein, as cited by David Brock in a review of *The End of the American Century* by Steven Schlosstein, *American Spectator,* April 1990, 41.

7. Bond, *Cauldron;* Anderson, *Japan Conspiracy;* Clancy, *Debt of Honor.*

8. Yergin, *Prize,* 632.

9. Ian O. Lesser, *Resources and Strategy* (New York: St. Martin's, 1989), 124.

10. *Washington Post,* 26 March 1991, A17.

11. Davis, "White House to Name 22 Technologies."

12. Quoted in Friedman and Lebard, *Coming War with Japan,* 9.

13. See, for example, John Crawford and Saburo Okita, *Raw Materials and Pacific Economic Integration* (Vancouver: University of British Columbia Press, 1978).

14. Gilder, *Microcosm,* 17.

15. Peterson, letter to author.

16. Sweeney, Oliver, and Leech, *International Legal System,* 281.

17. This is not to deny that there has been a decline in the relative strength of the U.S. economy. As this is being written, the United States accounts for slightly over 20 percent of the major forms of global activity. The United States produced 40–50 percent of the gross world product in the late 1940s and early 1950s. This of course was a postwar anomaly. However, as time passes, the U.S. share of the global economic market continues to decline.

18. Source is IFI/Plenum Data Corporation as reported by John Burges, *Washington Post,* 13 January 1994, D10.

19. "Central Planning," *Economist,* 6 November 1993, 7.

20. Richard Lacavo, "America's New Competitive Muscle," *Time,* 29 November 1993, 28.

21. Robert J. Samuelson, "The Great American Fantasy," *Washington Post,* 27 October 1993, A25.

22. National Security Institute, "Espionage in 90's Turns Economic," 1.

23. Lardner, "CIA Seeks to Define New Role."

24. National Security Institute, "Espionage in 90's Turns Economic."

25. Marlow, "Freebooter."

26. Thomas N. Thompson, "Dumping on Trade," *Washington Post,* 18 July 1994, A19.

27. Pat Buchanan, *Washington Times,* 5 May 1993, G1.

28. Eftimiades, *Chinese Intelligence Operations,* 71.

29. Schweizer, *Friendly Spies,* 46ff. It should be acknowledged that the authenticity of one espionage incident described by Schweizer has been challenged by David Leppard and Nick Rufford. (See "The Spy Who Wasn't There," *Washington Post,* 11 April 1993, C1.)

30. Cohen quoted in Lewis, "U.S. Panel Seeks Tighter Spy Laws"; Nelan, "New World for Spies."

31. Carroll, "Next for the CIA."

32. Gertz, "FBI Chief."

33. Lardner and Pincus, "CIA's Gates Opposed"; Gertz, "Friends, Foes."

34. Samuelson, "Spying Won't Boost U.S. Economic Competitive-ness"; Peterzell, "When Friends Become Moles."

35. Peterzell, "When Friends Become Moles."

36. Gertz, "French Probed."

37. Anderson and Binstein, "CIA's Hottest Question."

38. Buchanan, *Washington Times,* 5 May 1993, G1.

39. Gertz, "New Spy"; Gertz, "Japanese Intelligence Network."

40. Nelan, "New World for Spies."

41. Ibid.

42. Schweizer, *Friendly Spies,* 9.

43. Gertz, "French Probed."

44. Will Durant, *Our Oriental Heritage* (New York: Simon & Schuster, 1954), 55.

45. At least thirty-three U.S. companies were targeted, including such giants as TRW, Westinghouse, Texas Instruments, GTE, LTV, Boeing, and Hughes.

46. Mintz, "CIA: French Targeted Secrets."

47. Mintz, "Paris Air Show 'Plot.' "

48. Eftimiades, *Chinese Intelligence Operations,* 29.

49. Smith, "U.S. to Protest Industrial Spying."

50. Nelan, "New World for Spies," 30.

51. Frank Swoboda and Warren Brown, "GM Feud Becomes Test

Case," *Washington Post,* 29 July 1993, A1. By the time of this writing this allegation had been neither proved nor disproved, as an auditor's report failed to clear Mr. Lopez of the allegation of industrial espionage (per *Economist,* 4 December 1993, 5).

52. Gertz, "FBI Chief."

53. Samuelson, "Spying Won't Boost U.S. Economic Competitiveness."

54. Gertz, "World Economy New Focus."

55. Lardner, "CIA Seeks to Define New Role."

56. Ibid.

57. Ibid.

58. Gertz, "Friends, Foes."

59. Cooper, "Intelligence Goes Public."

60. Thomas W. Lippman, "U.S. Seeks to Halt Illegal Payments by Foreign Corporations," *Washington Post,* 3 December 1993, A10.

61. Lardner, "CIA Seeks to Define New Role."

62. Gertz, "World Economy New Focus."

63. Lardner, "CIA Seeks to Define New Role."

64. Wines, "Security Agency Debates New Role."

65. Lardner, "CIA Seeks to Define New Role."

66. William Branigan, "U.S. Pressured to Soften Panama Policy," *Washington Post,* 14 August 1988.

67. Steven Erlanger, *New York Times,* 9 June 1988, A1.

68. Pritchard, "Panama's Bishops."

69. Hoagland, "Sanctions: A Broken Arrow."

70. Pat Buchanan, *Washington Times,* 3 June 1991, D1.

71. Pichirallo and Goshko, "Anti-Noriega Sanctions."

72. Weymouth, "Panama."

Chapter 5: Legislation and the Morality Question

1. Carter, *International Economic Sanctions.*

2. Ibid., 235.

3. U.S. exporters do not all agree that they merit compensation for losses due to the United States' use of economic force. Gregor Peterson, former president and CEO of one of the world's leading banking software companies, writes, "I am opposed to providing compensation to those who are injured because of imposition of economic force. When I do business in foreign countries, I have to price my products and services based upon many risks—currency risk, political risk, legal risk, terrorist risk, economic

risk, etc. The government shouldn't insure me against any of these risks. Compensation for these risks should be included in my price and I should insist that my compensation curve is ahead of my costs and expense curve." Peterson, letter to author.

4. Peter Behr, "U.S. Holds Tight to Role of Trade Enforcer," *Washington Post,* 12 December 1993, A52.

5. Richard Gephardt, "How Dare I Criticize the President," *Washington Post,* 21 March 1991, A21.

6. Brown-John, *Multilateral Sanctions.* The navicert is a form of passport issued by a belligerent in a neutral country, which provides a guarantee—absent suspicious activity—that a vessel will not be subject to search and seizure by the belligerent once it sorties from the neutral port.

7. "The Use of Nonviolent Coercion: A Study in Legality under Article 2(4) of the Charter of the United Nations," 122 *University of Pennsylvania Law Review* 983 (1973); quoted in Sweeney, Oliver, and Leech, *International Legal System,* 1495.

8. 119 U.N.T.S.3; 2 UST 2394; as amended 27 February 1967, 21 UST 607.

9. Edward Mead Earle interpreted classical economist Adam Smith as supporting the use of economic force. To the question of "whether, when necessary, the economic power of the nation should be cultivated and used as an instrument of statecraft," Adam Smith's answer, Earle wrote, "would clearly be 'Yes'—that economic power should be so used." See Earle, *Makers of Modern Strategy,* 124.

10. Steinfels, "Beliefs."

11. Christiansen and Powers, "Unintended Consequences."

12. Hufbauer, Schott, and Elliot, *Economic Sanctions Reconsidered,* 548.

13. Douglas Farah, "Fuel Aid Sharpens Debate over Haiti," *Washington Post,* 15 January 1994.

14. Richard John Neuhaus, "Just War and This War," *Wall Street Journal,* 29 January 1991, A16. The bishops' appraisal of the use of economic force as "peaceful" is more defensible in light of the expectation that in the first twenty days of a shooting war U.S. forces would suffer thirty thousand fatalities.

15. George McGovern, "Stand up, but Seek Peace," *Washington Post,* 29 August 1990, A25.

16. Douglas Farah, "Timetable for Aristide Still under Revision," *Washington Post,* 9 June 1993, A21.

17. Christiansen and Powers, "Unintended Consequences."

18. Associated Press, "Iraq Sanctions Toll," *Washington Post,* 9 January 1994, A35.

19. James Schlesinger, "American Arrogance," *Washington Post,* 5 December 1993, C7.

20. Associated Press, "Ex-President Backtracks on Being Ashamed of U.S.," *Washington Post,* 9 September 1994, A31.

21. Matthew, "Dolphins, Tuna, and Free Trade."

Chapter 6: The Instruments of Economic Force

1. Nincic and Wallenstein, *Dilemmas of Economic Coercion.*

2. "Clinton Will Renew Favorable Trade Status to China for Year," *Winston-Salem Journal,* 28 May 1993, 8.

3. Brown-John, *Multilateral Sanctions,* 8; *New Encyclopaedia Britannica,* 15th ed., 10:405.

4. Hufbauer, Schott, and Elliot, *Economic Sanctions Reconsidered,* case 76-2, U.S. v. Taiwan, 422.

5. Carter, *International Economic Sanctions,* 84.

6. Perle, "Eastward Technology Flow"; Adler-Karlsson, *Western Economic Warfare,* xii.

7. Philip Shenon, "U.S. Firms Sidelined as Capitalism Runs Amok in Vietnam," *San Francisco Chronicle,* 4 October 1993, A14.

8. Ruth Marcus and Thomas W. Lippman, "Clinton Lifts Vietnam Trade Embargo," *Washington Post,* 4 February 1994, A1.

9. Carter, "Charge Iraq Oil Export Fees."

10. *Time,* 6 September 1993, 14.

11. Sue Anne Pressley, "On the Streets of El Paso, They're Feeling the Pinch," *Washington Post,* 14 November 1993, A3.

12. Cutler, "Creative Patent Stallers?"

13. T. R. Reid and Peter Behr, "A Software Fight's Blurred Battle Lines," *Washington Post,* 11 January 1994, D1.

14. Veigh, "India Misses U.S. Patent Deadline."

15. Brown-John, *Multilateral Sanctions,* 28.

16. Frankel, "The Other Gulf War."

17. Jim Hoagland, "To Bring Change to China," *Washington Post,* 3 June 1993, A25.

18. Schweizer, *Victory,* 73.

19. Anne Day, "Defying Cuba Travel Curb," *Washington Post,* 24 June 1994, A2.

20. *Oriental Economist* 8 (August 1940): 473, quoted in Friedman and Lebard, *Coming War with Japan,* 73.

21. Schweizer, *Victory,* 81.

22. Schelling, *International Economics,* 488.

23. Rosenfeld, "Development, Disarmament, Bribers."

24. Nelan, "New World for Spies."

25. Bruce Van Voorst, "The Ploy That Fell to Earth," *Time,* 30 August 1993, 26–27. Also see R. Jeffrey Smith, "3 'Star Wars' Tests Rigged, Aspin Says," *Washington Post,* 10 September 1993, A19.

26. Van Voorst, "Ploy That Fell," 27.

27. Stephen P. Gibert, *Soviet Images of America* (New York: Crane Russak, 1977), 65; Richard Pipes, ed., *Soviet Strategy in Europe* (New York: Crane Russak, 1976), 39.

28. Eugene Robinson, "Worldwide Negotiation Nears Crisis," *Washington Post,* 7 July 1993, A1.

29. William Drozdiak, "Embargo Said to Make U.S. Attack Less Difficult," *Washington Post,* 17 November, 1990, A9.

30. Schelling, *International Economics.*

31. Bill McAllister, "Overseas Counterfeiters Pose Threat to U.S. Currency," *Washington Post,* 18 April 1994, A16.

32. Shubik, "Unconventional Methods of Economic Warfare," F13.

33. Leslie Helms, "Many Japanese Skeptical of Clinton's Trade Policy," *Los Angeles Times,* 9 July 1993, A6.

Chapter 7: The Utility of Economic Force

1. Hufbauer, Schott, and Elliot, *Economic Sanctions Reconsidered,* 92.

2. Davis, "Squeezing Apartheid."

3. Nincic and Wallenstein, *Dilemmas of Economic Coercion,* 6; Reuther quoted in April 1993 Conference Summary "Economic Sanctions and International Relations," published by the Fourth Freedom Forum and Joan B. Kroc Institute for International Studies at the University of Notre Dame, 14; Torricelli, "Keep the Embargo," *Washington Post,* 11 September 1994, C7.

4. See, for example, Dobbs, "Soviet Reform Requires New Urgency."

5. Quoted in Martin Walker, "Britain's Uncommon Leader," *Washington Post,* 31 October 1993, Book World, 2.

6. Schweizer, *Victory,* xv, xviii–xix.

7. Garthoff, *Great Transition*.

8. "Cedras Thumbs His Nose," *Economist,* 6 November 1993, 43.

9. Douglas Farah, "Haitian Military Plans Years in Power," *Washington Post,* 28 November 1993, A1.

10. Werleigh, "Haiti and the Halfhearted."

11. John M. Goshko, "Saddam May Accept Terms for Oil Sale," *Washington Post,* 17 January 1994, A16.

12. Pipes quoted in Kramer, "Rung on the Ladder to War."

13. Friedman and Lebard, *Coming War with Japan,* 107.

14. William Matthews, "Leaders Say U.S. Not Prepared," *Navy Times,* 29 October 1990, 24.

15. Cernuda quoted in Shawn Miller, "Trade Winds Stir Miami Storm," *Insight,* 23 May 1993, 9; Pierre Salinger, "A Mistake and an Anachronism," *Washington Post,* 28 August 1994, C7.

16. Schweizer, *Victory.*

17. Jim Kolbe, "The Anti NAFTA 'Sovereignty' Follies," *Washington Times,* 14 September 1993, A23.

18. Baer, "Sanctions and Security," 178.

19. Friedman and Lebard, *Coming War with Japan,* 58.

20. "NAM Urges End to Use of Embargoes," *Washington Times,* 1 February 1983, 2A.

21. Thomas Jefferson to Horatio G. Spafford, 17 March 1814.

22. Pampel quoted in "The Battle Lines of Global Business Warfare," *Leaders,* October–December 1990, 86.

23. Douglas Farah and William Booth, "Efforts to Restore Aristide Tottering," *Washington Post,* 25 October 1993, A31.

24. Wilson quoted in Carter, *International Economic Sanctions,* 9; Brembeck quoted in April 1993 Conference Summary "Economic Sanctions and International Relations," i.

25. Lopez and Cortwright, "Sanctions: Do They Work?" 15.

26. Thurow, *Head to Head,* 23, 118.

27. Charles Krauthammer, "Europe's Future: Go West, Old Man," *Time,* 2 November 1992, 78; Friedman and Lebard, *Coming War with Japan.*

Chapter 8: Principles of Economic Conflict

1. These principles were originally discussed in Scharfen and Ball, "Principles of Economic War."

2. Nossal, "Trade Sanctions as Policy Instruments," 153–73.

3. James M. Lindsay, "Trade Sanctions as International Punishment," *International Organization* 43 (Spring 1989): 305.

4. Douglas Farah, "U.S. Tightens Sanctions on Regime in Haiti," *Washington Post,* 5 June 1993, A18.

5. Barber, "Economic Sanctions as a Policy Instrument," 368.

6. Cortwright quoted in April 1993 Conference Summary "Economic Sanctions and International Relations," 17.

7. Oznobistchev quoted in ibid., 5.

8. "Legality of the Blockade," *London Times,* 14 August 1990, 11.

9. Dusan Stojanovic, "Serbia Hurt by Sanctions," *Washington Times,* 31 May 1993, A7.

10. Ewing, "AF Chief," 26.

11. Quoted in Schelling, *International Economics,* 506.

12. *Washington Post,* 10 June 1982, A17.

13. Farah, "Timetable for Aristide."

14. Richard Stolz, "Too Late to Lift the Arms Embargo," *Washington Post,* 9 September 1993, A20.

15. Elliot quoted in April 1993 Conference Summary "Economic Sanctions and International Relations," 1; Joyner quoted in ibid., 4.

16. Mitterand quoted in *Washington Post,* 15 June 1982, A1; John Pomfret, "Neighbors Enforce Yugoslav Embargo," *Washington Post,* 14 September 1993, A8.

17. Miller, "Trade Winds," 27.

18. Schweizer, *Victory,* 105.

Chapter 9: The Dynamics of Economic Force

1. Konovalov, Oznobistchev, and Evstafiev, "Saying *Da,* Saying *Nyet,*" 30.

2. Morris Janowitz, *The Professional Soldier* (Glencoe, Ill.: Free Press, 1960), xii.

Chapter 10: The Role of Seapower in Economic Conflict

1. Minckler and Rebh, "Economic Conflict and National Security Research."

2. Friedman and Lebard, *Coming War with Japan,* 255.

3. Turn-of-the-century naval strategist Sir Julian Corbett classed blockades of ports as "tactical" while interdiction of commercial shipping at sea was "strategic." See Corbett, *Some Principles of Maritime Strategy,* 97.

4. Carter, "Blockade."

5. As pointed out by Roger Barnett, there are many fine legal distinctions to be made when defining a naval blockade. International lawyers recognize *pacific* blockades, which are not considered acts of war. There are also those who make "the fine distinction between committing an act of war and establishing belligerency. In the latter case, they argue that a blockade meeting the legal requirements *establishes the belligerency* of the states against whom it is targeted, but might not amount to an *act of war.*" Roger Barnett, letter to author, 18 January 1994.

6. Marjorie M. Whiteman, ed., *Digest of International Law* (Washington, D.C.: U.S. Government Printing Office, 1968), 10:861–69, quoted in Lowenthal, "Naval Restriction of Commerce against Iraq," CRS-2.

7. Ibid. Note that the embargo instrument defined here is in terms of import through and export from a target nation's ports. It does not address the exclusion of exports from the belligerent(s) invoking the embargo.

8. Valentine, "U.S. Naval Quarantine of Cuba," 23 *Federal Bar Journal,* 244, 246–247 (1963), quoted in Raymond J. Celeda, "Blockade: Some International and Domestic Legal Implications," Congressional Research Service, Library of Congress, 15 August 1990, CRS-2.

9. Mining is seldom an easy enterprise, however, for it demands great military superiority and is clearly an act of war.

10. O'Keefe, Kelso, and Mundy, "From the Sea."

11. See chapter 9 for a discussion of economic-conflict operations.

12. Stavridis, "To Begin Again."

13. Barnett, "Regional Conflict."

Chapter 11: Organizing the U.S. Bureaucracy for Economic Conflict

1. Moynihan, "U.S. Should Centralize."

2. Information on the activities of the FAC has been derived from a 21 June 1993 interview with Mr. R. Richard Newcomb, director, Office of Foreign Assets Control, and the following Treasury releases: R. R. Newcomb, prepared statement before the Subcommittee on Oversight,

Committee on Ways and Means, U.S. House of Representatives, 1 May 1991, and R. R. Newcomb, statement before the International Trade Committee, International Law Section, District of Columbia Bar, 15 October 1992.

3. Quoted in Lardner and Pincus, "CIA's Gates Opposed."

4. Lopez and Cortwright, "Sanctions: Do They Work?"

5. Dumas, "Organizing the Chaos."

Chapter 12: Conclusions

1. Quoted by Gavin Wright in a review of *The Work of Nations* by Robert Reich, *Washington Post,* 3 March 1991, Sunday Book Review, 1.

Glossary

Autarky. The process of achieving economic self-sufficiency. (May be used as a defensive economic instrument.)

Bidding wars. The competition between economic entities to win favor from a potential economic benefactor.

Blacklisting. The process of including a trade figure on a roll of those who are to be boycotted. (Normally the entity that is blacklisted is made aware of its status.)

Boycott. A refusal to deal with an adversary in an effort to punish or to influence the adversary's conduct.

Bribery. An illegal inducement to perform an economic favor.

Collateral damage. Harm done to a target, not intended, which may or may not contribute to the attainment of the objective and may be counterproductive.

Commercial disarmament. The agreement between economic entities, or a unilateral declaration, to forgo economic conflict.

Commercial warfare. A synonym for trade warfare.

Commodity dumping. The practice of charging a higher price—one that is not necessarily below cost—at home than for an export; international price discrimination.

Computer subversion. The practice of controlling or accessing a target's automated systems for the benefit of a hostile entity.

Credit system subversion. The practice of manipulating a credit system in such manner as to destabilize it, to punish, or to influence the behavior of an economic entity.

Currency subversion. The practice of manipulating a currency system to degrade or destabilize it.

Disinformation. Information known to be untrue, published or announced for a hostile purpose.

Doctrine. A collection of fundamental considerations that guide the formulation of strategies and tactics to achieve objectives.

Economic civil war. Economic strife between nations or between districts or cities of a single state.

Economic coercion. A limited use of economic force to achieve a limited objective, normally accompanied by the use of political force.

Economic competition. The natural contention between nations, cartels, and international industries and corporations to acquire markets, goods, and profits for national or commercial benefit. (Political or military force could play a minor role.)

Economic conflict. A state that includes either economic coercion, trade warfare, or economic warfare or any combination of the three. (May take place in concert with the use of military or political force.)

Economic force. The application of economic power.

Economic guerrilla warfare. The exercise of economic force by irregular, nongovernment entities against an adversary. May be sponsored and assisted by an established government.

Economic intelligence. The product resulting from the collection, evaluation, analysis, integration, and interpretation of all information that will have an impact upon conditions in economic competition or conflict.

Economic leverage. A synonym for economic power.

Economic nationalism. A concentration on the economic well-being of one nation to the exclusion of others (as opposed to economic internationalism).

Economic power. The capacity to influence the course of events, or to punish, using economic instruments.

Economic propaganda. The broadcast of economic information that will promote the aims of an economic entity.

Economic sanctions. A broadly interpreted popular term that includes the full spectrum of economic-coercion activities. (The term has value in communicating in popular, nontechnical works. However, it is too general to use in a detailed analysis of the dynamics of economic conflict. Barry Carter, in his book *International Economic Sanctions,* defines the term as follows: "Coercive economic measures taken against one or more countries to force a change in policies, or at least to demonstrate a country's opinions about the other's policies. The terms 'economic boycott' and 'embargo' are often used interchangeably with 'economic sanctions' " (p. 4).

Economic spectrum. The range of economic activities in terms of aggressive intent, from economic support to warfare.

Economic support. The award of economic benefits to influence the course of events using economic instruments.

Economic terrorism. An insurrectional strategy employing economic instruments that may or may not be state-sponsored.

Economic warfare. A major use of economic force to change the behavior of or to extract an advantage from an adversary, normally accompanied by the use of political force and sometimes by the use of military force.

Embargo. A restriction upon exports or imports that precludes the buying, selling, or bartering of goods from or to a target economic entity.

European Community. A group of twelve European nations committed to eliminating trade, investment, and other economic barriers among themselves as they establish a common trade policy with other nations. (May also be called European Union.)

Export/import licensing. A state's process for authorizing and establishing the conditions of the export or import of commodities across its borders.

Extortion. The process of influencing the behavior of a target by making threats as to the consequences should the target not do the extorter's bidding.

Food war. A term used to describe economic coercion in which food is the principal weapon used by the dominant adversary.

Force. The exercise of power.

General Agreement on Tariffs and Trade (GATT). A 1948 multilateral treaty that establishes rules for trade among the over one hundred member nations.

Graylisting. The process of covertly including a trade figure on a roll of those who are to be boycotted. (Normally the entity that is graylisted is not made aware of its status.)

Group of Seven. The seven leading industrial nations: the United States, Japan, Britain, Italy, France, Germany, and Canada.

Intelligence. Raw information that has been compiled and analyzed; informally, data acquired covertly from a classified source.

Limited extraction. A deliberate failure to produce a commodity to influence the behavior of a user or to benefit the producer.

Managed trade. A government practice of directing the industrial and trade policies and operations of its economy.

Military economics. The industrial potential, agricultural capabilities, military technology level, and strategic reserves of other nations.

Military war. Hostilities in which the major instrument of force is the military but that are likely to include the use of economic and political force.

Most-favored-nation status. A guarantee to one nation from another that it will have the right to trade equal to that of the most favored nation. (May be used as an instrument of economic conflict.)

National interests. Concerns for the well-being of the nation.

National objectives. The goals of a nation that are believed to ensure its well-being.

National power. The total of a nation's capabilities or potential provided by its economic, political, military, social, psychological, industrial, geographic, technological, and scientific resources.

National security interests. Concerns for the preservation of the nation.

National security objectives. Goals concerned with the preservation of the nation.

Nontariff barrier. Rules and regulations established to inhibit foreign goods competition with a domestic market.

Oil war. An economic war in which oil is the sole or major commodity being used as a weapon.

Patent denial. The practice of withholding approval of a patent application from, or the failure to recognize the patent of, another economic entity.

Physical sanctions. The use of military equipment and personnel to signal a threat. (Term used by international law scholar C. Lloyd Brown-John, in *Multilateral Sanctions in International Law.*)

Political warfare. The use of persuasion, threats, inducements, or other political instruments to achieve a political objective.

Power. A potential derived from strength.

Preclusive purchasing. A process of amassing a commodity of limited availability, to deny it to another economic entity.

Predatory capitalism. A term coined by critics of the Japanese to describe that country's economic system.

Principle. A fundamental truth that provides guidance for planning and operations.

Psychological warfare. The use of propaganda and disinformation to influence the conduct of an adversary.

Resource denial. The process whereby an important or essential commodity is denied to a using entity by a producing entity to punish or to influence behavior.

Senders. A term used by some analysts of economic conflict to describe a nation using economic force against another (target) nation.

Smuggling. The practice of bringing commodities over the borders of an economic entity to avoid tariffs or restrictions.

Stockpiling. The process of amassing and saving commodities on a meaningful scale for use in contingencies. (May be used as a defensive economic instrument.)

Strategy. The art and science of formulating and employing political, military, economic, psychological, and social force to support fundamental objectives.

Tactics. The employment of resources in operations to support a strategy.

Targets. A term used by some analysts of economic conflict to describe a nation that has been subjected to the use of economic force by another (sender) nation.

Tariff. A tax imposed by a state upon an import or export across its borders, often imposed to raise the price of an imported commodity relative to a domestic one.

Technology transfer. The process of conveying valuable technical information or commodities from one economic entity to another.

Trade battle. A definable phase or event in a trade war.

Trade warfare. The use of the economic instrument by two adversaries whose objectives are economic, normally accompanied by the use of political but not military force.

Selected Bibliography

This bibliography is divided into sections as follows: books, articles, reports, National Security Institute security awareness bulletins, military lessons plans and instruction manuals, television shows, statements, and interviews by the author.

Several sources have been useful in assembling this bibliography. Particularly helpful have been the Milner and Baldwin annotated bibliography and Schweizer's *Friendly Spies* (both cited in these pages). Milner and Baldwin summarize the state of scholarship on the subject of economics in national security with the statement, "The political economy of national security can be described as nascent." Even this thorough review of the literature failed to uncover enough titles to justify a separate category for the use of economic force. The categories that are identified follow: (1) theory, method, and concepts of national security analysis; (2) national security and the economy; (3) national security policy and policymaking; (4) economic statecraft; (5) 1945 and earlier studies.

Books

Adler-Karlsson, Gunnar. *Western Economic Warfare, 1947–1967: A Case Study in Foreign Economic Policy.* Stockholm: Almqvist & Wiksell, 1968.

Allen, Robert Loring. *Soviet Economic Warfare.* Washington, D.C.: Public Affairs, 1960.

Anderson, Jack. *The Japan Conspiracy.* New York: Zebra Books, 1993.

Ayubi, Shaheen; Richard E. Bissell; Nana Amu-Brafin Korash; and Laurie A. Lerner. *Economic Sanctions in U.S. Policy.* Princeton: Princeton University Press, 1985.

Baldwin, David A. *Economic Statecraft.* Princeton: Princeton University Press, 1985.

Bienen, Henry, ed. *Power, Economics, and Security: The United States and Japan in Focus.* Boulder: Westview, 1992.

Blechman, Barry M., and Stephen S. Kaplan. *Force without War.* Washington, D.C.: Brookings Institution, 1978.

Boltuck, Richard, and Robert E. Litan, eds. *Down in the Dumps: Administration of the Unfair Trade Laws.* Washington, D.C.: Brookings Institution, 1991.

Bond, Larry. *Cauldron.* New York: Warner Books, 1993.

Brice, Martin. *Axis Blockade Runners of World War II.* Annapolis: Naval Institute Press.

Brodie, Bernard. *A Layman's Guide to Naval Strategy.* Princeton: Princeton University Press, 1942.

Brown-John, C. Lloyd. *Multilateral Sanctions in International Law: A Comparative Analysis.* New York: Praeger, 1975.

Carse, Robert. *Blockade: The Civil War at Sea.* New York: Rinehart, 1958.

Carter, Barry E. *International Economic Sanctions.* 1988. Reprint, Cambridge: Cambridge University Press, 1989.

Clancy, Tom. *Debt of Honor.* New York: G. P. Putnam's Sons, 1994.

Clausewitz, Karl von. "On the Nature of War." In *War, Politics, and Power,* ed. Edward H. Collins. Chicago: Regnery, 1962.

Connelly, Philip, and Robert Perlman. *The Politics of Scarcity: Resource Conflicts in International Relations.* London: Oxford University Press, 1975.

Corbett, Julian. *Some Principles of Maritime Strategy.* 1911. Reprint, Annapolis: Naval Institute Press, 1988.

Cornwall, Hugo. *The Industrial Espionage Handbook.* London: Century Books, 1991.

Crichton, Michael. *Rising Sun.* New York: Alfred A. Knopf, 1992.

Daoudi, M. S., and M. S. Dajani. *Economic Sanctions: Ideals and Experience.* London: Routledge & Kegan Paul, 1983.

Davison, W. Phillips. *The Berlin Blockade.* Princeton: Princeton University Press, 1958.

Destler, I. M. *Making Foreign Economic Policy.* Washington, D.C.: Brookings Institution, 1980.

Doxey, Margaret P. *Economic Sanctions and International Enforcement.* London: Oxford University Press, 1971.

————. *International Sanctions in Contemporary Perspective.* New York: St. Martin's, 1987.

Earle, Edward Mead. *Makers of Modern Strategy: Military Thought from Machiavelli to Hitler.* Princeton: Princeton University Press, 1944.

Editors, Time-Life Books. *The Blockade: Runners and Raiders, The Civil War.* Alexandria: Time-Life Books, 1983.

Eftimiades, Nicholas. *Chinese Intelligence Operations.* Annapolis: Naval Institute Press, 1994.

Ellings, Richard J. *Embargoes and World Power.* Boulder: Westview, 1985.

Evans, Clark, ed. *Boycotts and Peace: A Report by the Committee on Economic Sanctions.* New York: Harper Brothers, 1932.

Figge, Harry E. *Bankruptcy 1995: The Coming Collapse of America and How to Stop It.* Boston: Little, Brown, 1992.

Freedman, Robert Owen. *Economic Warfare in the Communist Bloc: A Study of Economic Pressure against Yugoslavia, Albania, and Communist China.* New York: Praeger, 1966.

Friedman, George, and Meredith Lebard. *The Coming War with Japan.* New York: St. Martin's, 1991.

Garthoff, Raymond L. *The Great Transition: American-Soviet Relations and the End of the Cold War.* Washington, D.C.: Brookings Institution, 1994.

Gilder, George. *Microcosm: The Quantum Revolution in Economics and Technology.* New York: Simon & Schuster, 1989.

Gordon, David L., and Boyden Dangerfield. *The Hidden Weapon: The Story of Economic Warfare.* New York: Harper & Brothers, 1947.

Gray, Colin, and Roger W. Barnett, eds. *Seapower and Strategy.* Annapolis: Naval Institute Press, 1989.

Hanson, Phillip. *Western Economic Statecraft in East-West Relations: Embargoes, Sanctions, Linkage, Economic Warfare, and Detente.* London: Routledge & Kegan Paul, 1988.

Hufbauer, Gary Clyde, and Howard F. Rosen. *Trade Policy for Troubled Industries.* Washington, D.C.: Institute for International Economics, 1986.

Hufbauer, Gary Clyde; Jeffrey J. Schott; and Kimberly Ann Elliot. *Economic Sanctions Reconsidered: History and Current Policy.* 2d ed. Washington, D.C.: Institute for International Economics, 1990.

————. *Economic Sanctions in Support of Foreign Policy Goals.* Washington, D.C.: Institute for International Economics, 1983.

Hughes, Wayne P., Jr. *Fleet Tactics: Theory and Practice.* Annapolis: Naval Institute Press, 1986.

Jack, D. T. *Studies in Economic Warfare.* London: P. S. King & Son, 1940.

Kennedy, Paul. *Preparing for the Twenty-first Century.* New York: Random House, 1993.

Knorr, Klaus. *The Power of Nations: The Political Economy of International Relations.* New York: Basic Books, 1975.

————. *The War Potential of Nations*. Princeton: Princeton University Press, 1956.

————, ed. *Historical Dimensions of National Security Problems*. Lawrence: University Press of Kansas, 1976.

Knorr, Klaus, and Frank Trager, eds., *Economic Issues and National Security*. Lawrence, Kans.: Regent Press, 1977.

Leyton-Brown, David, ed. *The Utility of Economic Sanctions*. London: Croom Helm, 1986.

Lincoln, Edward J. *Japan: Facing Economic Maturity*. Washington, D.C.: Brookings Institution, 1988.

Losman, Donald. *International Economic Sanctions: The Cases of Cuba, Israel, and Rhodesia*. Albuquerque: University of New Mexico Press, 1979.

Luttwak, Edward N., and Stuart L. Koehl. *The Dictionary of Modern War*. New York: Harper Collins, 1991.

Lyons, Gene M., and Louis Morton. *Schools for Strategy: Education and Research in National Security Affairs*. New York: Praeger, 1965.

McLynn, Frank. *Invasion: From the Armada to Hitler, 1588–1945*. London: Routledge & Kegan Paul, 1987.

Medlicott, W. N. *The Economic Blockade*. London: Her Majesty's Stationery Office, 1952–59.

Milner, Helen V., and David A. Baldwin. *The Political Economy of National Security*. Boulder: Westview, 1990.

Milward, Alan S. *War, Economy, and Society, 1939–1945*. Berkeley: University of California Press, 1977.

Morgan, Dan. *Merchants of Grain*. New York: Viking, 1979.

Morgenthau, Hans. *Politics among Nations: The Struggle for Peace and Power*. 4th ed. New York: Knopf, 1967.

Morita, A., and S. Ishihara. *The Japan That Can Say No*. Trans. Frank Baldwin. New York: Simon & Schuster, 1991.

Morris, Eric. *Blockade: Berlin and the Cold War*. New York: Stein & Day, 1973.

Neff, Stephen C. "Boycott and the Law of Nations: Economic Warfare and Modern International Law in Historical Perspective." In *British Yearbook of International Law 1988,* ed. I. Brownlie and D. W. Bowett, 135–45. Oxford: Oxford University Press, 1989.

Nincic, Miroslav, and Peter Wallenstein, eds. *Dilemmas of Economic Coercion: Sanctions in World Politics*. New York: Praeger Special Studies, 1983.

Quinn, David B., and A. N. Ryan. *England's Sea Empire, 1550–1642*. London: George Allen & Unwin, 1983.

SELECTED BIBLIOGRAPHY

Renwick, Robin. *Economic Sanctions.* Cambridge: Center for International Affairs, 1981.

Rode, Reinhard, and Hans D. Jacobsen, eds. *Economic Warfare or Detente: An Assessment of East-West Relations in the 1980s.* Boulder: Westview, 1985.

Schelling, Thomas C. *International Economics.* Boston: Allyn & Bacon, 1958.

Schweizer, Peter. *Friendly Spies: How America's Allies Are Using Economic Espionage to Steal Our Secrets.* New York: Atlantic Monthly Press, 1993.

————. *Victory.* New York: Atlantic Monthly Press, 1994.

Singer, Max, and Aaron Wildavsky. *The Real World Order: Zones of Peace, Zones of Turmoil.* Chatham, N.J.: Chatham House, 1993.

Smith, Paul A., Jr. *On Political War.* Washington, D.C.: National Defense University Press, 1990.

Sun Tzu. *The Art of War.* Trans. and ed. Samuel B. Griffith. 1963. Paperback reprint, New York: Oxford University Press, 1973.

Sweeney, Joseph Modeste; Covey T. Oliver; and Noyes E. Leech. *The International Legal System.* New York: Foundation, 1988.

Thurow, Lester. *Head to Head: The Coming Economic Battle among Japan, Europe, and America.* New York: William Morrow, 1992.

Till, Geoffrey. *Maritime Strategy and the Nuclear Age.* 2d ed. New York: St. Martin's, 1984.

Tyson, Laura D'Andrea. *Trade Conflict in High-Technology Industries.* Washington, D.C.: Institute for International Economics, 1992.

Weintraub, Sidney, ed. *Economic Coercion and U.S. Foreign Policy: Implications of Case Studies from the Johnson Administration.* Boulder: Westview, 1985.

Wu, Yuan-li. *Economic Warfare.* New York: Prentice-Hall, 1952.

Yergin, Daniel. *The Prize: The Epic Quest for Oil, Money, and Power.* New York: Simon & Schuster, 1991.

Articles

Abbot, Kenneth B. "Coercion and Communication: Frameworks for Evaluation of Economic Sanctions." *New York Journal of International Law and Politics* 19 (1987): 781–802.

————. "Linking Trade to Political Goals: Foreign Policy Export Controls in the 1970s and 1980s." *Minnesota Law Review* 65 (June 1981): 739–890.

Alexander, Charles, with Lee Griggs, Abilene Lee, and Gary Lee. "Seething about Trade Sanctions, Farmers, Businessmen, and Scholars Call Them Self-Defeating." *Time,* 18 January 1982, 48.

Alexander, Michael. "High-Tech Boom Opens Security Gaps." *Computer World* 1 (April 1990): 119.

Allen, Michael. "Security Experts Advise Firms to Avoid Panic, Excess Zeal in Probing Data Leaks." *Wall Street Journal,* 20 September 1991, B1.

Amerongen, Otto Wolff von. " 'Commentary': Economic Sanctions as a Foreign Policy Tool?" *International Security* 5 (Fall 1980): 159–67.

Anderson, Jack, and Michael Binstein. "CIA's Hottest Question." *Washington Post,* 14 March 1993, C7.

Anderson, Jack, and Joseph Spear. "The Coming Cold Shower for Bush." *Washington Post,* 23 December 1988, E5.

Anderson, Jack, and Dale Van Atta. "Water as a Potential Weapon against Iraq." *Washington Post,* 3 December 1990, C15.

Andrews, Sally C. "The Legitimacy of the United States Embargo of Uganda." *Journal of International Law and Economics* 13 (1979): 651–73.

Arbetter, Lisa. "To Spy or Not to Spy." *Security Management,* 13 January 1993, 13.

Auerbach, Stuart. "Trade Curb Ineffective Study Says: U.S. May Be Hurt More Than Soviets by Embargo Effort." *Washington Post,* 9 May 1983, A1.

———. "U.S. to Aim Antitrust Laws at Japan." *Washington Post,* 22 February 1992, A1.

Awanohara, Susumu, and Melana Zyla. "United States: Spooks for Industry." *Far Eastern Economic Review,* 25 February 1993, 862.

Baade, Robert A., and Jonathan F. Galloway. "Economic Sanctions against the Union of South Africa." *Alternatives* 4 (March 1979): 487–505.

Baer, George W. "Sanctions and Security: The League of Nations and the Italian-Ethiopian War, 1935–1936." *International Organization* 27 (Spring 1973): 165–79.

Baldwin, David S. "The Power of Positive Sanctions." *World Politics* 24 (October 1971): 19–38.

Barber, James. "Economic Sanctions as a Policy Instrument." *International Affairs* 55 (July 1979): 367–84.

Barnett, Roger W. "Regional Conflict Requires Naval Forces." *Proceedings,* June 1992, 28–32.

"Beating the Sanctions on Serbia." *Economist,* 2 July 1994, 49.

Bequai, August. "The Industrial Spy: Red Flags and Recourse." *Security Management,* August 1985, 93–94.

Bialos, Jeffrey, and Kenneth Juster. "The Libyan Sanctions: Rational Response to State-Sponsored Terrorism?" *Virginia Journal of International Law* 4 (1986): 799–855.

Bienen, Henry, and Robert Gilpin. "Economic Sanctions as a Response to Terrorism." *Journal of Strategic Studies* 3 (3 May 1980): 89–98.

Blau, Thomas. "Strategic Economics: The Roots of Controversy." *Journal of Defense and Diplomacy,* June 1983, 45–49, 64.

Blustein, Paul. "Japanese Fear New Trade Disputes with U.S. in the Wake of Gulf War." *Washington Post,* 6 March 1991, A16.

―――. "Japanese Seek to Clip Wings of U.S. Airlines." *Washington Post,* 22 May 1993, A9.

Borrus, Amy. "Should the CIA Start Spying for Corporate America?" *Business Week,* 14 October 1991, 96–100.

Boykin, John. "With a Small Stick, Loudly." *Stanford Magazine,* Winter 1986, 43–46.

Briggs, Bruce. "The Coming Overthrow of Free Trade." *Wall Street Journal,* 24 February 1983, 28.

Brittan, Samuel. "Sanctions versus War: A Sober View." *Financial Times,* 17 September 1990, 19.

Buchanan, Patrick. "Current Glut Demonstrates Myth of Oil Weapon." *Alexandria Gazette,* 20 May 1981, A7.

Bulkeley, William M. "Voice Mail May Let Competitors Dial 'E' for Espionage." *Wall Street Journal,* 28 September 1993, B1.

Burgess, John, and John Mintz. "CIA, FBI Chiefs Warn Panel over Economic Espionage: U.S. Advanced Technology Is a Target." *Washington Post,* 30 April 1992, B11.

Burkhalter, E. A., Jr. "Soviet Industrial Espionage." *Signal,* March 1983, 15–20.

Burton, John, and Alexander Nicoli. "US Disarray over Policy on Sanctions for N Korea." *Financial Times,* 18 June 1994, 49.

Byrd, Harry F., Jr. "Rhodesian Chrome: The Myths vs the Facts." *Journal of Social and Political Affairs* 1 (Winter 1976): 289–306.

Canute, James. "Haiti Declares Emergency as UN Sanctions Tighten." *Financial Times,* 13 June 1994, 4.

Carswell, Robert. "Economic Sanctions and the Iranian Experience." *Foreign Affairs* 60 (Winter 1981): 247–65.

Carter, Barry E. "Charge Iraq Oil Export Fees." *Washington Post,* 4 March 1991, A13.

Carter, E. W., III. "Blockade." *Proceedings,* November 1990, 42–47.

Carver, George. "Intelligence and Glasnost." *Foreign Affairs* (Summer 1990): 147–66.

Chapman, Stephen. "Grain of Truth." *New Republic* 182 (19 January 1980): 14–15.

Choate, Alan G., and Michael L. Moore. "Bribes and Boycotts under the Tax Reform Act of 1976." *International Tax Journal* 4 (4 December 1977): 736–44.

Christiansen, Drew, and Gerard F. Powers. "Unintended Consequences." *Bulletin of the Atomic Scientists* 41 (November 1993): 41–45.

Clark, Lindley H., Jr. "Onward and Downward with Trade Warfare." *Wall Street Journal,* 15 March 1983, 27.

Clawson, Patrick. "Sanctions Can't Topple Saddam." *Washington Post,* 23 June 1991, B7.

Clinton, Bill. Executive Order 12917 (prohibiting certain transactions with respect to Haiti). *Weekly Compilations of Presidential Documents* 30 (30 May 1994): 1147.

"Clinton's China Decision." *Journal of Commerce,* 23 May 1994, 12A.

Cohen, Phyllis J. "The Constitutionality of New York's Response to the Arab Boycott." *Syracuse Law Review* 28 (Spring 1977): 631–63.

Cohen, Richard. "Embargo: Heads They Win, Tails We Lose." *Washington Post,* 7 September 1990, A15.

"Conference on Transnational Economic Boycotts and Coercion." *Texas International Law Journal* 12 (Winter 1977): 1–60.

Cooper, Kenneth J. "Intelligence Goes Public in the House." *Washington Post,* 9 March 1993, A17.

Cutler, B. J. "Creative Patent Stallers?" *Washington Times,* 11 November 1989, F4.

"Danger of Trade, Finance War Cited." *Journal of Commerce,* 28 December 1982, 23B.

Davidson, Gary E. "United States' Use of Economic Sanctions, Treaty Bending, and Treaty Breaking in International Aviation." *Journal of Air Law and Commerce* 59 (December–January 1993): 6.

Davis, Bob. "White House to Name 22 Technologies It Says Are Crucial to Prosperity, Security." *Wall Street Journal,* 25 April 1991, 2.

Davis, Jennifer. "Squeezing Apartheid." *Bulletin of the Atomic Scientists* 16 (November 1993): 16–19.

Deighen, Roderick P. "Welcome to Cold War II." *Chief Executive,* January–February 1993, 42–46.

Dobson, Alan P. "The Kennedy Administration and Economic Warfare against Communism." *International Affairs* 599 (Autumn 1988): 599–616.

Dodell, Sue Ellen. "United States Banks and the Arab Boycott of Israel." *Columbia Journal of Transnational Law* 17 (1978): 119–43.

Doi, Ayako, and Kim Willenson. "Japan: Back to the Past? The Idea of a Co-prosperity Sphere—Again." *Washington Post,* 11 August 1991, C1.

Dolan-Pearson, Maureen. "Pulling Purse Strings to Eliminate Purse Seiners: United States Protection of Dolphins through International Trade Sanctions." *De Paul Law Review* 42 (Spring 1993): 1085–124.

Doti, Hames. "The Response of Economic Literature to Wars." *Economic Inquiry* 16 (October 1978): 616–26.

Doxey, Margaret. "Economic Sanctions: Benefits and Costs." *World Today* 36 (December 1980): 484–89.

———. "International Sanctions: A Framework for Analysis with Special Reference to the UN and South Africa." *International Organization* 26 (Summer 1972): 527–50.

———. "The Rhodesian Sanctions Experiment." *Yearbook of World Affairs,* 1971, 142–62.

Dreyfuss, Robert. "Company Spies: The CIA Has Opened a Global Pandora's Box by Spying on Foreign Competitors of American Companies." *Mother Jones,* May–June 1994, 16–19.

Dulles, J. F. "Should Economic Sanctions Be Applied in International Disputes?" *Annals* 162 (1932): 103–8.

Dumas, Lloyd J. "Organizing the Chaos." *Bulletin of the Atomic Scientists* 46 (November 1993): 46–49.

Dupuy, T. N. "We Are Less Warlike If Not Kinder and Gentler." *Baltimore Sun,* 15 May 1992, 11.

"Economic Espionage Should Stay 'In the Cold,' Intelligence Consortium Analyst Says." *Corporate Security Digest,* 12 July 1993, 1–2.

"Economic Warfare Repudiated." *Wall Street Journal,* 31 May 1994, A16.

Eland, Ivan "Think Small." *Bulletin of the Atomic Scientists,* November 1993, 36.

Elliot, Kimberly. "A Look at the Record." *Bulletin of the Atomic Scientists* 32 (November 1993): 32–35.

Elliot, Kimberly; Gary Hufbauer; and Jeffrey Schott. "The Big Squeeze: Why the Sanctions on Iraq Will Work." *Washington Post,* 9 December 1990, K1.

Ewer, Sid R. "Protection of Trade Secrets and Intellectual Property." *Internal Auditor,* February 1993, 46–48.

Ewing, Lee. "AF Chief Praises 'Spectacularly Successful' Naval Blockade." *Navy Times,* 4 March 1991, 26.

Fairhall, David. "How Naval Chiefs Are Told the Limits." *Guardian,* 22 August 1990, 2.

Farer, Tom J. "Political and Economic Coercion in Contemporary International Law." *American Journal of International Law* 79 (1985): 405–13.

Feinberg, Kenneth R. "Economic Coercion and Economic Sanctions: The Expansion of United States Extraterritorial Jurisdiction." *American University Law Review* 30 (1981): 323–48.

Feldman, David H. "International Economic Sanctions." *Southern Economic Journal* 60 (January 1994): 768–77.

Fielding, Lois E. "Maritime Interception: Centerpiece of Economic Sanctions in the New World Order." *Louisiana Law Review* 53 (March 1993): 1191–241.

"Fighting Qaddafi with a Wet Noodle." *New York Times,* 10 December 1981, A30.

Fossedal, Gregory. "(How) Sanctions Work." *Washington Times,* 26 July 1982, A9.

Fox, Joseph C. "Our Gray War with Russia." *Retired Officer,* March 1982, 22–24.

Frankel, Glenn. "The Other Gulf War—Over Money." *Washington Post,* 19 August 1990, H1.

Fraumann, Edwin. "Drawing the Curtain on Economic Spying." *Law Enforcement News,* 15 November 1993, 8.

Fredman, Steven J. "U.S. Trade Sanctions against Uganda: Legality under International Law." *Law and Policy in International Business* 11 (1979): 1149–91.

Freeman, Nick J. "United States' Economic Sanctions against Vietnam: International Business and Development Repercussions." *Columbia Journal of World Business* 28 (Summer 1993): 12–22.

Friedman, Howard M. "Confronting the Arab Boycott: A Lawyer's Baedeker." *Harvard Law Journal* 19 (1978): 443–533.

Galtung, Johan. "On the Effects of International Economic Sanctions, with Examples from the Case of Rhodesia." *World Politics* 19 (April 1967): 378–416.

Gates, Robert M. Presentation to the Economic Club of Detroit, 13 April 1992. Quoted in "Gates Way: Intellinomics." *International Economy* 54 (July/August 1992): 54.

"General Motors and Volkswagen: Pistols at Dawn." *Economist,* 31 July 1993, 60.

Gertz, Bill. "FBI Chief: KGB up to Old Tricks." *Washington Times,* 26 October 1990, A3.

———. "FBI Expanding Spying to Cover Friendly Nations." *Washington Times,* 30 October 1991, A7.

———. "French Probed as Spies against U.S. Companies." *Washington Times,* 4 June 1993, A5.

———. "Friends, Foes Said to Employ Business Spies." *Washington Times,* 30 April 1992, A3.

———. "Japanese Intelligence Network Is All Business." *Washington Times,* 9 February 1992, A6.

————. "The New Spy: 90's Espionage Turns Economic." *Washington Times,* 9 February 1992, 1, 7.

————. "World Economy New Focus of U.S. Intelligence." *Washington Times,* 20 September 1989, 3.

"Getting in on the Action." *Journal of Commerce,* 22 December 1988, 8A.

Gigot, Paul A. (Potomac Watch). "President—Oops, Sen.—Nunn Sides with Gulf Doves." *Wall Street Journal,* 30 November 1990, 14.

Gilmore, Richard. "Grain in the Bank." *Foreign Policy* 38 (Spring 1980): 168–81.

Graham, Thomas R. "War & Peace." *Foreign Policy,* Spring 1983, 124–37.

Green, J. D. "Economic Sanctions as Instruments of National Policy." *Annals* 162 (1932): 100–102.

Greenberg, Paul. "The Power and Use of Trade." *Washington Times,* 27 May 1991, F4.

Grieve, Muriel J. "Economic Sanctions: Theory and Practice." *International Relations* 3 (October 1968): 431–33.

Haase, Rolf. "Why Economic Sanctions Always Fail: The Case of Rhodesia." *Intereconomics* 7–8 (1978): 194–99.

Harris, Joel B., and Jeffrey P. Bialos. "The Strange New World of United States Export Controls under the International Emergency Economic Powers Act." *Vanderbilt Journal of Transnational Law* 18 (1985): 71–108.

Harrison, Selig S., and Clyde V. Prestowitz. "Pacific Rim Shots: Trade War—Not the Cold War—Is Today's Threat." *Washington Post,* 8 July 1990, C1.

Heffernan, R. J., and D. T. Swartwood. "Trends in Competitive Intelligence." *Security Management,* June 1993, 42–46.

Hein, Steven L. "Coasties in the Persian Gulf." *Proceedings,* November 1990, 118–19.

Hoagland, Jim. "France Refuses to Wage Economic War on Soviets." *Washington Post,* 15 June 1982, A1.

————. "Sanctions: A Broken Arrow." *Washington Post,* 30 April 1988, A2.

————. "World Cop? No, World Customs Officer." *Washington Post,* 26 November 1991, A21.

Hoffman, Frederick. "The Function of Economic Sanctions: A Comparative Analysis." *Journal of Peace Research* 2 (1968): 140–59.

"How to Aim the Embargo Weapon." *New York Times,* 23 May 1991, 30.

Hufbauer, Gary C. "The Futility of Sanctions." *Wall Street Journal,* 1 June 1994, A14.

Hufbauer, Gary C., and Kimberly A. Elliot. "Sanctions Will Bite—and Soon." *New York Times,* 14 January 1991, 17.

Huntington, Samuel. "Trade, Technology, and Leverage: Economic Diplomacy." *Foreign Policy,* Fall 1978, 63–80.

Inderfurth, Rick. "Abolish the National Security Council." *Washington Post,* 21 June 1992, C7.

"Indiana Jim and the Temple of Spooks." *Economist,* 20 March 1993, 34.

Ishihara, Shintaro. "Teaching Japan to Say No" (interview). *Time,* 20 November 1989, 81.

Janssen, Richard F. "Rent-a-Spook." *International Business,* June 1993, 75–76.

Johnson, David Lawther. "Sanctions and South Africa." *Harvard International Law Journal* 19 (Fall 1978): 887–930.

Kennedy, Edward. "The Sanctions Are Working." *Washington Post,* 6 October 1987, A23.

Kissinger, Henry A. "International Trade: It's Time to Change the Rules." *Washington Post,* 22 October 1984, A21.

———. "Trading with the Russians: A Political Strategy for Economic Relations." *New Republic,* 2 June 1982, 14–16.

Knight, Jerry, and Peter Behr. "In U.S., Strategic Minerals Acquire New Prominence." *Washington Post,* 15 March 1981, H1.

Knorr, Klaus. "The Concept of Economic Potential for War." *World Politics* 10 (October 1957): 49–62.

———. "The Limits of Economic and Military Power." *Daedalus* 104 (Fall 1975): 229–43.

———. "Is International Coercion Waning or Rising?" *International Security* 1 (Spring 1977): 92–110.

Konovalov, Alexander; Sergey Oznobistchev; and Dmitri Evstafiev. "Saying *Da,* Saying *Nyet.*" *Bulletin of the Atomic Scientists,* November 1993, 28.

Koshel, Michael J. "Friendly Spies: How America's Allies Are Using Economic Espionage to Steal Our Secrets." *Security Management,* October 1993, 98–99.

Kraft, Joseph. "The Perfect Sanction." *Washington Post,* 30 December 1981, A15.

Kramer, Michael. "A Rung on the Ladder to War." *Time,* 13 June 1994, 31.

Krauthammer, Charles. "Sanctions Fallacy: They Are No Alternative to Military Force." *Washington Post,* 19 June 1992, A27.

Kunz, J. L. "Sanctions in International Law." *American Journal of International Law* 54 (1960): 324–48.

"Labor Letter: Business Espionage." *Wall Street Journal,* 28 June 1994, B7.

Lacavo, Richard. "Mixed Signals on Sanctions." *Time,* 17 December 1990, 32.

SELECTED BIBLIOGRAPHY

Lardner, George, Jr. "CIA Seeks to Define New Role." *Washington Post,* 13 November 1990, A1.

Lardner, George, Jr., and Walter Pincus. "CIA's Gates Opposed to Commercial Spying." *Washington Post,* 12 December 1991, A18.

————. "KGB Defector Predicts an Increase in Moscow's Industrial Espionage." *Washington Post,* 29 October 1991, A11.

Lamont, James. "As Red Menace Cools, Spies Go Corporate." *Wall Street Journal,* 22 April 1991, A12.

Lenway, Stefanie Ann. "Between War and Commerce: Sanctions as a Tool of Statecraft." *International Organization* 42 (Spring 1988): 397–426.

Lewis, Flora. "Japan's Looking Glass." *New York Times,* 8 April 1989, A31.

Lewis, Neil A. "U.S. Panel Seeks Tighter Spy Laws." *New York Times,* 24 May 1990, 22.

Lindsay, James M. "Trade Sanctions as Policy Instruments: A Re-examination." *International Studies Quarterly* 30 (June 1986): 153–73.

Lippman, Thomas W. "Wisdom of Trade Sanctions Widely Questioned." *Washington Post,* 17 January 1982, G1.

Lissakers, Karen. "Money and Manipulation." *Foreign Policy* 111 (Fall 1981): 107–26.

Longo, James. "CGd's Law Enforcement Detachments Share Knowhow on Boardings." *Navy Times,* 12 November 1990, 20.

Longworth, R. C. "Sanctions Are the World's Cure-all, but They Rarely Heal." *Charlotte News and Observer,* 7 August 1994, 15A.

Lopez, George A., and David Cortwright. "Sanctions: Do They Work? Introduction." *Bulletin of the Atomic Scientists* 14 (November 1993): 14–15.

Losman, Donald. "International Boycotts: An Appraisal." *Politics* 37 (December 1972): 648–71.

Lowenthal, Mark M. "Keep James Bond out of GM: Why Economic Spying Won't Solve America's Problems." *International Economy,* July/August 1992, 52–54.

Luttrell, Clifton B. "The Russian Grain Embargo: Dubious Success." *Federal Reserve Bank of St. Louis Review,* August 1980, 2–8.

Luttwak, Edward N. "America's Setting Sun." *New York Times,* 28 September 1991, 17.

McCarroll, Thomas. "Next for the CIA: Business Spying?" *Time,* 22 February 1993, 60–61.

McCloskey, Robert J. "Unfinished Business." *Washington Post,* 24 August 1982, A18.

MacDonald, R. St. J. "Economic Sanctions in the International System." *Canadian Yearbook of International Law* 7 (1969): 61–91.

MacDonald, Stuart. "Nothing Either Good or Bad: Industrial Espionage and Technology Transfer." *International Journal of Technology Management* 8 (1993): 95–105.

McGovern, George. "The Elements of 'McGovernism.' " *Washington Post,* 31 May 1993, A19.

McGurn, William. "I Hear Asia Calling." *American Spectator,* May 1993, 24.

Marcy, Carl. "Will Sanctions Sway the Soviets? No—'Unless We Act as a Group, the Effect Is Simply to Offend Our Allies.' " *U.S. News and World Report,* 11 October 1982, 27–28.

Marlow, Gene. "Freebooter: Spies Shifting to Private Sector." *Winston-Salem Journal,* 30 May 1993, A10.

Mastanduno, Michael. "Strategies of Economic Containment: U.S. Trade Relations with the Soviet Union." *World Politics* 37 (July 1985): 503–31.

———. "Trade as a Strategic Weapon: American and Alliance Export Control Policy in the Early Postwar Period." *International Organization* 42 (Winter 1988): 121–50.

Matthew, Jessica T. "Dolphins, Tuna, and Free Trade." *Washington Post,* 18 October 1991, A21.

———. "Redefining Security." *Foreign Affairs* 68 (Spring 1989): 162–77.

Miller, Judith. "When Sanctions Worked." *Foreign Policy* 39 (1980): 118–29.

Mintz, John. "CIA: French Targeted Secrets of U.S. Firms." *Washington Post,* 27 April 1993, F1.

———. "Paris Air Show 'Plot' Gets Lost in Translation." *Washington Post,* 30 April 1993, F1.

Moyer, Homer E., and Linda A. Mabry. "Export Controls as Instruments of Foreign Policy: The History, Legal Issues, and Policy Lessons of Three Recent Cases." *Law and Policy in International Business* 15 (1983): 1–171.

Moynihan, Daniel Patrick. "U.S. Should Centralize Trade Responsibility." *Journal of Commerce,* 28 December 1982, 4A.

Nelan, Bruce W. "Can Sanctions Still Do the Job?" *Time,* 21 January 1991, 40–41.

———. "How the World Will Look in 50 Years." *Time,* special issue, Fall 1992, 36.

———. "A New World for Spies." *Time,* 5 July 1993, 29.

Nicoloff, Olivier. "Value of Food as Weapon More Symbolic Than Real." *International Perspectives* 31 (July 1979): 471–94.

Nitze, Paul H., and Michael F. Stafford. "War Whether We Need It or Not? A Blockade—Plus Bombs—Can Win." *Washington Post,* 6 December 1990, C1.

Nossal, Kim Richard. "International Sanctions as International Punishment." *International Organization* 43 (Spring 1989): 301–22.

———. "Trade Sanctions as Policy Instruments." *International Studies Quarterly* 30 (1986): 153–73.

Nunn, Sam. "War Should Be a Last Resort." *Washington Post,* 10 January 1991, 21.

O'Keefe, Sean; Frank B. Kelso III; and Carl E. Mundy, Jr. "…From the Sea: Preparing the Naval Service for the 21st Century." *Proceedings,* November 1992, 93–96.

Olson, Richard Stuart. "Economic Coercion in World Politics, with a Focus on North-South Relations." *World Politics* 31 (July 1979): 471–94.

Passell, P. "Economics: Reading Your Way out of Chaos." *New York Times,* 29 October 1989, Book Review section, 1.

Peterzell, Jay. "When Friends Become Moles." *Time,* 20 May 1990, 50.

Phillips, Kevin. "Troops Must Come Home to Win the Economic War." *Los Angeles Times,* 4 March 1990, M3.

Pichirallo, Joe, and John M. Goshko. "Anti-Noriega Sanctions: No Quick Knockout." *Washington Post,* 16 May 1988, A1.

Pipes, Richard. "Will Sanctions Sway the Soviets? Yes—Kremlin Would 'Shift Resources out of Defense into Capital Investment.' " *U.S. News and World Report,* 11 October 1982, 27–28.

"Pressuring North Korea." *Seattle Times,* 21 March 1994, B4.

Pritchard, Bill. "Panama's Bishops Call U.S. Sanctions 'Immoral.' " *Arlington Catholic Herald,* 14 December 1989, 13.

Pyatt, Rudolph A. "No Way to Win in Economic Civil War." *Washington Post,* 12 April 1993, Business section, 3.

Randol, Mark A., and Wallace J. Thies. "The Opportunity Costs of Large Deck Carriers: Naval Strategy for the 1990s and Beyond." *Naval War College Review,* Summer 1990, 9.

Rankin, Peter J. "The Grain Embargo." *Washington Quarterly* 3 (Summer 1980): 141–53.

Raspberry, William. "Fly on the Wall in Japan." *Washington Post,* 29 December 1989, A19.

"Reagan Team Favoring Tougher Export Laws." *Journal of Commerce,* 3 March 1983, 5A.

Redman, Charles. "A Brief Guide to Friendly Spying." *Economist,* 7 December 1985, 44.

Robinson, James D., III. "Progress toward Commercial Disarmament." *Washington Post,* 5 January 1989, A25.

Roney, John C. "Grain Embargo as Diplomatic Lever: Fulcrum or Folly?" *SAIS Review,* 1982, 189–205.

Rosen, Allen. "Canada's Use of Economic Sanctions for Political and Human Rights Purposes." *University of Toronto Faculty Law Review* 51 (Winter 1993): 1–53.

Rosenfeld, Stephen S. "Development, Disarmament, Bribers." *Washington Post,* 5 October 1991, A23.

———. "Sanctions: A Washout." *Washington Post,* 17 June 1988, A25.

Rositzke, Harry. "The Ultimate Weapon." *New York Times,* 23 July 1982, 23.

Rowen, Hobart. "Missing an Economic Strategy." *Washington Post,* 22 October 1984, A21.

Safire, William. "Staying a Superpower: Create a Council on Economic Intervention." *New York Times,* 5 February 1990, A19.

Samuelson, Robert J. "Books I Didn't Read." *Washington Post,* 20 December 1989, A25.

———. "Sanctions' Problem Is They Don't Work." *Washington Post,* 13 September 1983, D7.

———. "Spying Won't Boost U.S. Economic Competitiveness." *Washington Post,* 11 July 1990, A19.

———. "Why Are We Fighting with Japan?" *Washington Post,* 16 June 1993, A21.

"Sanctions against Moscow." *Baltimore Sun,* 30 December 1981, A6.

"Sanctions: Do They Work?" (selective reporting of the proceedings of the Spring 1993 conference of the Joan B. Kroc Institute for International Peace Studies at the University of Notre Dame and the Fourth Freedom Forum in Goshen, Indiana). *Bulletin of the Atomic Scientists,* November 1993, entire issue.

Scharfen, John C. "The Efficacy of Economics as an Instrument of Force." *Washington Times,* 25 January 1983, C1.

———. "Military Power: How Much Is Enough?" *Baltimore Sun,* 29 October 1979, Sunday Perspective section.

Scharfen, John C., and William R. Ball. "The Principles of Economic War." *Proceedings,* December 1983, 59–69.

Schrage, Michael. "High Technology Won't Be the Main Battleground in Future Trade Wars." *Washington Post,* 4 December 1992, B3.

Schreiber, Anna P. "Economic Coercion as an Instrument of Foreign Policy: U.S. Economic Measures against Cuba and the Dominican Republic." *World Politics* 25 (April 1973): 387–413.

Schultze, Charles L. "The Economic Content of National Security Policy." *Foreign Affairs* 51 (April 1973): 522–40.

Scott, Alexander. "Economic Warfare: How to Play Hardball with the Russians." *Armed Forces Journal International*, 17 March 1980, 67–69.

Shear, Jeff. "Japanese Tract Rankles Americans." *Insight*, 20 November 1989, 44.

Shubik, Martin. "Unconventional Methods of Economic Warfare." *Conflict* 1, no. 3 (1979): 211–29.

Smith, Bruce. "Espionage a Factor in Hughes' Pullout." *Aviation Week & Space Technology*, 3 May 1993, 24–25.

Smith, Geoffrey N. "The French Connection." *Financial World*, 16 February 1993, 6.

Smith, Jeffrey R. "U.S. to Protest Industrial Spying by Allies." *Washington Post*, 30 April 1993, A39.

"Some Sanctions That May Not Work." *Time*, 21 December 1981, 24–26.

"Soviet Says Sanctions Must End." *New York Times*, 17 November 1982, D1.

"Spies?!! At the Show?!! Naturally!" *Air Transport World*, June 1992, 224.

Squitieri, Tom. "New Course May Be Economic Espionage." *USA Today*, 25 April 1991, 11A.

Stavridis, James. "To Begin Again." *Proceedings*, July 1993, 36.

Steiner, H.; L. Kestenbaum; and P. Areeda. "International Boycotts and Domestic Order: The American Response to the Arab Boycott." *Texas Law Review* 54 (November 1976): 1353–437.

Steinfels, Peter. "Beliefs—Three Years after the Gulf War, a Question Lingers: Would Economic Sanctions Have Been Moral?" *New York Times*, 8 January 1994, National section, 9.

Thurow, Lester C. "The Trouble with Sanctions." *Newsweek*, 26 July 1982, 20.

"Trade Warfare: Can Sanctions Ever Work?" *Time*, 25 October 1982, 68–69.

Train, John. "When Can Sanctions Succeed?" *Wall Street Journal*, 14 June 1989, 14.

Tuan, Bui Anh. "Trade Embargo Debate Unending." *Washington Times*, 3 August 1982.

Ullman, Richard H. "Human Rights and Economic Power: The United States versus Idi Amin." *Foreign Affairs* 56 (April 1978): 529–43.

Unger, Harlow. "The Spies of Silicon Valley: How Industrial Espionage Is Hurting the Computer Business." *Canadian Business* 15 (25 December 1980), 25.

"US Should Centralize Trade Responsibility." *Journal of Commerce*, 28 December 1982, 4A.

"US Viewed as Timid in Trade War with Japan." *Journal of Commerce,* 19 January 1983, 3A.

Veigh, Anne. "India Misses U.S. Patent Deadline." *Washington Times,* 27 January 1992, C1.

Walker, Tony. "Strategic Waterway Well Suited to Blockade Ships." *London Financial Times,* 22 August 1990, 3.

Wallenstein, Peter. "Characteristics of Economic Sanctions." *Journal of Peace Research* 3 (1968): 248–67.

Werleigh, Claudette Antoine. "Haiti and the Halfhearted." *Bulletin of the Atomic Scientists* 20 (November 1993): 20–23.

Weymouth, Lally. "Panama—The May '88 Option." *Washington Post,* 31 December 1989, C1.

Wickersham, Mark. "Reconcilable Differences? United States–Japan Economic Conflict." *Yale Journal of International Law* 19 (Winter 1994): 303–4.

Will, George F. "Blaming Japan First." *Washington Post,* 1 January 1992, A27.

———. "Needed: A Policy of Punishment." *Newsweek,* 12 September 1983, 32.

———. "Turning the Trade Weapon against Ourselves." *Washington Post,* 15 October 1981, 29.

Wilson, Christopher. "Economic Sanctions Credited as Big Factor behind Reform." *Washington Times,* 12 February 1990, A9.

Wines, Michael. "Security Agency Debates New Role: Economic Spying." *New York Times,* 18 June 1990, A1.

———. "U.S. Urged to Emphasize Economic Strength." *New York Times,* 4 April 1990, A5.

Woodward, Susan L. "Yugoslavia: Divide and Fail." *Bulletin of the Atomic Scientists* 24 (November 1993): 24–27.

Zalud, Bill. "Economic Espionage: Friends as Business Enemies." *Security,* August 1993, 26.

Zolton, Marc. "Quiet Step in Victory, Navies Choked off Iraq's Livelihood." *Navy Times,* 25 March 1991, 12.

Zumwalt, Elmo R., and Worth H. Bagley. "Machinery for Economic Warfare Seen as U.S. Need." *Cincinnati Enquirer,* 14 June 1981, G3.

Reports

Ayars, Benjamin N. "Economic Warfare." Carlisle, Pa.: U.S. Army War College, Carlisle Barracks, 26 March 1956.

Brancato, Carolyn Kay, and Jeffrey P. Brown. "An Economic Embargo of Iran." Congressional Research Service Report no. 80-4 E. Washington, D.C.: Library of Congress, 13 December 1979.

Cate, Penelope C.; A. Ellen Terpstra; and Jasper Womach. "The U.S. Embargo of Agricultural Exports to the Soviet Union: Agricultural Impact." Congressional Research Service Report no. 80-14 ENR. Washington, D.C.: Library of Congress, 21 January 1980.

Celada, Raymond J. "Blockade: Some International and Domestic Legal Implications." Congressional Research Service Report no. 90-386 A. Washington, D.C.: Library of Congress, 15 April 1990.

Levine, Herbert S., et al. "Study of the Political and Military Utility of U.S.-USSR Economic Relations." SRI Project 5087. Menlo Park: Strategic Studies Center, Stanford Research Institute, 1976.

Losman, Donald L. "Economic Sanctions in the 1990's." Report ACN 80027. Carlisle, Pa.: Strategic Studies Institute, U.S. Army War College, Carlisle Barracks, 30 October 1980.

Lowenthal, Mark M. "Naval Restriction of Commerce against Iraq: Historic Background, Implications, and Options." Congressional Research Service Report no. 90-388 RCO. Washington, D.C.: Library of Congress, 14 August 1990.

Minckler, Rex D., and Richard G. Rebh. "Economic Conflict and National Security Research: A Report on the Proceedings and Results of a Workshop for the Office of Naval Research." GE 77 TMP-5. Washington, D.C.: General Electric Center for Advanced Studies, 1977.

Phillips, Charlotte A. "The Arab Boycott of Israel: Possibilities for European Cooperation with U.S. Antiboycott Legislation." Congressional Research Service Report no. 19-215F. Washington, D.C.: Library of Congress, May 1979.

National Security Institute Security Awareness Bulletins

The following are from *The Employee Security Connection,* published quarterly by the National Security Institute, Framingham, Mass.

Bader, William. "The New Global Environment in Defense Industry." January 1992, 23–25.

"Espionage in 90's Turns Economic." April–June 1992, 1, 7.

Gwash, Greg. "A View from Industrial Security." April 1990.

Webster, William H. "Intelligence Issues of the New Decade." April 1990, 10–12.

Military Lesson Plans and Instruction Manuals

"Economic Mobilization Studies, Economic Warfare." Industrial College of the Armed Forces, Washington, D.C., February 1956.

"Merchant Vessel Documents." U.S. Fleet Training Group, San Diego, Calif., undated (assumed 1990).

"Middle East Maritime Intercept Ops Boarding Team Information." Commander Fleet Training Group, San Diego, Calif., undated (assumed 1990).

"Tactical Sweep Procedures." Fleet Training Group, San Diego, Calif., undated (assumed 1991).

"Visit, Board, Search, and Seizure: Sample Log Entries." Fleet Training Group, San Diego, Calif., undated (assumed 1991).

"Visit, Board, Search, and Seizure: Theory Brief." Fleet Training Group, San Diego, Calif., undated (assumed 1991).

Waterman, B. S. "Introduction to Economic Warfare" (speaker's text). Industrial College of the Armed Forces, Washington, D.C., 1950–51.

Television Shows

Transcripts of the following bibliographic citations may be secured from the cited network or from television show monitor services.

ABC, *Adam Smith's Money World*. "The Gulf Crisis—Blockade's Last Chance." Do sanctions work? Will sanctions drive Saddam Hussein out of Kuwait? What are the historical lessons of sanctions? 23 November 1990.

ABC, *Adam Smith's Money World*. "The Gulf Crisis—Can Embargoes Work?" Historically, have embargoes ever worked? Will they drive Saddam Hussein out of Kuwait? 19 October 1990.

ABC, *Business World*. "Japan and Unfair Trade Practices." Carla Hills discusses administration's position on imposing trade sanctions on Japan. 7 May 1989.

ABC, *Business World*. "Semiconductors Lead to Trade War." Secretary of Commerce Malcolm Baldridge comments on allegations that Japan is dumping semiconductors and what the U.S. response might be. 29 March 1987.

ABC, *Business World*. "Trade War." A discussion of the possibilities of imposing economic sanctions on Japan for unfair trade practices. 5 April 1987.

ABC, *Frontline*. "Losing the War with Japan." 1 December 1992.

ABC, *Nightline*. "Bush Lifts Sanctions against South Africa." Even though all U.S. conditions established for the lifting of sanctions have not been met, the administration removed economic sanctions against South Africa. 10 July 1991.

ABC, *Nightline.* "Japan—Trade Sanctions." Secretary of Commerce Malcolm Baldridge, Japanese Economic Minister Peter Sato, and Professor Arthur Laffer discuss the imposition of high tariffs on Japanese semiconductor chips to protect American industry. 27 March 1987.

CNN, *Crossfire.* "Out of the Penalty Box." Representatives Charles Rangel and Dan Burton discuss the administration's announcement that the United States is preparing to lift the sanctions against South Africa. 10 July 1991.

CNN, *International Hour.* "Spies Turn Attention to Business Secrets." U.S. businessmen operating overseas are targets for industrial espionage. U.S. intelligence services may refocus their efforts to this area. 17 April 1992.

CNN, *Larry King Live.* "What Is the Role of the CIA in the '90s?" Should CIA resources be reoriented to gather information on foreign competitors (i.e. engage in industrial espionage)? A debate between a former director of the agency and an intelligence expert. 5 August 1992.

CNN, *Moneyline.* "Spies Turning from Military to Corporate Secrets." Business leaders express concerns about the security of their corporate secrets. 29 April 1992.

CNN, *News Day.* "Croatian Official Applauds U.N. Sanction." Zelko Sikic, president of the Dubrovnik Municipality in Croatia, welcomes the U.N. sanctions despite hardships on the populace. 31 May 1992.

CNN, *Worldwide Update.* "UN Sanctions Won't End War in Yugoslavia." The United Nations maintains control of the Sarajevo airport to ensure access for humanitarian purposes. Peacekeeping forces are attacked. There appears to be little hope that sanctions will resolve conflict. 6 June 1992.

Statements

The following statements by R. Richard Newcomb, director, Office of Foreign Assets Control, Department of the Treasury, are available from the Department of Treasury, telephone (202) 566-2041.

Prepared statement before the Subcommittee on Oversight, Committee on Ways and Means, U.S. House of Representatives, 1 May 1991.

Presentation before the Kuwait Economic Society, "Economic Resistance to Iraqi Aggression," 24 February 1992.

Presentation to victims of Pan Am Flight 103, 28 March 1992.

Prepared statement before the Committee on Foreign Affairs, U.S. House of Representatives, 8 April 1992.

Presentation before the International Trade Committee, International Law Section, District of Columbia Bar, "Vietnam: The U.S. Economic Embargo," 15 October 1992.

Interviews by the Author

Bugner, Douglas (director, Policy Programs, SRI International). Interview and briefing, 22 December 1992.

Comiez, Maynard (director of policy analysis, Office of the Assistant Secretary of the Treasury, Economic Policy, United States Department of the Treasury). Interview and briefing, 4 August 1989.

Connolly, Gerald E. (vice president, SRI International). Interview and briefing, 17 August 1992.

Earnest, Peter (chief, Media Relations, Central Intelligence Agency). Telephonic discussion and briefing, 23 February 1993.

Foss, Robert (emergency coordinator, United States Department of the Treasury). Interview and briefing, 4 August 1989.

Frazier, Gregory (Office of Congressman Dan Glickman). Telephonic discussion of economic conflict concept paper, 11 March 1993.

Leach, Gerald (director of science and technology affairs, National Security Council). Interview and briefing, 28 June 1989.

Levine, Robert D. (United States Department of the Treasury). Interview and briefing, 21 June 1993.

Mathieson, John A. (director, International Policy Center, SRI International). Interview and briefing, 22 December 1992.

Merrill, John P. (Office of the Secretary of Defense, Undersecretary of Defense for Policy). Discussion of economic conflict concept paper, 20 August 1981.

Murdock, Clark (staff, U.S. House of Representatives Armed Services Committee). Discussion of economic conflict concept paper, 17 June 1991.

Newcomb, R. Richard (director, Office of Foreign Assets Control, United States Department of the Treasury). Interview and briefing, 21 June 1993.

Paugelinan, Eddie (administrative assistant, Office of Congressman Ben Blaz of the House Armed Services Committee). Interview and discussion, 6 June 1991.

Salmon, Jeffrey (executive director, George C. Marshall Institute). Interview and briefing, 9 March 1992.

Togo, Kazuhiko (minister, United States Embassy of Japan). Interview and briefing, 25 August 1993.

Trainor, Bernard E. (director, National Security Program, Kennedy School of Government, Harvard University). Multiple discussions between 1991 and 1994.

Welch, Thomas J. (associate director, Science and Technology, Office of the Secretary of Defense, Net Assessment). Telephonic discussion concerning economic conflict concept paper, 23 February 1993.

Winterling, Grayson (national security adviser to Senator John Warner). Briefing and interview, 18 April 1989.

Woolsey, James R. (prospective director of Central Intelligence Agency). Interview, briefing, and discussion, 12 July 1988.

Index

immigration control as, 92, 120, 121; incitement of work stoppages as, 120; indebtedness as, 114; industrial espionage as, 55–68, 119; and international law, 105–6; limited extraction as, 117; list of, 101; MFN status as, 95, 100, 102, 119; nationalization of assets as, 115; patent denial as, 111, 112; preclusive purchasing as, 117, 118; resource denial as, 118; sabotage as, 124; sanctions as, 104; smuggling as, 123; stockpiling as, 116, 140, 149; tariffs as, 41, 108, 123; technology transfer as, 65, 118; travel limitations as, 108–10; the withholding of payments as, 114, 159

intelligence, 67, 173, 181

International Economics (Schelling), 24, 25

International Economic Sanctions (Carter), 25

International Emergency Economic Powers Act (IEEPA), 71, 114. *See also* legislation

international law: and commodity dumping, 41; and definition of blockade, 9, 164, 166; discussed, 82–85; effect of, on use of economic force, 104–6; as guarantee of freedom of commerce, 95; and MFN status, 100. *See also* instruments of economic force

International Trade and Security Policy staff, 29

International Trade Commission, 110

intranational economic conflict, 34

Iran: as a counter to Iraq, 133; and EKTA, 28; during hostage crisis, 114; and military spare parts, 107; and U.S. petroleum reserve proposal, 116; as target of private-sector embargo, 141; wages economic war against U.S., 12

Iraq: and compensation for Gulf War, 116; and effectiveness of sanctions, 129, 144; just cause for use of force against, 88; and oil export tariffs, 108; and smuggling, 123; suffers collateral damage, 92; supported by Jordan, 113; as target of blockade, 19, 163, 167, 168; as target of economic espionage, 67; as

target of punitive economic force, 141; as target of UN economic pressure, 4, 132; and use of finance as weapon, 112, 113; use of French computer virus against, 122; value of oil exports of, 106; vulnerability of, to damming of Euphrates, 118

Irish Republican Army (IRA), 125

Ishihara, Shintaro, 10

Israel, 52, 58, 103, 114

Jackson-Vanik Amendment, 102

Japan: in Asian economic sphere, 48, 117; boycott of Aeroflot by, 109; in economic competition, 39, 137; as economic giant, 48, 55, 56; and economic war scenarios, 21; engages in industrial espionage against U.S., 58–60; food agency of, 28; imposes penalties on aviation industry, 141; as OECD signator, 95; as potential member of UN sanctions committee, 177; purchasing power of, 56; scenarios for coercion by, 49–51; and Sonno group, 51; as target of economic war following World War II, 133; as target of economic war prior to Pearl Harbor, 135; as target of U.S. counter-intelligence, 68; as target of U.S. economic coercion, 141; and trade surplus, 125; in trade wars, 42, 44; and U.S. trade imbalance, 41; and U.S. trade limits, 128; and use of economic power, 80; vulnerability of, to oil embargo, 53–55

Japan Aviation Electronics Industry Ltd., 141

Japan Conspiracy, The (Anderson), 21, 51

Japan That Can Say No, The (Morita and Ishihara), 10

Joyner, Christopher, 151

just war: Aquinas and, 87; and competent authority, 93; and discrimination, 92; general theories of, 87–93, 95; and just cause, 88, 89, 93; as last resort, 74, 90, 93; principles of, 93; and probability of success, 90, 93; and proportionality of

National Security Council, 29, 173, 175
National War University, 23
Ngobi, James, 20
Nincic, Miroslav, 10, 14, 100, 129
Noriega, Manuel: indicted by U.S., 71, 75; rise to power of, 70, 72; as saboteur, 124; as target of coup attempt, 71, 74; as true objective of U.S. economic force, 11, 70, 73, 76, 114, 145; vulnerability of, 75, 153
North American Free Trade Agreement (NAFTA), 38, 134
North Atlantic Treaty Organization (NATO), 32, 99, 118, 137, 144
North Korea, 12, 20, 67, 105, 143

objectives of economic force, 45, 90, 140, 141, 180. *See also* principles of economic conflict
Office of Foreign Asset Control (FAC), 31, 33, 172, 175, 176. *See also* organization for economic conflict; Treasury Department, U.S.
On Political War (Smith), 27
Operation Blockade, 109
organization for economic conflict, 28–32, 171–77
Organization for European Economic Cooperation (OECD), 95, 96
Organization of American States (OAS), 85, 86
Overseas Security Advisory Council, 32, 59
Oznobistchev, Sergey, 144, 156

Panama, 11, 69–77, 114, 133, 181
Pan Am flight 105, 109
Paris Air Show, 61. *See also* economic espionage
Passell, Robert, 7
Patolichev, Nikolai, 11
Perle, Richard, 11, 12, 106
Permanent Court of International Justice, 95
Persian Gulf War, 91, 92. *See also* Desert Storm; Hussein, Saddam; Iraq; Kuwait
Peterson, Gregor, 31, 42, 54
Philippines, 50, 139

Point Four program, 38
Poland: and carrot-and-stick approach, 142; and cod war, 40; economic bureaucracy of, 28; 1981 crisis in, 109; possible default of, on debt payments, 143, 147
policy for economic conflict: lack of, in U.S. bureaucracy, 25, 128, 172, 173, 180; and nationalistic economics, 19; in overall framework, 156; "straw man" approach to, 157, 158
political force: combined with economic force, 3, 34; cost of, compared to economic force, 138; and international law, 84; as an instrument before last resort, 90; and resource allocation, 33; responsibility for, in U.S. bureaucracy, 28; synonymous to diplomatic force, 14. *See also* diplomatic force
postulates of economic conflict, 3, 5
Power, Economics, and Security, 25
Power of Nations, The (Knorr), 25
Powers, Gerard, 19, 87
principles of economic conflict: are seldom addressed, 6; concentration, 146, 147; diversity, 140–43; flexibility, 147, 148; lack of, 1; and magnitude of effort, 148, 149; objectives of, 143–46; resilience, 153; security, 149; stability, 152; in spectrum of economic activities, 140; time, 149, 150; unity, 150–52; universality, 139; value, 139. *See also* objectives of economic force
Prize, The (Yergin), 52
psychological force, 14, 84, 90–93, 159
Puppets of Nippon (Choate), 59

Reagan, Ronald: charged with escalating the arms race, 11; denies waging economic war against USSR, 11, 12; enlists NATO support, 144, 151; imposes Aeroflot embargo, 109; and Polish debt crisis, 147; uses economic instrument against Panama, 70, 71; uses economic instrument against USSR, 113, 129, 130; uses War Powers Act against Panama, 11
Recon/Optical, 58

About the Author

While on active duty in the Marine Corps, Col. John C. Scharfen held a number of senior planning positions, including that of general war planner on the staff of the U.S. Commander in Chief, Europe. He has written and lectured extensively on national security affairs.

He holds a bachelor's degree from Stanford University and a master's degree from Georgetown University. He and his wife, Nancy, live in Alexandria, Virginia. They have five children and nine grandchildren.